The mother of Maurice Ravel

Maurice Ravel

Variations on
His Life and Work
by
H. H. Stuckenschmidt

Translated from
the German by
Samuel R. Rosenbaum

NORTHWEST COMMUNITY
COLLEGE

Calder and Boyars
London

First published in Great Britain 1969
by Calder and Boyars Ltd
18 Brewer Street London W1

© Samuel R. Rosenbaum 1969

Translated from the German
Maurice Ravel;
Variationen über Person und Werk
© Suhrkamp Verlag
Frankfurt am Main 1966

SBN 7145 0024 0 Cloth edition
SBN 7145 0025 9 Paper edition

PICTURE CREDITS: Bettman Archive; Pierre Petit;
Francoise Masson & L'Oeil Magazine; Wide World Photos;
Bibliotheque Nationale, Paris; Leopold Stokowski;
Mme. Roland-Manuel; Culver Pictures Inc, New York;
Studio Harcourt, Paris

ACKNOWLEDGMENTS

In the preparation of this book the help I received from Roland-Manuel, the best informed and the most accurate of Ravel's friends, was invaluable. For many other helpful hints I am also indebted to conversations with Maurice Delage, Manuel Rosenthal, Hélène Jourdan-Morhange, Francis Poulenc, D. E Inghelbrecht, Igor Stravinsky, and Marguerite Long, to name only the most intimate friends in Ravel's circle. Léon Leyritz, who accompanied Ravel, then already a sick man, on his last trip abroad, gave me a comprehensive account of his physical condition. Mlle Marie Gaudin, the friend of his youth, told me about his summer vacations in Saint-Jean-de-Luz.

However, nothing can compare, in their direct influence on me, with the insights I gained from the many hours spent in Ravel's house in Montfort-l'Amaury. M Durand, his publisher, allowed me to study his manuscripts and also many details of his correspondence, though some of this concerned works that were never completed or performed, such as the setting of Gerhart Hauptmann's *Sunken Bell*.

I must also give sincere thanks to the German Research Institute for aid extended me on one of my study trips into France.

The principal source of the letters quoted is the collection of Ravel autographs in the Bibliothèque Nationale in Paris. Several were quoted from French books and magazines, including René Chalupt's *Ravel au miroir de ses lettres*, Robert Laffont, Paris, 1965; Hélène Jourdan-Morhange's *Ravel et nous*, Éditions du Milieu du Monde, Geneva, 1945; the collection *Maurice Ravel par quelques-uns de ses familiers*, Éditions du Tambourinaire, Paris, 1939; Roland-Manuel's *Ravel*, Éditions Gallimard, Paris, 1948; the special Ravel issues of *Revue Musicale*, Paris, April, 1925, December, 1938, and January–February, 1939; Misia Sert's autobiography *Misia*, Insel-Verlag, Wiesbaden, 1958. Roland-Manuel made available to me the text of Ravel's postcard about Stravinsky's *Les Noces*.

Other works I consulted were: Jules van Ackere, *Mau-*

rice Ravel, Elsevier, Brussels, 1957; Armand Machabey, *Maurice Ravel,* Éditions Richard Masse, Paris, 1947; Roland-Manual, *Maurice Ravel et son œuvre dramatique,* Éditions musicales de la Librairie de France, Paris, 1928; Norman Demuth, *Ravel,* J. M. Dent and Sons, Ltd., London, 1947; Vladimir Jankelevitch, *Maurice Ravel,* Éditions du Seuil, Paris, 1956; *Catalogue de l'œuvre de Maurice Ravel,* published by the Maurice Ravel Foundation with Durand et Cie., Paris, 1954.

Grateful acknowledgment is also made to the following for permission to quote from:

Bolero by Madeleine Goss, Holt, Rinehart and Winston, Inc.

Misia and the Muses: The Memoirs of Misia Sert. Copyright 1953 by Boulos. Reprinted by permission of The John Day Company, Inc.

CONTENTS

INTRODUCTION

In France music has a different purpose and a different aspect than it has in non-French-speaking lands. Its ancient ties with primitive calls, words, speech, and articulate utterance have never been entirely broken. It tries to reduce emotion to form, it feels related and obligated to the dance, it seeks to elevate feeling, not deepen it. In many ways related to the theater, and of service to it, music has at the same time freed itself from their common cultural bonds and yet come closer to it in spirit.

To the Latin, for whom *serenitas* is a quality inborn, the concept of entertainment does not have a lowly connotation. Just as comedy is considered to be one of the higher forms of art, so even tragedy can and should entertain.

The nature of French music betrays the influence of what may be termed a Faustian philosophy only where it encounters strains impinging on it from the East, and when these have come into conflict with its essential character. It may be a more fruitful and creative encounter than that with the music of the Ars Nova of the fourteenth century, or with that of Hector Berlioz, or, in our own time, with Pierre Boulez. But it always causes an aberration of the compass needle that makes its course uncertain. France, the land of the most highly developed interweaving of thought and spirit, has never been favorable to the Faustian struggle of the symphony. One must be born or reared in the region of the more easterly High Alps to be free of the ideal of moderation and clarity in which France's spiritual strength is rooted.

For this reason, Maurice Ravel is a French musician of purest strain. He never really experienced the impact of romantic pathos. His artistic progress is neither a battle nor a tournament. The giant shadow of Richard Wagner, which had loomed over French music since the 1850's, hardly touched him. Therefore, conflicts that inspired creative reactions in contemporaries like Claude Debussy were to Ravel commonplace experiences which called for no change in his course and brought on no crises. The discovery of exotic sources of music during the 1889 Paris World's Fair, the fascination exerted by Russian nationalism in art, as displayed in the symphonies of Aleksandr Borodin and the tone poems of Nikolai Rimski-Korsakov, left traces in Ravel's music, without actually changing his mode of speech.

Ravel never became involved as an active partisan in any movement for or against any doctrine. He hardly ever concerned himself with the discussion of the artistic problems of his time, unless it were to defend the rights of the spirit against external powers or to restore to its rightful place those truths he felt had suffered debasement by the machinations typical of the times. In this manner he came to the defense of Debussy whenever he felt it necessary, but, on the other hand, he pointed out his own preeminence if the followers of Debussy might question it.

In World War I, when the outbreak of nationalistic hatreds on both sides of the Rhine threatened to destroy all objective judgment, even in the arts, it was Ravel who spoke up for the enemy aliens Bartók and Schönberg, an act of civil courage he likewise manifested when he rejected the offer of the Legion of Honor in 1920.

Ravel's music has, during the last few decades, gone through a reappraisal of value. It was at first regarded simply as one element in the entire complex of neo-French art, in which, without true differentiation, the works of Paul Dukas, Claude Debussy, Florent Schmitt, and several others were all included. The rubric of "Musical Impressionism" was applied as a usefully indefinite and indefinable title for quite a variety of musical phenomena, grouped together because they resisted more accurate analysis.

With the distance of historical perspective, their differences, not only in relative merit but also in modes of thought and expression, have become clearly recognizable, so that today the chief personalities in this superficial grouping, Debussy and Ravel, are identified no longer as twins in spirit, but indeed as opposites. Now it can be seen that Ravel was, from the beginning, the more sensitive personality, and, in this sense, the more consistent.

If it were possible to name the most conspicuous qualities of his many-sided output, the two words "polish" and "preciseness" would be the most appropriate. In his very beginnings Ravel felt the stimulus that ordinarily comes from the possibilities of conflict between these two concepts. For every refinement contains within itself the urge toward complexity and, also, toward clarification. On the other hand, the desire for clarification of the complex strives toward the ideal of simplicity. To reconcile these two tendencies, or, in certain cases, to limit their differences, is the innermost effort of all Ravel's music. One sees it not only in the larger forms, but also in the many smaller units of which they are composed. Refinement operates, in a general cultural sense, as a synthesis of superior achievement. In this way the contributions of more distant cultures enter the picture, those remote in geographical as well as in historical origins. On the other hand, this very cultural manysidedness must be taken into consideration in the search for clearer definition, as when Spanish folk themes or baroque composition forms are merged with the unmistakably modern post-romantic thought of a Frenchman of today.

There is an element of the enigmatic, a residue of unsolved riddles, in Ravel's music, as in his personality. This diminutive, odd little man, constantly alternating between intellectuality, elegance, and childlike playfulness, never let even his most intimate friends peep into the secrets of his private life. The circle of his friends was composed of people of most dissimilar tastes and origins. The homes that Ravel furnished for himself in Paris and in Montfort-l'Amaury are full of riddles, grotesque notions, and arbitrary collections of treasures and trash.

The titles he gave his works show the same unaccountable capriciousness that his little private reference library discloses. There we find strains of strict classicism alongside romanticized ghost stories, copies and imitations of entire musical models such as, for instance, a slow movement of Mozart, alongside fully original inventions and musical "gags" like the buildup of the *Bolero*. Cool and apparently dispassionate exercises in the realm of harmony and rhythm present a curious contradiction to the often violent eruptions of dynamic and rhythmic sound that appear in their background. Ravel, indeed, did everything he could to make the riddles in his music even more puzzling. Many of his titles, and of the musical interpretations he offered of them, just do not make sense. Admittedly, the apparently senseless and paradoxical was a spur to Ravel's creative fantasy. There is a sort of esthetic philosophy to this upside-down world, and this elegant, rather undersized man with the large handsome head seemed to be intoxicated by it.

Ravel was a man of many acquaintances. There were a large number of friendships in his life, all of which did not endure for long, but he did manifest a strong attachment to his friends, even if it were only for a limited time. If one can say of Beethoven that there never was a time in his life when he was without love, one can also assert that Ravel could not have survived, probably could not even have created, without strong attachments to friends.

There are not many great artists who have left behind so few documents casting light on their private and creative existence as has Ravel. This is of a piece with the peculiar shyness, confirmed by all his friends, of exhibiting his feelings. Not that he was incapable of feeling emotion, but he resisted giving such sentiment expression except in his music. Therefore, his not too numerous letters are often marked by a reflex of excess caution when he speaks of his emotions. They avoid telling anything that moves him inwardly, and only if one knows the biographical circumstances and knows how to read between the lines can one often decipher the real content and motive of the written words. At the same time, an emotion often emerges from his music like a flaming signal. Indeed, these little outbursts of flame exert the strongest fascination in the study of a style that almost invariably displays the same spotless and elegant exterior as did the outward appearance of the man who created it.

The era between 1890 and 1932, to which Ravel's creative life belongs, was the most colorful period in French life since the beginning of the Third Republic. The national rebirth after the collapse of the Second Empire in 1871 brought to fruition thousands of tendencies that had been spawned in the late romantic period of the mid-century. What passed for, and felt itself to be, French culture was more a synthesis of all the arts, and had its spiritual headquarters in Paris. Maurice Ravel, like so many other creative French artists, was not by birth a Parisian, but he was, from childhood, formed and polished by the metropolis. Without being himself what one calls an intellectual, he submerged himself instinctively and drank in all the experiences of the artistic life. He traveled in bohemian circles and with the culture-loving nobility, just as did many artistic figures in the novels of Marcel Proust (whom he met personally without, however, belonging to his circle of friends).

No knowledge of Ravel's art and its sources is possible without an illumination of the course of his development. However, the threads that link his life and *œuvre* are often hardly visible. The dedications he inscribed on his compositions seem to have been a result of chance as much as of the actual interplay of his life and his work.

The literature about Ravel, however rich it is in details of musical analysis, has not succeeded in closing the gaps in the events of his career and in understanding their significance. This book sets itself the task of analyzing the known connections between them and disclosing what up to now has had to remain hidden.

Maurice Ravel

Dedicated to my friend Josef Rufer

I 1875–1895

FAMILY BACKGROUND, 1875–1887

Men of the mountains have customs different from those of the coast. In the presence of perpetual snows, men's thoughts are turned back on themselves, on the sedentary virtues. Preciseness in little things, love of fine handiwork flourish here in the seclusion of long winters spent without contact with the outside world. In the little Swiss valleys they speak their dialects, preserved for centuries, which are not understood even in the next valley. The settlement becomes a microcosm. Whoever wishes to survive in it must do so in this narrowest circle. Therefore a special diligence is applied to artisanry. This balances any restlessness by seeking and achieving its highest objectives in the making of clockworks for small watches that have a worldwide reputation.

A different type of man grows up on the seacoast. He is averse to limitations. He wants to embrace the whole earth, seeks the distant, the difficult to attain, where legendary treasures lure him on. He does not flee the elements that menace him. He goes into combat with them, he defies them at sea in fishing boats and on sailing vessels. It is the catch of fish that bounds his existence, the unexpected windfall squandered or bestowed on him by chance. There is always a touch of adventure in the man of the seacoast, hankering for the unknown, the riddle, the exotic, a residue always of longing to be elsewhere, as, by contrast, there is always in the man of the mountains a homesickness that draws him back to the silence of his valleys.

Running obliquely southwest through southern France there is a road called the *Route d'Argent,* the Silver Highway. It starts near Lake Geneva, that silver droplet among the peaks of the Jura, the glaciers of Savoy, the snow massifs of Mont Blanc, and the gentle meadows of the Canton

1

Vaud. The best watchmakers in the world work there. This industrious artisanry is at home in the villages around Geneva, where they speak a broad, resonant French. It produces little miracles of precision and dependability, weighing only a few ounces, assembled out of tiny metal wheels and jewels. They are dwarf machines that measure a little bit of eternity and last longer than the life of a man, often more than a century, in their unceasing labor.

The Silver Highway follows the course of the Rhone, leads through the Beaujolais and the country of the black earth. From Toulouse it wanders westward through the dominion of two regions: that of the Pyrenees, whose peaks to the south overshadow vineyards, and that of the ocean, whose expanse is signaled by sky and clouds over the fields and the fruit orchards of the Armagnac. Beyond the Adour the Basque country begins. Hot springs gush forth from the rocks and perform the miracles of Lourdes. Gypsies live in the ravines and on the passes that lead across to Spain.

Near the border, where the Highway terminates, lie Saint-Jean-de-Luz and its twin city Ciboure. The mouth of the Nivelle opens into a little cove, protected from the storms of the Bay of Biscay. Fishermen and pirates have settled around here for thousands of years. Huge catches of tuna fish founded the fortunes of the locality.

Ciboure is the more modest of the twin sisters, but both have well preserved their Basque character. Their chalk-white houses are neatly built on red or green timber frames. They have galleries and balconies, sometimes a large courtyard, and wide overhanging steep sloping roofs for protection against rain. Every house has a name, generally that of a flower, a woman, or a favored season of the year. But the names are Basque, like the word "etch" which precedes them. It means "the house." The Basque language, generally spoken in the interior of the Basque country, has nothing in common with French or any other Latin or Teuton tongue. It has stubbornly withstood all Europeanizing influences, as have the costumes, the dances, and the music of its people.

The house in which Maurice Joseph Ravel was born in 1875 stands on the quay at Ciboure. It is a proud middle-class house sturdily built of stone, three tall stories high. Its wing-shaped spreading roof overtops all the houses in the neighborhood. It might seem that its architect had the intention of having his more modern urban building contrast with a little gem of a Basque cottage that had stood on the neighboring lot for centuries.

The child that came into the world here had two very dissimilar parents. Chance had brought them together in a Spain strange to both of them. They married in 1874. Both were strikingly handsome. The father, from a peasant and artisan family in Collonges, near Lake Geneva, was more than a gifted engineer. As a child he had a passionate love of music. In addition to pursuing his studies in the sciences, he attended the Geneva Conservatory, where he won a first prize in the piano class. Incidentally, the name Ravel appears in a variety of spellings: Ravex, Ravet, and Ravez. Apparently, Ravel is a mutilated version.

Pierre-Joseph Ravel led a restless, wandering life, quite the opposite of people of his race and region. In September, 1868, the engineer Ravel had a petroleum engine patented, with which he could set a vehicle in motion. With this, and with the later invention of a two-stroke motor, he belongs among the pioneers of the automobile. The pictures of him that have survived show an expressive face with a high forehead, dark wavy hair, a strong pronounced nose, keenly observant eyes, and a luxuriant full beard. The throat is decorated by a large cravat tied in an artistic knot.

Pierre-Joseph Ravel never lost his love of music, despite the thoroughness and brilliance of his engineering and

3

mechanical knowledge. It was natural that he should wish to realize in one of his sons the career he himself was denied. Fate fulfilled his wish in rich measure.

This expert mechanic met a Basque girl, Marie Deluarte, in the early 1870's. Her name, probably originally Eluarte, was later gallicized and eventually turned into Delouart. The family came from the Pyrenees, and Marie's birthplace seems to have been Ciboure. She, too, came from a modest background and undoubtedly was brought up in the old national traditions of the Basque race. The songs and dances of her people must have been as familiar to her as to every healthy young girl of her country.

We have no documentation as to the time she was sent to central Spain. However, it is certain that there, in 1873, in the province of New Castile, she met the Swiss engineer Pierre-Joseph Ravel. Born in Versoix in 1832, he was fifteen years older. He immediately fell in love with the beautiful twenty-six-year-old young woman with the slender Roman nose and the clear, well-modeled oval face that radiated kindliness and cheerfulness.

With a reputation already established, he had been sent to Spain in 1871 to work on building railroads. Immediately after the wedding the Ravels moved to Ciboure to stay in the house of the young bride's aunt.

Local gossip has it that Marie Ravel wanted to have her baby born in Spain, that she meant to travel south for this purpose in 1875, but had passport difficulties, and that only for this reason gave birth instead in Ciboure. However little confirmation there is for this legend, it shows that the stay of the Ravels in Ciboure was only by chance and was not meant by them to be a permanent residence. In fact, Pierre-Joseph Ravel went to Paris to look for employment, so he was not able to assist his wife when her difficult hour arrived. He was absent when his first son came into the world on March 7.

4

In his place Marie's aunt went to the registry office in the little baroque castle where the mayor's office was located, only a few hundred steps from her house, and gave notice of the event. It bears the number 21 in the register for the year 1875. The entry follows:

In the year one thousand eight hundred seventy-five, on the eighth March, appeared before us, the burgomaster and registrar of the town of Ciboure in the Canton of St. Jean de Luz, Department of Lower Pyrenees, as a witness, Gracieuse Billac, 50, fish dealer, resident in this town, who declared to us that Marie Delouart, 28, temporarily resident in Ciboure, lawful wife of Pierre-Joseph Ravel, yesterday at six o'clock in the evening at No. 12 rue du Quai, gave birth to a male child, which she exhibited to us, and declared that she wished to give it the first name Joseph Maurice; the said declaration and statements were made in the presence of Haramboure Renaud, 43, teacher, resident in Ciboure, and the witness, and we witnessed the aforementioned entry, but not the declarants as they cannot write, after it was read back to them. Harispuru Haramboure, the Burgomaster.

And five days later the infant was held over the baptismal font by the same fifty-year-old aunt Gracieuse Billac, who made her living as a fishmonger but could not write. It was no ordinary church where this solemn event took place on March 13, but the beautiful old basilica of St. Vincent. It stood opposite the rear of the house of birth. They had only to walk out the rear door of the house, cross the medieval rue Pocalette, and they were in the side court of the church, where, next to the portal carved in sandstone in 1579, a huge stone cross had been erected in 1760 in the center of the courtyard.

The inside of the church has its mysteries. From the flat roof there hangs a model of a two-master, decorated with pennants, symbol of the Seafarers' Guild, whose weather-beaten members take their seats on the three-tiered wooden platforms, their round black berets in their tough fists. Here is the altar, which the nuns approach from a side door, with silent, hidden faces, to say their prayers. A wrought iron screen and gilt ornaments soften the bare interior of this House of God. Its three-tiered steeple nestles among the hills and treetops of the rising hills around it; a little stair leads from the courtyard past the gardens of the houses that lie just above it. Their stone enclosures are covered by a plaster coping, as are the parapets of the quay in Saint-Jean-de-Luz. From above, at a distance, they resemble a mosaic of gay pebbles that combine to present a gleaming nonobjective composition.

Marie Ravel lived with her newborn son for three months on the Ciboure Middle Quay. For three long months she watched the bay in its changes from spring to summer, saw the harbor from which the little blue fishing smacks ran out and to which they returned from their short or long journeys in search of the spoils of the sea. During these months the child heard the cradle songs of his mother's Basque homeland. His eyes took in the first objects they glimpsed in the special, bright, almost shadowless sunlight of the Basque coast. Odors of seaweed, fish, and tar lay in the air.

All this must have left traces deep in the subconscious of the child, possibly faint traces, but strong enough for the yearning toward these coasts to remain lively in his memory.

Of the two heritages given to Maurice Ravel, the Swiss-Savoyard of his father, the Basque of his mother, the latter prevailed throughout his active life. Everything that related to the senses, the eyes, the ears, the nose, the taste (in the widest psychological sense of the word), was guided by the maternal inheritance, by the province and the people from which she sprang. The paternal influence made itself felt in the imagination. But Ravel was a Basque in all that

6

directly affected his work and his person. He consciously cultivated his Basque reactions. He came back constantly to his home surroundings, either as a summer sojourner who came to the beach at Saint-Jean-de-Luz for recuperation, as a creator who fled the big city to find peace and concentration in the little twin villages, or as an invalid, in the closing years of his life, to enjoy their pure air and strong sunlight.

His friends accompanied him often to Saint-Jean-de-Luz and to Ciboure. They were Ricardo Viñes, comrade of his youth and pianistic champion of his works; the violinist Hélène Jourdan-Morhange; the sculptor Léon Leyritz; his biographer Roland-Manuel; and, above all, his nearest and dearest friend, his younger brother by three years, Edouard Ravel, who later purchased the Villa Mayatza (where he died).

The contour of the house that Maurice Ravel later acquired in Montfort-l'Amaury, the Villa Belvédère, with its decorative turrets and its large wooden balcony, is reminiscent of a Basque villa of the nineteenth century.

Entirely different forces and capabilities can be traced to his father. His was the more positive nature, more versatile, transmitting to his son more of his inner qualities and creative processes. He was a restless Promethean spirit who tracked down the secrets of mechanics, physics, and chemistry. In more favorable circumstances, and with a stronger mercantile endowment, Pierre-Joseph Ravel might have become an Edison. He was a typical son of the second generation, the firstborn of a father who rose from simple farm-servant to owning a bakery and his own home. All the family's drive for economic improvement seems to have run out with this grandfather, Aimé Ravel. His sons were highly gifted but less concerned with possessions than with creativity, which for them was a sufficient end in itself. A younger brother of Pierre-Joseph Ravel, Edouard, achieved some prestige as a painter. Some of his paintings have come into the possession of French and Swiss museums.

Pierre-Joseph was undoubtedly the most interesting representative of his generation in the family. Inventiveness showed itself in him even in his childhood. But he obviously never understood how to turn the little timesaving gadgets and the practical results of his pottering about to commercial advantage. The inheritance he received from his father's estate gradually slipped through his fingers. The inventor of a device so prophetic of the future as a two-stroke internal combustion engine had to be satisfied with quite modest employment. Even a machine gun that he designed and put together found no favor in the eyes of a general to whom he was permitted to demonstrate it.

It was Joseph Ravel who decided that his son should be a musician. He found the lad gifted and promoted this gift as early as it was possible to do so.

The family left Ciboure in June, three months after Maurice's birth. They took up residence in Paris at 40 rue des Martyrs, not far from Montmartre. In 1882 Joseph found a piano teacher for Maurice. He was Henri Ghys, who had a good name as a musician and composer. Ghys kept a diary in which he made an entry on May 31 that mentions "the intelligent child Maurice Ravel." The boy was seven. A photo taken the year before shows him painstaking in his dress, his sailor collar buttoned, his hands rather shyly on his knees, collar and cuffs snow-white. The face is round, serious, and tense from posing, the eyes with a faraway look and a bit inquisitive, just as they often seemed later in his life.

Another picture, taken perhaps four years later, shows him with his father and his brother Edouard. The boy is more self-conscious. The head is framed by luxuriant curly hair. As in the earlier photo, the forehead is concealed by bangs. One foot is coyly pushed forward across the other in their high shoes. The expression of the face is cheerful, with a restrained smile, very like his father who sits with his arms happily around his two sons. The physical resemblance between Joseph and Maurice is unmistakable. The picture, probably an amateur snapshot, is evidence of the family's happiness, for the completeness of which only the presence of the mother is needed.

In fact there were hardly ever any misunderstandings among the Ravels. All four members of the little household, from whom the cares of existence could never have been far removed, clung to each other with the most sincere affection. The sons idolized their parents and received from them all the care and attention that their circumstances allowed.

There were two incursions of fate into Maurice Ravel's life that he felt as terrible blows, true catastrophes. For a time these laid his creative processes low. One was the death of his father after a long illness, on October 13, 1908; the other, the loss of his mother, who passed away January 5, 1917.

Edouard Ravel, who survived his brother Maurice by many years, felt his grief for the loss of his brother so keenly that he would break into sobs when reminded of it, even as an old man. The two brothers lived together for years when they were grown men. Their last house together was in Levallois, on the outskirts of Paris, in the rue Desmoulins. It was furnished for them in a bizarre, modernistic style by Maurice Ravel's friend, the sculptor Léon Leyritz, who selected bull's-eye panes of glass for it that had to be ordered from Germany. The house belonged to Edouard and his wife, who also lived in it. It stands next to a factory Edouard established and ran.

The volume of letters Maurice wrote his brother is large, especially when one considers how rarely they actually were separated. On the tour through the United States he wrote regularly every few days. In that correspondence artistic matters play practically no part at all; it is the outward life, colorful and varied, that the traveling musician shares with his brother. This seemed deeply necessary to him. He felt the need for his family, and, after the death of his parents, all the more for his brother, as so essential a part of his existence that he could not allow the contact ever to be interrupted.

This close tie with the family tree from which one has grown, this never-loosened link with the bonds of blood and the warmth of the family hearth, is common in France. But with Ravel this intimacy reached a level of influence on his creative and spiritual powers far beyond that in the average man. One might say that this sensitive individual, so disposed to defy, and, in unexpected ways, to oppose the outside world, was never able to part from his mother's bosom. The realm of his imagination remained all his life a specially personal kind of children's nursery, peopled by fairy-tale characters, magicians, strange animals with human ways, and fabulous creatures from Arabia, China, and Africa. It is a world of fantasy where humans can share in the marvels, the delights, and the surprises of the world beyond reality, the realm of wonders, of boundaries that disappear.

Ravel entered and inhabited this world of magic with his eyes wide open and with complete understanding of it. He was able to lay his hands on the objects in it, to model their mythical figures to his own measure, to dress them in gay garments, decorate them with rich ornament, which he himself had conjured up out of sound and rhythm in music.

MUSICAL BACKGROUND, 1887–1895

From his childhood Maurice Ravel had been stimulated and guided by his father into habits of methodical work. He was given a half-franc extra pocket money for each half hour of piano practice. This premium helped the child to make progress, though he was not by nature overly keen about playing scales. At age twelve Maurice was able to take a longer step along the road of his training as a musician. Beginning in 1887, he was taught by Charles-René how to analyze and invert chords. This new teacher, himself young, had been a winner of the Prix de Rome and a pupil of Léo Delibes, the ballet composer. He guided Maurice into the study of harmony, from harmony to counterpoint, and from counterpoint to composition. He taught on the shrewd principle of letting his pupils, from the beginning, compose passages of their own. According to Ravel's own account, during the two years of this period of study he wrote a set of variations on a theme from a song by Schumann, which show many traits that manifested themselves in his later works.

In a letter to Roland-Manuel, Charles-René speaks of Ravel's innate musical fecundity. This judgment was correct. Like Chopin, Ravel did not, fundamentally, once he had demonstrated his mastery at a very early stage, go through a period of growing development. He was one of those creative natures that bloom suddenly and unforeseen and emerge as a complete phenomenon. For them the achievement of artistic perfection is not a process of slow, painful growth and self-improvement. It is there as an inherent quality.

Meanwhile Ravel's parents had moved from the rue des Martyrs and taken lodgings temporarily in the rue Lavall. From there they moved again, in 1889, to a house at 73 rue Pigalle. Maurice was fourteen. His father Joseph then sent him to the Conservatory in the rue de Madrid, where he passed the entrance examination and was enrolled in Anthiome's piano class.

Love of the exotic was widespread in that genera-

11

tion. Paul Gauguin, the painter, succumbed so completely to the magic of the East that he left France for good to go and live among the simple, beautiful creatures of the South Seas. What was ostensibly primitive in music was accepted as the sign of an ancient culture unspoiled by contact with Occidental conventions. It confirmed the nostalgic yearnings of the most modern musicians who were striving to escape from the hundred-fold bonds of Rameau's cadences. The intoxication with color into which Ravel was transported by exotic music showed aftereffects in his orchestra all through his life, but he drew conclusions from it quite different from those of Debussy or Rimski-Korsakov.

Besides, he appreciated associations between tone color and harmony that were never analyzed, much less taught, in any conservatory or school of music anywhere in the world. The modest upright piano in the rue Pigalle that Maurice played began to produce effects that seemed to defy the laws of harmony. A more pronounced use of the damper pedal made the penetrating sweetness of successive sevenths in a piece by Chabrier overpowering. A shifting of the soft pedal conjured up a mysterious clarity so that a chord succession of Liszt, which had before been unintelligible, now made sense.

And Wagner? Naturally he was known, in fact very well known. Ravel knew his way around the score of *Tristan* at least as well as Debussy did. He understood, as did few Frenchmen, the riches of the chromatically extended chordal language and polyphony that Wagner had created as a flexible instrument to give voice to his philosophy.

But Ravel's youth began in the decades after the War of 1870, at a time of national and cultural self-appraisal for the French, especially for musicians who aspired to freedom from the thralldom of Wagnerism. These were the highly cultivated successors of Baudelaire and Théophile

Gautier who had passed through a thousand schools of taste. As the line goes in *Tristan*: "Deadly poisons need strong antidote." (*Für böse Gifte Gegengift.*) They needed antidotes for the strong poison of Wagnerian pathos that was still so clearly perceptible in the Knights of the Grail in Debussy's *Proses Lyriques.*

Admittedly their resistance was only hypothetical at first. They conspired together, slandered him, drew back to the safe bastions of "French good taste," from behind which they could safely attack Wagnerian standards as barbaric and questionable. To stimulate self-pride against Wagner's frightening conquest, they resorted to the esoteric, the culture of the anti-popular.

Even in his youth Ravel felt and loved Mozart as the authentic antithesis to high romanticism. Mozart was not the least of those who figured in the bouts of two-hand and four-hand piano music that Viñes and he looked through together and, so to speak, put under their microscope. Besides the Russians and Chabrier there were as many classics and romantics among them as moderns: Mozart, Schumann, Weber, Chopin, and Mendelssohn; Liszt, Gounod, Grieg, and Saint-Saëns.

This repertory is not too remarkable in and of itself. It becomes so only if the list of poets set to the music is perused: Mallarmé, Baudelaire, Huysmans, Edgar Allan Poe, and still others of these fantasts and satanists, glorifiers of opium intoxication and erotic eccentricity. There is no doubt of it: Ravel's literary taste went into directions different from his musical predilections. In his own province he was more conservative, one could almost say more middle-class, than when, in solitude, he was drawn into the realm of fantasy. He very plainly rejected in music what his literary leanings would have led him into: the Wagnerian philosophy of ecstasy and its complex psychology.

Meanwhile the long-haired page boy of the rue Pigalle was growing up into artistic apprenticeship. In 1891 he won a medal for his piano playing. He was able to graduate from Anthiome's preparatory class and was accepted in Charles de Bériot's piano class. He received his theory training from a very conservative professor, Émile Pessard. Later he dedicated his *Rapsodie Espagnole* to his piano teacher Bériot as a testimony of his respect and affection for him. Pessard is only casually mentioned in one of his autobiographical memoranda. Among his other theory teachers were such unyielding academicians as Napoléon-Henri Réber and Théodore Dubois. The latter would retire from his office as Director of the Conservatory because of the notorious "Ravel Affair." What Ravel got from his instruction was mostly the strength that develops from resisting it.

This does not mean he was a rebellious pupil. He did his assignments superbly. He found it easy never to break the rules that were prescribed as gospels of the art not to be questioned. Indeed, he exceeded the severity of his teachers by his own diligence.

This in itself should not have been enough to cause mistrust in those who encountered him in the corridors of the Conservatory. But there are indications that the young man with bobbed hair and a faraway look was not regarded as so upright and harmless a scholar as his school record and his exercise books would lead one to believe.

He openly cultivated the acquaintance of characters who espoused ideals entirely different from those of the professors at the Conservatory. It might have been understandable that Ricardo Viñes, the Spanish pupil of Bériot, an unruly and gifted pianist from Lérida, had the freedom of his parents' home. The two boys made music together. While it was not known exactly what they were playing, it was evident they were making progress. However, one day the rumor got around that the two of them had paid Emmanuel Chabrier a visit and had pounded out for that jovial, stout individual his own *Trois valses romantiques* for four hands, pieces that were known to contain dangerous, subversive tendencies. In general, this Chabrier was a musician under suspicion, in spite of the success of his *Roi malgré lui* at the Opéra Comique, in the building that subsequently burned down. Émile Pessard was not a bit pleased when, one day, Ravel brought him in class a copy of the *Chanson pour Jeanne*. In any event, Ravel and Viñes came back from their visit to Chabrier more sobered than proud.

But an association then began that was even more reprehensible. In his regular weekly rummagings through the stock at Durand's and Lerolle's, the big music dealers, Ravel had discovered a composer whose name no one knew. This was Satie, with his first name Erik ending in an atypical "k." Two albums of his piano music had appeared in print. The first was called simply *Sarabandes,* the other by the almost unintelligible title *Gymnopédies.* Was the latter supposed to deal with Greek youths dancing? The music itself was no less enigmatic. It went beyond the boldness of Chabrier and Grieg by a giant step. In a somewhat heavy-footed and unpolished piano style, it carried along parallel sevenths and ninths without even giving a thought to any resolution. At the cadences it avoided the leading tone, and by that device seemed to try to approach the spirit of ancient Greek modes.

Ravel was deeply impressed by this music. He immediately expressed a wish to meet the composer, of whom all that was known was that he lived in Paris. Now, more than ever, his father Joseph Ravel showed himself to be his son's best and most understanding comrade. Any small-minded, cautious parent would have timidly tried to keep his son far away from any such bizarre and unknown acquaintance. But the engineer and inventor, to whom, since 1868, people in Neuilly had referred as "the man who made the first gasoline vehicle run," at once arranged to bring Maurice and that queer chap Satie together. They met first in the Café Nouvelle Athènes in 1895. Ravel was then twenty. He was delighted to accept the unconventional advice given him by this new acquaintance, who was about ten years his senior and sported a velvet jacket and a pointed beard.

Satie had been a member of the Rosicrucian Order, a personal favorite of Sar Joseph Péladan, the leader of the sect, a pornographic romancer and fanatical pilgrim to Bayreuth, from whom, however, Satie did not conceal his aversion to Wagner. After he parted company from Péladan, Satie founded a sect of his own. The aura of bohemianism and talented dilettantism that surrounded Satie was as opposite to that in which the academic and brilliantly cultivated young Ravel moved as one could imagine. Probably it was just this that fascinated Ravel.

Satie had a complete lack of prejudice and an indifference to every rule of orderly life that impressed Ravel immensely. The distance from the Parnassians to the gypsies is great, but the two were united in Satie's rather questionable, unstable, ironic, and disrespectful personality. This composer of church music for a religious order without adherents, which was founded by and whose tenets were preached by himself, played piano at night in the Auberge du Clou and the Chat Noir to make a living. He had enrolled at age forty in the counterpoint class at the Schola Cantorum and passed the course with a good mark. He was famous, even notorious, for piano pieces with grotesque names, such as *Embryons desséchés (Dried Embryos)*, or *Véritables prèludes flasques pour un chien (Authentic Flabby Preludes for a Dog)*. In 1917, with Jean Cocteau and Pablo Picasso, he staged the ballet *Parade,* which inspired a change in the musical taste of Paris. In 1919, with his *Socrate*, he founded the movement toward neoclassicism that was joined by Igor Stravinsky.

DANDYISM AND PARADOX;
MENUET ANTIQUE, 1895

In most of the descriptions of Ravel we have from his friends, we encounter the idea of "dandyism." It is typical of *fin-de-siècle* France. Literally, it comes from a Hindu word *dandy*, which signified an upper official of the British Indian administration, aristocrats with exclusive habits of life and dress. To distinguish themselves from other Europeans, these "dandies" carried a small stick known as a swagger stick. In England itself dandyism had its best-known representative about 1800 in the beau George Brummell. The dandy type became a favorite figure in English novels of the period, which, in Germany, was contemporaneous with that of the much more solid-citizen style of Biedermeier furniture.

A little later dandyism produced a mental attitude that set artists and intellectuals apart from the average of ordinary humanity. Out of a background of fops and flirts there developed an intellectual aristocracy whose favorite concepts included "art for art's sake" and "the ivory tower." In England Lord Byron early showed traits of such literary dandyism. In France artistic spirits of the quality of Charles Baudelaire appropriated the same tradition of alienation and aloofness. Romantic elements are hidden in the impulse toward literary dandyism. The spiritual basis of Parnassianism and symbolism, which are indebted to dandyism, is likewise romantic.

Just as the symbolists conceal their thought behind symbols, so literary dandies love to make use of formulations that turn the sense of ideas to be expressed upside-down, but at the same time let their true meaning be apprehended. Out of this mental device there grows a manner of speech intentionally obscure, such as is practiced at its highest pitch in the poems of Stéphane Mallarmé and the plays of Maurice Maeterlinck. In this environment of ideas and figures turned on their heads, paradox becomes the preferred form of expression. When two mutually contradictory ideas or word meanings enter in combination, a new truth emerges in the form of an inner perspective, for which way must be made. This device of speaking in paradoxes is characteristic of the late romantic era. It reaches its most dazzling form in Oscar Wilde, who in himself embodies the latest type of Anglo-Irish dandy. Lord Henry Wotton, in Wilde's *Picture of Dorian Gray*, is an unmistakable dandy, not only in his outward appearance, but also in the witty paradoxes he utters.

We have pictures of Ravel as a boy of fourteen, after he graduated from the musical preparatory course and was sent by his parents to take the entrance examination at the Conservatory in the rue de Madrid. The clear eyes gaze out inquiringly at the world; a noble Roman nose forms the center of a long face with wide cheekbones that narrow down to a strong chin. The mouth, with thin lips, is serious, with only the faintest trace of the smile the camera might expect of him. Maurice is no longer a merry lad. His demeanor is made up of measured movements and expresses a youthful dignity such as is often met in musicians of his age. Later he experimented with his outward appearance, possibly because he never grew to the height of the average, normal man. He certainly suffered from the knowledge that his stature would always remain less than that of his friends.

His attractive, masculine, strongly developed head was poised on much too small and slender a body. Even as a youth he began to try to compensate for this painfully realized defect by cultivating elegance in his dress. He tried a whole series of styles of beard, until he finally decided to keep his face clean-shaven, as we know it in his later pictures. The little swagger stick he loved to carry was much remarked on by many contemporaries who met him about the turn of the century.

Roland-Manuel, his oldest pupil and friend, writes that when he first met Ravel he thought he was a jockey. The writer Colette, who later worked closely with him, constantly compared him to a squirrel. These contradictory comparisons tell much about Ravel's physical appearance. They keep cropping up in a variety of descriptions.

For him elegance was not merely an external habit, but, as with many Latins, a way of life, an outlook on the world. Only those not familiar with this type are surprised at actions such as his friends often mention. For instance, when he came to the premiere of *L'Heure Espagnole,* he remarked to a friend: "Have you noticed that we are the only ones here not wearing midnight-blue evening jackets?" On his tour of America in 1927, Ravel took along fifty shirts. In all questions of dress his urge toward the extreme would assert itself.

The paradoxical became a part, an inseparable element, of his artistic existence. Everything he came across in the way of artistic or creative phenomena that was beyond conventional powers of comprehension aroused his admiration and charmed him into increased activity.

In 1889, and for the fourth time, Paris experienced the enormous turmoil of a World's Fair. Once more the nation, humiliated and sorely wounded by the catastrophe of 1871, lay at the focus of world interest. It not only enjoyed this role, it drew varied intellectual and economic benefits from the colorful parade of goods, production methods, and cultures that were put on display.

The encounter with Japanese and Chinese art was

as much a revelation to the painters of the school of impressionism as was the experience to the musicians of hearing North African and Hindustani singers and instrumentalists, the Annamite theater, the dances and the gamelan music of Indonesia. While the work of building the steel Eiffel Tower three hundred meters high excited the technical imagination of twenty-eight million visitors, these exotic arts drew the attention of the young intellectuals and awakened them to cultural possibilities outside modern Western civilization. Young composers like Claude Debussy and Erik Satie, just arrived at manhood, stood transfixed before the apparent freedom and the revolutionary strangeness of musical forms from the Far East. What they had only vaguely apprehended as an exotic and, as it were, perpetual background in the scores of the Russian nationalist innovators—in the piano and the orchestral works of Balakirev, Borodin, Moussorgsky, and Rimski-Korsakov—now lay open before them: a world of unknown sounds, incomprehensible rhythms, instruments never before heard, and forms without restrictions.

All this must have had the effect of a thunderclap on a sensitive youth like Ravel. An unusual, hypnotic music penetrated him, without tonality in the European sense, but strictly tied to a tonal center that is never abandoned, without harmony or polyphony as taught by the rules and without the metric straitjacket of bar lines. Beautiful brown-skinned people played an assortment of instruments of bizarre shape: lutes, bronze kettles, metal discs, ringing wood blocks, and trumpets built like an hourglass. A sea of sounds, never before heard, surged out of a tinkling, bright-colored gurgling orchestra in dynamically rising and falling waves. In a short autobiographical text that Ravel later wrote, he says: "Even as a small child I was receptive to every kind of music." '

The composing experiments of those early years

have been forgotten. We have only a slight knowledge of Ravel's inner attitude at that time from remarks of a friend of his youth. Ravel entered the piano class of Charles de Bériot in 1891 after leaving Anthiome's preparatory class. It was then that he met a Spanish youth with a long narrow countenance, thick black eyebrows, and nervous hands. The Spaniard played the piano magnificently and had a clear, quick Latin mentality. He was Ricardo Viñes, born in the same year as Ravel. He set great store in being a Catalan, from Lérida, the seat of an old bishopric with a famous cathedral.

The boys introduced their mothers to each other. Madame Ravel, the Basque, was delighted to meet another woman who, like herself, was not entirely at home in Paris. They spoke Spanish to each other. The sons played the piano together. Viñes later developed into a pianist with an individual style, a tireless champion of modern French music from Debussy and Ravel to Messiaen, Jolivet, and Daniel-Leseur. From him we get our first description of the decisive years 1889 to 1895 in Ravel's youth. At that time, according to Viñes, the stamp of Ravel's individuality was already seen most markedly. He consciously cultivated a style of his own, a style, to quote the expressive phrase of Viñes, *"à la manière de lui-même."* Only after puberty did Ravel become simpler, more natural, more companionable, more spontaneous in his utterance. Only with increasing reputation did he learn to set aside a certain affectation that was almost natural to him.

At that time Ravel's intellectual leanings were all toward everything rare, unusual, and delicate, turned toward every form of poetry and fantasy, the opposite of all that would interest a classically trained mind. "Receptive to every kind of music," he had said of himself—receptive, one should add, to the choicest utterances of the spirit, that is, in literature. In this respect he was unlike the somewhat older Debussy, who was more susceptible to visual impressions, therefore more strongly attracted than was Ravel to the graphic arts of his own time.

As did so many young artists of the time, Ravel loved to strike the pose of the bored esthete. He wanted to be misunderstood, another mad poet full of contempt for everything popular, even for popularity itself if his own artistic efforts had the slightest chance of being well received.

Although thirsty for literature as were few others, Ravel as a young man displayed a most remarkable, almost enigmatic strain in his intellectual shyness. He never carried books about with him or left them lying around in his room. He read incessantly, but what he read he hid away with cunning, even from his closest friends. The books were, as could be ascertained later, almost without exception those of authors who could be considered among the decadents of their day: Stéphane Mallarmé, Joseph de Maistre, Charles Baudelaire, Joris Karl Huysmans, Edgar Allan Poe, Barbey d'Aurevilly, Villiers de l'Isle Adam, Paul Verlaine, and possibly Oscar Wilde as well.

The intellectual dandyism and the aloofness of his literary taste are reflected in the titles he gave his earlier music. There are piano pieces and songs with names like *Sérénade Grotesque* or *Ballade de la Reine morte d'aimer* or *Sites Auriculaires.*

The earliest published piano piece of that period is dated 1895. It was printed three years later by Enoch in Paris. It bears the unusual title *Menuet Antique.* The name is a paradoxical anachronism. There were no minuets, at least by that name, before the sixteenth century. They were then a variety of bransles, old French dances. In the seventeenth century the minuet became current as a folk dance from Poitou. Needless to say, the ancients knew nothing of minuets, and Ravel was very well aware of this. What was his reason for this anachronistic name? In an inset square, the title-page shows a picture sketched by P. Borie. It pictures a Greek shepherd, surrounded by vine tendrils, playing an aulos, a double reed instrument like those represented on many ancient Greek vases. His hands also grasp a posy of roses. The pseudoantique character of the illustration is plain. The music, too, has similar traits, without pretending, however, to be an imitation of Greek models in its polyphony and harmony. It is only the consistent avoiding of the leading tone, of the raised seventh in minor, that indicates its pretonal character. It might just as readily have been modeled on church modes as on ancient systems of tonality.

The tempo is very slow for a minuet. The marking *majestueusement* is more appropriate to a sarabande than to a *bransle à mener*. Perhaps in that very manner Ravel wished to differentiate his piece from classic minuets, that is, the type cultivated by composers from Lully to Mozart. The broad 3/4 measures first contain figures in sixteenths, later, in the middle section, dotted or regular eighths. Characteristic of Ravel's thinking in dissonances is the first chord with the constricted harmony B–D–E sharp–F sharp. The basic key is F sharp minor; the tonic appears at once together with the neighboring half tone, E sharp, the subdominant B and its third, D. The very fact that the lower neighboring step, E sharp, is here coupled with the tonic evidences how little Ravel feels it as a leading tone.

Characteristic also is the rapid modulation, first to C sharp, then to D sharp, finally to F minor. In the closing section of cadences the leading tone is always replaced by the lower seventh degree, and the major tonic is linked with the dominant. This gives an effect borrowed from the world of old church modes. The piece ends Mixolydian. Sequences, repetitions of similar phrases on successively lower steps, are carried out in antiquated fashion with contrary motion in the middle voice. Even the notation of the sixteenths, from the fifth measure on, shows a paradoxical tendency, as Ravel beams groups of four sixteenths against the downbeat and the bar lines.

The piece is in the ternary song-form, A–B–A. The middle section is in F sharp major. The exactly specified dynamic markings and pedal directions are extraordinary, especially the passage in the middle section where, in triple piano, both pedals are applied and each pair of chords is to be played *sans aucune accentuation*. With its abruptly changing dynamics, the piece requires an uncommonly experienced performer despite the absence of technical difficulties. It is dedicated to Ricardo Viñes.

Ravel wrote other minuets later, such as that on the name of Haydn in 1909, and the one in the *Tombeau de Couperin* in 1917, which are closer to the spirit of the baroque dance but are never copies of its familiar type. This is consistent with his inborn nonconformism, his inclination to appear to submit to the rules but all the more emphatically to disobey them.

In French music of the time, the affixing of paradoxical titles was not infrequent. Erik Satie in 1913 published an album named *Croquis et Agaceries d'un gros Bonhomme en Bois* (*Sketches and Annoyances of a Big Fat Wooden Man*), including a piece with the bizarre name *Tyrolienne Turque*. Ravel himself followed his *Menuet Antique* with a little piece that rapidly became famous, which had the unusual name *Pavane pour une Infante Défunte*. When he was asked what he meant by the title, he replied: "I let myself be led into writing that title because of the pleasure I got from the assonance of the words."

CHABRIER AND SATIE

The piano brought Ravel constant stimulation from manifold and varied sources. His friendly companionship with Viñes assured him that there never was a lack of objectives for their joint exploration. When intellectual interests bind them together, there is an easy, attractive, and generous rivalry in discovery among young friends through which they conquer worlds of new artistic expression. Viñes has informed us what music kept the two of them occupied, entranced, and disturbed—works of the Russian innovators, piano pieces and scores of Franz Liszt, bold harmonic departures by Edvard Grieg and by several French contemporaries.

They discovered sevenths and ninths as new, inexhaustible, and hardly explored charms. To be sure, they had always existed, in romantic as well as in classic music, but, like all other intervals and chords, they had been understood and taught, since Zarlino and Rameau, as elements in a canonically fixed technical esthetic system. To write a seventh presupposed, to every composer who abided by the rules, the understanding that it must be resolved since it occupied a definite station in the hierarchy of harmony, that its wide interval span sounded two degrees within the key, and that this key must take precedence over all other things in the world of harmony. And the same went for ninths, although even less freedom was accorded to them than to sevenths, because an ancient law forbade their being inverted.

But this was completely different with Franz Liszt, with the Russian innovators, above all with Edvard Grieg, and naturally with Emmanuel Chabrier, whom Ravel admired so greatly. In their work the dangerous dissonant intervals stood as entities valued for themselves. One could probe, could taste, could listen to their caustic euphony, let them enter one's imagination, let them die away to nothingness on the piano by holding down the pedal.

In such a context, they no longer found or needed any resolution. Indeed, they were hardly even sensed as elements of a key, but stood independently as glowing color complexes in an impressionistic painting, or as enigmatic and unexplained words and sound sequences in a poem by Mallarmé or Baudelaire. Just as in contemporary lyric poetry, vistas were opening out in music toward a world of shapes without demonstrable origins, the strict logic of which was nevertheless asserted by a highly developed feeling for form.

All these precious discoveries found their way to Ravel and his friend Ricardo Viñes through their music-making together. They ploughed through whole libraries of four-hand music tirelessly and with insatiable curiosity and listened to each other just as endlessly. Among the Russian rarities that Viñes played for his colleague was the formidable *Islamey* fantasy of Mili Balakirev, the exotic and virtuoso style of which made a deep impression on young Ravel. Among contemporary French works he was especially taken with the *Gymnopédies* of Erik Satie and the *Valses Romantiques* and *Menuet Pompeux* of Chabrier, which he orchestrated in 1918.

Ravel expressed himself about this period in his autobiographical text:

My first compositions, which remained unpublished, date from about 1893. I was then in Pessard's harmony class for instruction. The influence of Emmanuel Chabrier was evident in the *Sérénade Grotesque* for piano, and of Erik Satie in the *Ballade de la Reine morte d'aimer*. In 1895 I wrote my first published works: the *Menuet Antique* and the *Habanera* for piano. I consider that this work contains in the bud several elements that would govern my later compositions.

The development he underwent in his early years at the Conservatory was much more thorough than he would later credit or, out of modesty, he would admit.

Chabrier certainly occupied first place in the treasure trove unearthed by the two friends playing music of French origin for four hands. This musician had lived mostly in Paris, from 1841 to 1894, his training in law equipping him for a position as an official in the Ministry of the Interior. However, he was a brilliant pianist and composer in whom the early influence of Wagner could not diminish the unique and individual talent he possessed. Paul Verlaine wrote two libretti for him. The French gift of gaiety was inborn in him and explained the European success of his opera *Le Roi malgré lui,* which, shortly before the burning down of the Opéra Comique, delighted the Paris public, a success that was confirmed on the Berlin stage, where it was played from 1889 to 1931 as *Der König wider Willen.* Chabrier's *España* is counted among the most successful products of French hispanicism of the late nineteenth century. Chabrier, indeed, was the first, after Bizet, to continue the exploration of musical Spain. A whole tide of compositions ensued, often of lighter content, which finally ebbed in 1913 with the lightsome banter of Erik Satie's piano piece *España.*

That came, to be sure, long after the young Satie had disconcerted and upset the good solid Parisian citizens with his early efforts in composition and his highly irregular mode of life. Ravel became acquainted with Satie's unusual *Sarabandes* in 1890, when the velvet-jacketed composer was already under the influence of Sar Péladan and ensnared in the mysticism of the Rosicrucians. This was something he, for a while, regarded as quite compatible with his activity as the house pianist in Paris nightclubs. Young Ravel brought the *Sarabandes* enthusiastically into Pessard's harmony class, where, presumably, it aroused more interest among his fellow students than with the professor himself.

Debussy later orchestrated the first and the third of these *Sarabandes*. The third, in its spare original version for piano, is the one that, above all, was important to Ravel in the development of his musical speech, in which the accents of Chabrier and Satie were somewhat softened, never losing, however, their inner keenness.

UN GRAND SOMMEIL NOIR, 1895; SITES AURICULAIRES (HABANERA), 1895; SAINTE, 1895–1896

In his autobiographical summary Ravel fails to mention a song that was written (it bears the date, August 6, 1895) at about the same time as the *Menuet Antique*. The deeply depressing poem to which it is composed is by Paul Verlaine. Its opening words, *Un grand sommeil noir,* also gave the song its title. Roland-Manuel published it in 1953, the manuscript having been in the possession of Ravel's friend Lucien Garban. Like Ravel, Garban had been educated in Fauré's class. He was a man of sure taste and dependable judgment, and his friendship with Ravel lasted all through the composer's later years.

Verlaine's poem pictures a life about to be extinguished and calls it a cradle rocked by a hand from a tomb. For this disconsolate mood Ravel finds an astonishingly suitable expression. The alto voice intones the entire beginning of the song on the low note, G sharp, sung twenty-three times; this note is also repeated seven times at the ending.

The song is governed by an esthetic of repetition that affects the first eight measures at once. These are completely identical, repeating the triads E major–F minor–C sharp minor–F minor over the bass notes B, G sharp, C sharp, G sharp.

In the middle section, where in a narrow space the voice rises two octaves from A to A″, the chain of chords lies just at the limits of the key and makes unrestricted use of the right to apply dissonance without resolution. The melody exhibits a marked alternation between recitative-like tone repetition and excited rocket-propelled ascents upon which the drop from the peak imediately follows. Toward the end the melodic line condenses into a sequence in which a falling figure with the compass of a fourth is repeated, each time on a lower degree.

The dynamic changes are as violent as the melodic. The song begins piano, then increases in volume until it reaches the middle section, which begins pianissimo only to be driven in a mighty crescendo to triple forte. After this, the intensity decreases, until the whole piece is brought to a conclusion on the word "silence," dying away from a triple piano.

The composition captures the whole of Ravel's aloof dandyism, and with it the deep groundless melancholy that only young men feel. At that time one spoke of such feelings as the mood of *fin-de-siècle* if one did not prefer the English word "spleen," difficult to translate into French. In its literary application we know this phenomenon as depressive symbolism. Roland-Manuel accurately speaks of the completeness and the self-sufficiency of this song. It goes far beyond a youthful effort.

Just as Ravel's leaning toward unconventional harmony and dissonant half tone combinations is evident in *Menuet Antique* and in the Verlaine song *Un grand sommeil noir*, his love of Spanish rhythms makes itself felt in another work of the same year, 1895. Its earliest document is the *Habanera,* first composed as a piece for piano four hands, accompanied by another called *Entre Cloches.* Both pieces obviously sprang from the musical association with Ricardo Viñes. Together they bear the contradictory name *Sites Auriculaires. Entre Cloches,* actually written in 1896, has remained unknown and unpublished, but both pieces were given their premiere, from extremely illegible manuscripts, by Ricardo Viñes and Marthe Dron on March 5, 1898.

This was at one of the regular concerts presented by the Société Nationale de Musique under the sponsorship of the Schola Cantorum. The audience was overwhelmingly conservative. This was consistent with the tone of the Cantorum, which cautiously adhered to the oldest traditions. In its circle they respected the old polyphony, took pains to know Bach's works thoroughly, and gave a hearing only to that new music which was produced by César Franck and his followers.

So it was not surprising that the first public performance of such music as Ravel's met with complete lack of understanding and was greeted with protests. Claude Debussy was one of the listeners at this unsuccessful performance. He was so captivated by the *Habanera* that he asked Ravel to lend him the manuscript. Five years later Debussy wrote his three *Estampes,* the second of which, *Soirée dans Grenade,* shows a striking consistency with the principal harmonic concept of Ravel's *Habanera* and even follows its rhythmic structure. The result was a lawsuit between the two composers over the claim of priority. Although it was settled out of court, it became the subject of lively gossip in Parisian music circles. Today we can no longer doubt that Ravel was the originator, Debussy the imitator. At any rate, the harmonic effect is too striking to make it possible to speak of casual coincidence in the inventions. It consists of a cluster of three adjacent chromatic tones. (This frequently recurs in Ravel's writing.) A chord of the second, B sharp–D–F sharp–A, is associated with the tonic C sharp, which is rhythmically repeated in octaves so that the neighboring tones B sharp, C sharp, and D sound together. The same combination is repeated later on different steps such as the dominant G sharp and the subdominant F sharp. It is not difficult to advance an explanation of this according to the laws of traditional harmony if one knows the historical development of modern harmony. The chord of the Neapolitan sixth, which Henry Purcell had applied as early as 1691 in his *King Arthur*—therefore somewhat earlier than the Neapolitan opera composers—is a triad on the lowered second degree, e.g., D flat major in the key of C major, and stands directly beside the tonic. It can, however, also be resolved through a dominant triad, omitting the tonic, so that D flat major (in the first inversion, F–A flat–D flat) and G major (in the 6/4 position, D–G–B) follow each other. The tonic C, closed in from above and below, then appears to be a resolution.

Tonal cadences often appear in this form in Schubert, even more frequently in Anton Bruckner, who, for example, constructs the main theme of his Ninth Symphony on this span of a half tone. In view of the historic law that melodic formations, that is, formations in horizontal sequence, later are transformed into harmonic formations, that is, in vertical arrangement, the occurrence of the three tones together in one chord is easily understandable. Incidentally, one can, in any event, point to such combinations in older compositions over pedal points.

But in the daringly radical form used by Ravel in the *Habanera* the phenomenon is new. It corresponds to the desire of his harmonic thought to make use of the keenest dissonance while, at the same time, never to violate the basic sovereignty of the tonic, that is, of the tonality. This chord structure, which made so great an impression on Debussy that he had to follow it, appears all through Ravel's entire output. It does not diminish Debussy's greatness to assert that he was unusually receptive to such impressions. In his writing he frequently copied, unaltered, from the work of other composers, chord combinations that struck him. The most interesting of such instances is the sequence of five quartal chords that he took over without alteration in his *Six Epigraphes Antiques* and in the piece *Pour la Danseuse aux Crotales* from a song by Alban Berg that had previously been published.

Ravel later orchestrated his own *Habanera* and incorporated it in his *Rapsodie Espagnole* as its third movement. In doing so he emphasized the 1895 date of its original composition by having it printed at the top of the orchestral version, as the latter did not come out until 1907.

There have been many habaneras in French music since Bizet's *Carmen*. The piquant rhythm of this dance, which emigrated from Spain to the West Indies and then remigrated, enriched by some exotic features, to the land of its origin, consists of a combination of dotted eighths plus sixteenths and eighths in triplets, to which an evenly measured motion in eighths is added. We are, therefore, dealing here with an instance of polyrhythms within the narrowest scope, the numberless possibilities of which both Ravel and Debussy exploited, as have Manuel de Falla and the majority of modern Spanish composers. In 1907 Ravel wrote a *Pièce en forme de Habanera* which was first sketched as a vocalise, that is, a piece for a singing voice without words, but later reworked for a large orchestra.

In 1896 Ravel wrote his first song to a text by Stéphane Mallarmé. This was seventeen years before the *Trois Poèmes,* which occupy such an isolated position in his entire output. The youthful song is called *Sainte.* Mallarmé's poem is about a picture of a saint in a gold frame, into which viols, a flute, and a mandolin are carved. The saint holds a book; over her an angel plays on a golden harp. The last words of the poem are: *Musicienne du silence,* so this song, too, closes with the same word that ended *Un grand sommeil noir.* Ravel applies the same device, the repetition of identical measures, that we find in the earlier song, but from the very beginning he gives the voice a quiet, undulating movement. In it both archaic-sounding and pentatonic aspects are juxtaposed. Only in the last three measures, over the words just quoted, does the device of psalmody appear on the single note F, which is sung eight times. The song is in an archaic G minor without leading tone, but closes with the ninth chord E flat–G–B–D flat–F.

SHÉHÉRAZADE OVERTURE, 1898;
THREE SHÉHÉRAZADE SONGS: ASIE,
LA FLÛTE ENCHANTÉE,
L'INDIFFÉRENT, 1903

It appears that at about this time Ravel abandoned the idea of preparing himself for a career as a piano virtuoso. Bériot became dissatisfied with his gifted pupil because, while Ravel performed his assignments, he was not working at his piano with enthusiasm. His teacher is said to have called him, in an access of fury, a "criminal" because, while he was capable of leading the class, he was the lowest in it. Viñes advances, as an excuse for Ravel's pianistic negligence, the congenital and obviously incurable smallness of his hands, which certainly would have hindered him from reaching the top as a virtuoso. But it is also certain that Ravel's artistic aspirations were toward creation, not interpretation. This was evidenced by the eagerness with which he dissected music and then applied the results of his analyses.

In 1897 he reached the goal he coveted, to be accepted in the advanced class at the Conservatory for young students of composition. Here he met others of his own generation like Charles Koechlin and Florent Schmitt. In his autobiographical sketches he writes:

> In the year 1897, while I was studying counterpoint and fugue, under the direction of André Gédalge, I entered Gabriel Fauré's composition class. I am happy to say that I can thank André Gédalge for the most worthwhile elements of my handiwork. As for Fauré, the encouragement I received from his artistic counsel was no less profitable. My unfinished and unpublished opera *Shéhérazade*, which was very strongly controlled by Russian influences, stems from this period.

Gédalge, of the vintage of 1856, had studied composition under Giraud at the Conservatory, and won his second Grand Prix de Rome in 1885. Jules Massenet entrusted the teaching of counterpoint and fugue to him. He was one of the pedagogues who inspired a whole generation of highly gifted French musicians. He was uncommonly active in all spheres of music, but as a composer (he even wrote operas) he never gained recognition. Among his pupils were Ernest Bloch, Georges Enesco, Roger-Ducasse, Jacques Ibert, Arthur Honegger, Darius Milhaud, and many others. Darius Milhaud has written an engaging description of his teaching methods, which, apparently, were strict but free of convention.

Fauré, on the other hand, depended, more than anything else, on the authority of his reputation as a composer. He sprang from the group around Camille Saint-Saëns, who brought him up in the spirit of Wagnerian and post-Wagnerian music. He first became a professor of composition at the Conservatory in 1896 as a successor to Massenet. Through his classes, too, passed the most highly gifted among the music students of the time, among others Émile Vuillermoz (who later became a musicologist) and Nadia Boulanger, the most prominent composition teacher of all. Fauré's influence on these young people who entrusted themselves to his artistic leadership was much stronger than one would surmise from his gentle, almost feminine, and conciliatory manner. The master, whose songs aroused the same admiration and affection in France as did those of Schumann fifty years earlier in Germany, found his own musical development outside the Conservatory. He was as familiar with Gregorian melody and singing methods as with the romantic music of Germany, and, as teacher, he acknowledged no prejudices. In harmony he belongs to the generation of great explorers before Debussy and Ravel. In his mastery of form he shows some similarity to his teacher Saint-Saëns, whom Ravel learned to admire through him. In Fauré's music the element one terms "atmospheric" plays an important role. It was just this quality that he knew how to develop in each one of his pupils.

Shéhérazade is the legendary narrator of the tales in the *Thousand and One Nights*. The name is Persian. It means "of noble countenance." Her appearance in legend, associated with both love and death, has appealed to the imagination of many composers. Nikolai Rimski-Korsakov, in 1888, wrote an orchestral suite about this teller of tales. Through its choreographic embodiment by Sergei Diaghilev and its performances by the Ballet Russe it subsequently became famous. Ravel composed parts of an opera on the same theme in 1898. He himself conducted the premiere of the Overture a year later at a concert of the Société Nationale, where it evoked both applause and catcalls. In 1903 he composed a cycle of three songs to texts by Tristan Klingsor which bears the same name as the unfinished opera but is independent of it.

During these years Ravel forged a close bond of

friendship with Florent Schmitt, who became his most serious partner in an exchange of ideas that went on for years. In 1899 Schmitt entered the period of complete seclusion required to compete for the Conservatory's Prix de Rome. This meant that for a time he was completely without direct contact with the outside world. Therefore, Ravel had to write him a report of the disputed success of the *Shéhérazade* Overture. It is the oldest letter from him now preserved:

You have every right, dear friend, to regard me as quite negligent, but I have some excuses ready at hand. The first is that I got your letter only last Monday, because I had not gone to the Conservatory the week before. The second is that I am busy on entr'actes, with which I am not yet reaching port. How I envy you, being submerged in the bliss of writing your cantata!

Let me speak a little about the Nationale evening. Koechlin's piece succeeded very well, as we expected. The impression he makes is really enchanting; it was the part of the concert that seemed to me the most original. No doubt it was just for this reason that G. V. [abbreviation for Gauthier-Villars] allotted him only three lines. As that . . . (choose your own epithet) correctly wrote, *Shéhérazade* was violently whistled at. But there was a lot of debate as well, and my love of truth obliges me to recognize that those who applauded were much more numerous than the protesters, for I was called out twice.

D'Indy, whose attitude toward me was perfect, exulted over the fact that the public could still get excited over anything. As far as I could judge from the podium, I was satisfied with the orchestration. The critics found it rather picturesque. *Ménestrel* went so far as to call it "unique."

I could not remind Koechlin about the visit he owes you, as I have not seen him since I got your letter. I wish you courage, dear friend, for your last days in seclusion. Greetings to all the friends. Hearty handshake.

If one may now appraise the Overture in light of the songs, written five years later, its impact must have been striking, for in the songs we hear already the first unmistakable colors of the Ravel orchestra, which always sounds clear and transparent in spite of all its blending. For instance, do not the woodwind solos of the song *La Flûte Enchantée* express the same mood as the flute passages of Chloë's dance in the ballet *Daphnis and Chloë?* The three songs are usually performed in the same sequence as in the printed version: *Asie, La Flûte Enchantée, L'Indifférent*. However, Émile Vuillermoz asserts that when Ravel himself conducted them he put *La Flûte Enchantée* at the beginning and *Asie* at the end, so that *L'Indifférent* became the middle section of the triptych.

Tristan Klingsor, one year Ravel's senior, had been his friend since the turn of the century. He describes Ravel as spare of build and stubborn, outwardly enjoying fun, but inwardly inflexible. To Klingsor he seemed secretive because he was too shy to let his inner thoughts become apparent. His humor helped him to mask his true feelings. This ambitious dreamer loved to pretend that he was interested only in externals. It gave him pleasure to play the dandy. With the most serious face in the world he would allow his cravats and socks to be admired and he would discuss their colors. Klingsor was a member of a group with which Ravel also associated, the "Apaches," centered around the painter Paul Sordes. It was there that, at Klingsor's suggestion, Ravel read the poem *Asie*. Its free rhythms arrested his attention. The same freedom in musical rhythm governs the *Shéhérazade* songs, and they possess the same predominantly recitative-like melody we have previously observed in the song *Un grand sommeil noir* of 1895.

Prosody, that is, the relationship of the melody to the words, has been a subject of much controversy in France ever since the Middle Ages. In French different laws are observed in song from those for speech. For instance, the silent ultimate syllables are made audible in song. Under the influence of Wagner, occasional efforts were made to replace the artificial prosody of song with one more natural to speech. Debussy took important steps in this direction in *Pelléas et Mélisande*. Such tendencies are hardly visible in *Shéhérazade*, but obviously the recitative parlando style was just the medium in which he could avoid the problem. The end syllables are very seldom suppressed, as, for instance, in the verse: *En des peaux jaunes comme des oranges*. In other instances the preceding note is merely repeated on the ultimate syllable, the melodic structure taking no notice of it.

Ravel's music even this early bore his special personal stamp as coming from a world apart, of having grown hidden in a place far from human reality, an esthetic cultivation attainable only through esoteric detachment. It shows the point of view of Mallarmé, full of contempt for success, for popularity, for the academic as well as for the respectable. Beyond that, it is most painstakingly elaborated. Ravel takes the trouble not to leave the slightest detail to chance.

In the quotation from the letter to Schmitt the name of the critic Henri Gauthier-Villars is indicated by the initials G.V. In fact, Gauthier-Villars was not very well disposed toward young Ravel. He is the source of some of the most severe rejections of Ravel's earlier works. Later he frequently wrote over the pen name "Willy." His wife, who frequently met Ravel during his aristocratic period, was the famous novelist Colette. It was the irony of fate that she became his collaborator in one of his greatest masterpieces, the ballet–opera he wrote for the stage, *L'Enfant et les Sortilèges*, although by that time she was no longer married to Gauthier-Villars.

In the battle over music written after the last decade of the nineteenth century, Willy always stood on the side of the reactionaries. The letters he published in *Echo de Paris* from 1895, signed *Ouvreuse du Cirque d'Été,* aroused the indignation of Erik Satie, who was then the leader of a sect he had himself founded, the *Église Métropolitaine d'Art de Jésus Conducteur.* In a kind of house journal of the sect named *Cartulaire,* Satie pronounced his ban against the critic, whom he insulted in the coarsest manner because of an article G.V. had written ridiculing Wagner. This was not necessarily because Satie was all for Wagner but because such an incompetent critic had dared to publish an appraisal that only he, Satie, was capable of writing. Gauthier-Villars' scoffing effusions were also directed against Debussy's early works.

What seems noteworthy in this attitude of the Paris daily press at the end of the century is only that it was hiding behind the pseudonym of an anonymous and fictitious usherette, intended to be a representative of the lower classes. This realistic gesture was in distinct contradiction to the then current level of criticism in Paris, the most prominent representatives of which were more disposed to give expression only to aristocratic points of view.

Pierre Lalo was also one of the faultfinders at that time. He censured the structural shortcomings of works by Grieg, Rimski, and Balakirev for the same lack of cohesion in their basic plan and in their tonal relationships.

Was Ravel cautious enough in his dealings with his critics? Hardly. He never paid the customary round of visits then expected of any debutant. He never flattered them, but, on the contrary, spoke with dangerous frankness in society about the accepted authorities of the day, to whom he attributed ignorance and worse. The critics repaid him in kind. It was a long time before Ravel obtained in the press of France the recognition to which he was entitled, and which, for instance, Debussy had always enjoyed in spite of the phalanx of his powerful enemies. The critics also found confirmation in the Conservatory, where the teachers were not sufficiently independent of the opinions of the leading critics to ignore their occasional condemnation.

In the winter of 1898 Maurice Ravel met the singer Jane Bathori. She wrote about their meeting in the large Memorial Edition that the *Revue Musicale* issued in December, 1938, after Ravel's death. She was then in the chorus in the Conservatory concerts, the Saturday morning rehearsals of which composition students were permitted to attend. She said:

I can still see him, with his little Basque-type beard, his black, sparkling imaginative eyes, his refined and equivocal smile. He spoke about the composition class, and mostly about Claude Debussy, who at that time occupied a great place in the opinion of the young. He even lent me the *Proses Lyriques* (first edition) with the green drawings on its white title page, which then seemed to me the most extreme example of modernity. . . .

The first work of his I sang was the premiere of *Noël des Jouets,* at an evening party given by his friend Benedictus. I was, I think, fated to sing the premieres of Ravel's songs, either because he chose me to do so, which often happened, or because at the last moment circumstances made it necessary for him to send for me.

For instance, for the premiere of the *Shéhérazade* songs, I read the manuscript for the first time at three o'clock and had to sing them at five o'clock at a concert organized in 1904 by Vuillermoz at the Bouffes-Parisiens.

This, in essence, settled her career. The impression made by this new music was so great that it left its stamp on her life and her art. She became the first interpreter of most of Ravel's songs and courageously rejected all the protests that the premieres usually aroused.

PAVANE POUR UNE INFANTE
DÉFUNTE, 1899

Though so far Ravel had made use only of modern texts in his lyrics, such as poems of Verlaine and Mallarmé, yet, in his *Deux Épigrammes* he now turned to Clément Marot, a poet of the Renaissance, the Protestant protégé of Margaret of Navarre. The "Marot style," medieval forms blending with a foreshadowing of the rococo, had, in French literature, become the fashion for a special kind of mannerism.

In the two songs *D'Anne jouant de l'espinette* and *D'Anne qui me jecta de la neige* Ravel attempted to approach the spirit of the text through allusions to the musical language of the fifteenth century. This was one of the first steps on the road of archaism and classicism, which French artists later loved to tread so often, especially in the period between the two World Wars.

Ravel early adopted these procedures in his work. They reached their high point in 1917 in *Le Tombeau de Couperin.*

The essence of this spirit flavors the piano piece *Pavane pour une Infante Défunte* composed in 1899, which contributed so largely to the establishment of his reputation. Here again Ravel writes an antique dance, older than the minuet or the habanera. He moves in the courtly Spanish past of an imaginary baroque.

The origins of the word "pavane" are mysterious. We do not know if, as *pavana* it refers to a stately peacock dance (*pavone* in Italian, *paon* in French), or if it can be traced back to the name of the city of Padua (in Italian, Padova). The name *Padovana* (Paduan) appears historically in the same period as the word *pavana*. In one of the source books of information about the early sixteenth century, Ambrosio Dalza's *Tabulatura de Lauto* of 1508, four of the dances included are entitled *pavanas*. But the title of the collection speaks of *Padoane diverse*. Later publishers and authors also use the names interchangeably. The dance was most popular in Spain, where, in its earliest origins, it was in a slow triple meter, which, however, soon yielded to duple time. As a slow and solemn court dance it displaced the older *basses danses* of the Burgundian school. It joined agreeably with the more rapid triplemeter gailliard, a coupling that forms the basis of the later suites.

Ravel adopted a slow, grave tempo; the quarter notes carry the metronome indication 54, and, on the whole, the piece has a dragging rather than a forward tendency. Later Ravel spoke very slightingly and rather unjustly about the piece, the form of which apparently did not satisfy him. Actually, it displays in its form a compactness and elegance that is almost too smooth and makes a coquettish contrast with the melancholy theme. The G major with which it begins, and to which it returns, comes close, by various little devices, to the feeling of church modes. It does use the leading tone F sharp in the cadence, which then, however, does not rise to G, as the rule would require, but glides down over E to D.

Ravel subsequently orchestrated the pavane. In that garb it became even more popular than in its original form for piano. But it is not the only pavane in his output. Besides those that are not expressly defined as such but display the same characteristics, there is the piece that came out in 1908 as the first movement in *Ma Mère l'Oye*, the *Pavane de la Belle au bois dormante*.

Later Ravel made light of the sonorous title of the earlier pavane. Actually, the title carries several ambiguities.

The double meaning of the word "pavane" itself is linked with the royal title of Spanish and Portuguese princesses. The concept of youthfulness and minority is given the mournful contrast of a vision of death.

Do we not see here references to the legend of the maiden, bewitched into a deathlike sleep, who likewise is of royal blood and who, in a happy ending, is brought back to life by a handsome prince? *The Sleeping Beauty* is French in origin. The fairy tale is found in Perrault's collection earlier than in that of the Grimm brothers. In Nordic circles the material is analogous to the concept of Brunhild, which Richard Wagner in turn associated with his Siegfried figure.

With the *Pavane pour une Infante Défunte* Ravel ended his period of youthful dependence. He was now artistically adult and ready for his entrance into mature society. The little man with aristocratic leanings would have been quite eligible for one of those salons of the rich and noble that are described by Marcel Proust. The great houses of the Faubourg St. Germain offered to open their doors to him as soon as the first beams of a Paris reputation picked him out. But all such tenders were rejected by this remote, elegant, cynical, and obviously gifted musician.

Incidentally, Proust knew Ravel but did not regard him as highly as he did Reynaldo Hahn, the friend of his youth, who, although he never did share Proust's admiration for Wagner, became his personal adviser in all questions relating to music. Apparently Proust, the writer and chronicler of high society, did not have enough musical understanding to tell the difference in quality between the much stronger inner fire and originality of an artist like Ravel and the talented gossip who had a gift for grinding out operettas and little tastefully perfumed ballads in limitless quantities.

In the same year (1899) that saw the birth of the

Pavane and in which the *Shéhérazade* Overture met with both approval and catcalls from the public, there came also the song *Si morne,* after a text by Émile Verhaeren.

MADAME DE SAINT-MARCEAUX, 1901

The century was drawing to its close. It was a century of great transformations, departures, and decisions in scholarship and the arts. The authority of older traditions had begun to totter as a result of undermining by skepticism and the penetration of rationalism. Youth offered more determined combat to prejudice and convention than it had since the days of the French Revolution. Proponents of one view of life followed hard on the heels of another.

Among these were the socialists, led by spirits like the incorruptible Émile Zola, whose example in the Dreyfus case would soon lend a new dignity to the views of writers and intellectuals. The reforms advocated by these political leaders invaded even the areas reserved for pure art. Indeed, they decreed that there was no such area as pure art, creators being, they asserted, the voice of the society to which they belong. Writing, painting, the plastic arts, and music have a right to exist only if they surrender their splendid isolation and decide to place themselves at the disposition of the newly rising society, that of the workers. Through this gospel, industry, machines, and factories were exalted to a mystical level of nobility. A new beauty was discovered in poverty and the daily routine, which found adherents even in circles quite remote from all these social doctrines.

However, there was no lack of an opposite party, a phalanx, equally powerful, of pure esthetes, who had no wish to know anything about such reforms. The literature of the *fin-de-siècle* period, that of the Parnassians as well as of the

44

symbolists, adheres to a totally unsocial cult of form, pure beauty, and art for art's sake alone. In these circles it was a hundred times more important to discover novel nuances of expression, of rhyming technique, and of characterization than to satisfy the wishes of wide circles of customers with questionable works of art. The search for the *mot juste,* the suitable word, the only exact, irreplaceable noun or adjective was, they said, the most sacred task of the artist. To appeal to the mass public with his efforts was not desirable. The future belonged to those who could touch new strings in the heart and soul of those who had taste, who could produce a *nouveau frisson.*

As a young man and a Conservatory student Ravel belonged, without reservation, to the "art for art's sake" persuasion. His writings confirm this, as do the titles he selected for his piano works and the texts he chose for his songs. The artistic dandyism Viñes ascribes to him would not permit his joining any other cult but that of pure form. And what could it be but the *nouveau frisson* that these new alchemists in sound were seeking so tirelessly to find in the scores of the Russians, the Norwegians, and their own contemporaries and countrymen?

There were nevertheless border areas between the two hostile camps. There were some who began to believe in the possibility of an alliance between the art of social significance and that of the Parnassians. Had not impressionistic painters represented heads of cabbages and butcher shops in such revolutionary media that the leaders of established society had visited their exhibitions, albeit with ridicule and resentment? Even Ravel himself became intoxicated with the beauty of glowing blast furnaces.

For the time being, however, he was content with exclusiveness in artistic matters and even in social intercourse. His earlier comradeships had a common interest in

45

music as their basis. The friends of his youth were, like himself, Conservatory students, men and women like Ricardo Viñes, Florent Schmitt, Jane Bathori. Or they were creators to whom he felt himself spiritually related and by whose standards he guided himself, such as the grotesque Erik Satie, *Monsieur le Pauvre,* as he liked to dub himself.

There were two groups of people out of the ordinary run who attracted Ravel at the turn of the century. One was composed of intellectuals without aspirations in the field of the arts. The other was made up of the socially exclusive, who maintained the type of classic and romantic Parisian salons that were inspired by great curiosity about artistic creation and had an authentic respect for it and for artistic fame.

The novelist Colette has described the environment in which Ravel came into contact with the upper levels of aristocratic society. She had met him during the early years when his reputation and hers were beginning to grow, several decades before this led to their collaboration on the opera *L'Enfant et les Sortilèges.* Madame de Saint-Marceaux received her friends Wednesdays after the evening meal. The men arrived when it pleased them, in business clothes, the ladies in high-necked dresses. They met in two middle-sized drawing rooms: members of the upper nobility, musicians, music lovers, and critics. The hostess herself was mad about music. She listened attentively when her guests played or sang, but she never forced anyone to do so, and this included her husband, who did not share her pleasure in the arts. Interruptions were not tolerated.

Among the regular guests were Gabriel Fauré, the conductor André Messager, and the pianist Edouard Risler. Fauré, gifted in many media, showed himself adept as a caricaturist and, in three strokes, could whip up a silhouette. Or he and Messager improvised crashing chords for four hands, parrying each other's thrusts to outdo each other until the gaiety would reach a high point in a quadrille on themes from Wagner's *Der Ring des Nibelungen.* Colette also stresses in her description the incongruity between Ravel's oversized head and his rather undersized body. Not unkindly she speaks of his *favoris,* the stylish side-whiskers that he let grow at that time. She also mentions his striking cravats and pleated shirts. All in all, he appears in her description as excessively shy, aloof in bearing, and sober in conversation.

At Meg's (this was the Shakespearean style in which she was addressed by her friends) one would also meet the Prince and Princess de Polignac, who enjoyed spending their wealth, derived both from America and from the champagne cellars of Rheims, for the support of rising celebrities. One evening when Vincent d'Indy performed, the painter Jacques Émile Blanche was carrying on a conversation with Claude Debussy. Blanche was a portraitist from a rich family and a close friend of Proust, whose group of friends included painters like Aubrey Beardsley, James McNeill Whistler, and the poet Oscar Wilde. He later painted excellent portraits of Claude Debussy and Igor Stravinsky.

"Who is the little man turning the pages of the score?" he asked his neighbor. "He is Maurice Ravel," answered Debussy. Blanche looked hard at the young musician and noticed that he was visibly high-strung and looked, in his tight, short jacket, like a jockey. It happened that at this time the rich music-loving painter was searching for a partner to play piano duets with him. He proposed to Ravel that the latter should come to his studio twice a week and make music with him. Ravel could have made good use of this sure income, but he imposed one condition on which the whole project foundered: that they should play no Beethoven, no Schumann, no Wagner, or any other romantic music, but must restrict themselves to Mozart. Blanche later realized how very characteristic this demand was, how indicative of Ravel's determination to resist every outside influence on the indulgence of his taste.

It is unfortunate that Blanche never painted Ravel's portrait. There are few good pictures of the composer, either from the time of his youth or after he achieved world fame. When he was young he experimented with various styles of beard, and a picture by Ouvre shows him at the turn of the century with his wavy hair parted, a neatly curled moustache, and his chin framed by a carefully trained and trimmed full beard. Very few photos trace the development of his facial appearance.

Maurice Ravel never grew in bodily stature enough to make him acceptable for military service. He was underweight by four pounds. In fact, his appearance was that of a half-grown man, almost on the border of dwarfism. Napoleon was larger. Just as with Napoleon, and all too short, undersized people, the impulse to compensate for this defect was lively in Ravel. He became increasingly self-conscious, especially as a young man. This, combined with his excessive intellectual snobbishness, created an impression of precocious arrogance, which made for him as many enemies as he had admirers.

Some have supposed that the composer Vinteuil in *À la Recherche du temps perdu* embodies traits of Ravel's character. The error is very obvious, for Vinteuil is a wholly invented character. The music that Proust ascribes to him combined aspects of Reynaldo Hahn and of César Franck, especially in terms of the latter's violin sonata. The conception is really derived from the musical recollections of Proust's youth.

Façade of the house of Ravel's birth, March 7, 1875. From a postcard picture made at Ciboure about 1940.

First and last pages of Ravel's original manuscript of his piano composition *Jeux d'Eau*. It bears the motto "Dieu fluvial riant de l'eau qui le chatouille. H. de Regnier," and his signature at the end, dated November 11, 1901.

PAUL SORDES; THE APACHES;
JEUX D'EAU, 1901

The other circle, which Ravel entered some years later, was considerably more youthful, more artistic, and consequently more interesting. Maurice Delage, immensely gifted both as composer and as writer, and later one of Ravel's most intimate friends, has described it. Born in Paris four years later than Ravel, he became his chief pupil, and Ravel taught very few. As a composer of songs of very special character, he leaned toward the East—Asiatic exoticism that attracted many Frenchmen of his generation. His *Quatre poèmes hindous* and *Sept Hai-Kais* are singular examples of European importations of varying Indian and Japanese moods. Delage also wrote a work for orchestra on Indian themes.

His account begins in 1903, at two o'clock on a December morning, before the house at 39 rue Dulong. Paul Sordes, a painter and passionate amateur musician, lived in a studio on the fourth floor. He received friends every Saturday. One of them, on this occasion, was Léon-Paul Fargue, a melancholy newspaper columnist with the look of a poet, who was known as the *piéton de Paris*. He knew and wrote masterful little pieces about the minor tragedies and broader comedies that took place in every corner of the city. After three volumes of verse, he wrote other books, including *Pour la Musique* and *Phantômes de Rilke*.

There were also present two young critics, enthusiastic devotees of modern music. One, of Greek origin but writing in French, was Michel Dimitri Calvocoressi, who was born in Marseilles in 1877 and died in London in 1944. His numerous published books include studies of Russian music as well as biographies of Franz Liszt, Modest Moussorgsky,

Mikhail Glinka, Robert Schumann, and Claude Debussy. Another of those dedicated avant-gardists was Émile Vuillermoz, a musician and musicologist of wide versatility and cultivation. Born in Lyons in 1878, he was a pupil of Fauré at the Conservatory, but later became exclusively a music critic and author. He wrote biographies of Mendelssohn, Debussy, and his teacher Fauré, as well as a book on the love life of Frédéric Chopin.

There, too, was Désiré-Émile Inghelbrecht, the conductor-composer, born in Paris in 1880. He joined the Paul Sordes circle just as he was beginning his military service and passed his leave with these comrades. Naturally, Ricardo Viñes was another member, his face divided by an enormous moustache, the face of a peaceable policeman in the caricature by Fargue.

In Sordes' studio there was a spirit of friendly equality, which was one of the most attractive attributes of life in bohemian Paris. They were all of one mind in their enthusiasm for new, problematical, and unpopular experiments in products of the imagination. Ravel occupied a special place in the little gathering. He rapidly became its central personality. He had, by that time, outrun that status of gifted beginner in which the drawing room of Madame de Saint-Marceaux had taken him up.

In 1901 he produced a piano piece in Saint-Jean-de-Luz that became the subject of the highest admiration in the Sordes group. With it Ravel's pianism suddenly stepped into the twentieth century. Ravel himself says of it in his autobiographical sketches:

The *Jeux d'Eau,* which appeared in 1901, stands as the point of departure for all new pianistic expressions one may find in my works. This work, inspired by the bubbling of water and the musical sounds of fountains, waterfalls, and brooks, is built on two themes in the manner of the first movement of a sonata, without, however, being subjugated to the classic tonal formula.

Ravel himself must have played it fascinatingly. We can imagine how his friends were enraptured by it. The score is headed by a motto quoted from Henri de Régnier: "The river god laughing at the water that tickles him."

It is dedicated to his "beloved master Gabriel Fauré." Not only in the amount of technical difficulties but in the searching out of instrumental sonorities, the model of Franz Liszt is clearly recognizable. However, Liszt is left far behind. The return to the opening key of E major reconciles the spread of certain modulations with the original harmonic idiom, which, however, always preserves the diatonic element through all its chromatic changes.

Vlado Perlemuter and Hélène Jourdan-Morhange, two music analysts from Ravel's inner circle, have tried, in their book, to describe Ravel's own rendition of this piece. They rely on Fargue, who was present the first time it was played at a Sordes gathering. He wrote that "There was an unfamiliar fire in it, a whole spectrum of undulations and delicacies that could come from no other composer."

Perlemuter declares that Ravel wanted the beginning to be not too fast, melodious but not sentimental, cheerful and smooth, soft and connected, not overly hurried. The pedal markings are just as specific as the dynamics. Viñes states that Ravel recommended pedaling for the upper voice, so as to give the impression of vibrations in the air, rather than to stress the clarity of individual notes. Ravel specifically wished the close to be without any retard. The piece is to die away gradually, as it were.

The ease with which such a masterpiece flowed from his pen prevented Ravel from appreciating the unique quality it had. He did not press his publisher Demets to have it printed and even deterred him from protecting the American copyright. *Jeux d'Eau* came out in 1902, so it has priority over all the impressionistic piano music that appeared in the first decade of the twentieth century. With it Ravel reached the front rank of innovators and inventors of pianistic sound effects and instrumental tone colors. Next to Debussy, Scriabin, and Schönberg he contributed the most to freeing pianistic idiom from a romanticism that had become rigid. Consistently and with even sharper definition he followed the path Franz Liszt had begun to outline in the 1870's.

About the time the *Jeux d'Eau* was being written, Ravel's friend and classmate Florent Schmitt was living in the Villa Medici of the French Institute in Rome as a winner of the Prix de Rome. Schmitt was an industrious and faithful correspondent, more dependable in this regard than Ravel, who always kept him waiting for an answer. However, at last, on April 8, 1901, the negligent Ravel wrote detailed news to Rome:

My dear Schmitt: How can I excuse my conduct to you? I would rather spare you such annoyance. My hindsight provides me daily with excellent reasons to stifle my conscience. The strongest, though the poorest, is my unconquerable indolence when it comes to writing letters. Now I have some others to add to that one, choruses, fugues, looking toward the contest, as well as transcriptions of the admirable *Nocturnes* of Debussy in collaboration with Raoul Bardac. After I demonstrated a certain skill in this kind of work, an assignment came my way to rework the third, the *Sirènes,* all by myself, probably the most beautiful of them, but certainly the most difficult, especially as I have never heard it. How I regret, dear friend, that you are too far away from Paris to hear such things. Those, and also Liszt's *Faust,* that astounding symphony, in which the most noteworthy themes of the *Ring* are to be found much earlier, and so much better orchestrated.

Meanwhile, in spite of the deep sympathy I feel for you, I would very much wish to be (who knows?) where you are. Does Rome inspire you with delightful ideas? Is your *Peau de Chagrin* making good progress? And will it be your *Damoiselle Élue* for us? Or (Phoebus forbid) your *Impressions d'Italie?* These are questions which I hope you will answer soon.

There is reason to doubt that you will ever get a letter from Miss T. . . . , as a young lady is not supposed to correspond with a young man. This injunction, pronounced by the young woman's mother, seems to be somewhat peculiar, because I have always regarded a woman who writes fugues as a bit of a hermaphrodite.

Now I must end this epistolary effusion, or I shall be late to dinner at Mme D's . . . , where I expect to circulate some still unpublished slanders about you.

Expecting early and detailed news from you, a hearty handshake from

> Your devoted
> Maurice Ravel

This letter is filled with allusions. It does not surprise us that the master of *Jeux d'Eau* idolized Liszt and recognized the Mephisto theme in the Faust Symphony as the model for a theme in Wagner's *Walküre*. His reference to invitations from fine people is in the true style of the Sordes milieu, just as is his disrespect for Gustave Charpentier's Prix de Rome work, his *Impressions d'Italie*. More interesting than this little show of malice is his admiration for Debussy, not only for his *Nocturnes* but also for his *Damoiselle Élue*.

Debussy was the man with whom he spoke a common language, the man he honored all his life in spite of all the tensions that were stirred up between himself and the older master. It was fate and the malicious joy their contemporaries took in brewing trouble between them that caused Ravel to be represented over and over as an imitator, even as a plagiarist, of Debussy. What Ravel chalked up, in jest, against Wagner for copying Liszt was used seriously as an argument to question Ravel's own originality.

There is no doubt that the young Ravel knew and spoke Debussy's idiom. That was done by nearly all the young French composers. It was the idiom of the new France, just as certain ways of laying on colors, the splitting up of rays of light into the various colors of the spectrum, formed precisely the idiom of impressionistic painting. In any event, the determined turning away from Wagner and from all of German romantic music limited the choice of new melodic and harmonic forms.

And was Debussy himself without forerunners? Did he not stand on the shoulders of Moussorgsky, Grieg, Chopin, and Borodin? Had he not learned a certain boldness from Chabrier and Satie, just as he acquired certain melodic tendencies from Fauré and Massenet? To these were added in 1889 the same East-Asiatic influences that affected Ravel himself.

At the turn of the century France was developing a new musical style. It came along a broad front, in the same fashion as 120 years earlier with the classical masters in Vienna. The same relationship in utterance existed between Haydn and Mozart, and it tended toward a complete identity in forms and idiom. The young Beethoven is often interchangeable with either of the two older composers. And as for painting, did not cubism come forward in 1908 as a group movement, so that we have difficulty in distinguishing works of that period by Pablo Picasso or Georges Braque, and sometimes by Juan Gris, from each other?

These problems also animated the discussions in the

Saturday meetings at Paul Sordes'. Soon these gatherings acquired a name. One evening, after a concert they all attended in a group, they were strolling back down the rue de Rome. We can imagine how these intellectual gypsies looked, with their wild beards, their extravagant hats and waistcoats, their esthetic rantings, and their execrations upon respectable society. A news vendor, encountering them, wanted to sell them copies of *L'Intransigeant,* but, on seeing their eccentric appearance, called out: "Beware the Apaches!" This tag was immediately adopted by them, and from then on the group at Paul Sordes' was called the "Apaches." Meeting under the new sobriquet, their musical debauches extended even longer into the night.

Ravel regularly gave them extra impetus, bringing along heaps of new Russian music, which they ploughed through tirelessly at the piano. At that time Russian music was the bright ideal among the younger generation of French painters, writers, and composers. They learned about Nikolai Rimski-Korsakov from his concerti. They began to take an interest in Tchaikovsky. They idolized Modest Moussorgsky and Aleksandr Borodin. The Russian modernists had been cultivated frequently and quite methodically at the Concerts Pasdeloup ever since the 1880's. In fact, as early as November, 1879, Tchaikovsky wrote to Nadezhda Filaretovna von Meck a letter from Paris criticizing works of César Cui and Modest Moussorgsky, members of "The Mighty Five," but conceding that they showed elegance and good taste.

Among all these Russians it was Borodin who exerted the greatest influence on Ravel. The group all heard the B minor Symphony together. After the concert they adopted as the identification call for the members of the Apaches Borodin's characteristic theme with the Russian alternation between major and minor.

There were constant difficulties in the apartment house with other tenants who could not tolerate the weekend nocturnal music sessions in Sordes' studio. It was Maurice Delage who came to the rescue. He rented a garden cottage out in Auteuil, remote from anyone's dwelling, and installed first one piano in it, then soon after, another. From then on the gatherings of the Apaches took place there. Ravel was delighted with the isolated house. He often spent the rest of the night there on a little cot. Nobody bothered the bohemian band any more. They could even keep up their musical orgies until Sunday forenoon. The Apaches spent their days, or rather their nights, in Delage's house all through the year. Countless artists sought the group out or belonged to it. Among them were Manuel de Falla, Igor Stravinsky, Tristan Klingsor the poet, Lucien Garban, who later became Ravel's publisher at Durand, and the young Abbé Léonce Petit, whose friendship with Ravel did not hinder the composer from remaining a freethinker all his life.

Sometimes strangers pushed their way into the club, tiresome and undesired participants, of whom the members had to rid themselves somehow. They did not wish to seem discourteous. What to do? Ravel found a solution characteristic of his imagination. He created out of whole cloth a personality no one knew. He called him Gomez le Riquet. "What a shame," they would say when they found themselves burdened with an importunate bore. They were just about to adjourn to visit this legendary Spaniard, who had invited the gathering for a cup of tea or a glass of wine. They must not keep him waiting or fail to arrive. They were exceedingly sorry to have to depart, but Gomez le Riquet was very sensitive . . . a typical Spaniard. "Adieu!" Even in creating this mythical figure, the Spanish element that was so constantly in Ravel's thoughts and feelings played a role.

STRING QUARTET, 1903;
STYLISTIC OBSERVATIONS

During these years, shortly after the turn of the century, Ravel created his first chamber-music work, the *String Quartet,* that made his name famous among a wholly different circle of music lovers. In his autobiography he says of it very briefly: "My *Quartet in F,* 1902–1903, responds to a desire for musical construction, which undoubtedly is inadequately realized but which emerges much more clearly than in my preceding compositions."

This is a very modest description of music that can be reckoned among Ravel's most successful and most perfect productions. It is one of the first works to which he assigned no programmatic or literary title, merely *String Quartet in F major,* in four movements (as the schools require) : a rapid first movement in the two-theme sonata form; a scherzo in A minor and G sharp minor, with a slow trio of wavering tonality; a very songlike slow movement in free form, harmonically and structurally bolder than the others; and a finale in a quintuple meter that probably derives from Russian rhythms.

The character of this music is bright, ardent, and youthfully vigorous as are few others of his works. In many ways it bears the impress of Debussy's musical speech. Debussy was delighted with the score when Ravel played it for him. On the contrary, Gabriel Fauré, to whom Ravel dedicated it, had some reservations, especially as to the last movement, which seemed to him too short. The kindly old master probably did not recognize the astonishing unity that makes this work appear as though it had been poured into its mold in one continuous stream.

Ravel achieved this unity by means of the mono-thematic process, which also hovered over the thoughts of the Viennese classic composers from Haydn to Beethoven. This means that all the themes and all the motives used in the four movements of the work grow out of a common seed and are elaborated by little rearrangements and by a phenomenal variety of changes in perspective and lighting. There is variety in the effects produced and in the actual forms, a masterpiece of the will of the artist to take everything apart and, having done so, to reassemble it differently.

Ravel left the premiere of the piece to the Société Nationale. It took place March 5, 1904, and was received with great enthusiasm. There were naturally still some contrary-minded listeners, not only among French musicians and critics. The Paris correspondent of the New York *Tribune* in 1906 said that the theme of the *Quartet* reminded him of the wailing of clarinets in a Chinese theater and that the general feeling of the four movements was that of a lesson in arithmetic. But others realized that Ravel had taken equal rank with Debussy and now stood beside him as one of the young masters of French music.

Delage, Ravel's lifelong friend, came to him at Sordes' with the request for musical instruction. Ravel agreed. He listened to the efforts of the young dilettante and handed him the score of the *String Quartet* so he might copy out the bass part. Under Ravel's influence Delage developed into a composer of high individuality. His exotic pieces preceded by thirty years what Olivier Messiaen later created with his amalgam of Indian and European musical esthetic ideas.

Ravel was never an outspoken intellectual. He had a strong leaning toward contradictory formulations and, in his youth, a rather affected manner of expressing himself. He made use of intellectual means only as a musician, from an urge of his nature to play with them, but always only for their effect on sound and rhythm. This explains the impact of a title like *Pavane pour une Infante Défunte,* which signifies nothing. There is evident in it, however, the intention to urge the listener in advance into a prepared state of mind merely from reading the title. This he had also done earlier in the *Menuet Antique,* and here he even applied the device of a conscious anachronism.

Such syntheses as these point in the direction of surrealism and the uniting of incompatible elements, which came fifty years later. On the other hand, the title of *Sites Auriculaires* expresses a thoroughly romantic sentiment, which stemmed from the old ideal of synesthesia that E.T.A. Hoffmann, Baudelaire, Nietzsche, and Aleksandr Scriabin, in their various ways, tried to bring to artistic realization.

JOSEPH RAVEL; THE GODEBSKIS, 1904

In the circles that received him and seemed to cultivate him, although in fact he rather ruled them, Ravel's personality blossomed. The garden cottage of Maurice Delage in Auteuil, with its spare, simple furnishings, its wood and cardboard partitions, and its two pianos, suited his entirely nonconformist desire for uncompromising freedom and his hostility to ordinary conventions. Here, in the circle of musicians, painters, and writers his equals in age and ambition, he found confirmation of what Erik Satie and Emmanuel Chabrier, the autodidacts, had awakened in him earlier. The Apaches spurred on his inventive instinct, his joy in what was novel and never before heard. If Léon-Paul Fargue, who may have just come home after roaming through some of the most unsavory alleys of the great metropolis, knocked on their door at two in the morning, he would find the group in excited argument over Wagner or Debussy or Yvette Guilbert. Ravel would sit at the piano, his narrow bony hands with their stiff fingers and splayed thumbs conjuring daring flights of arpeggios out of the fresh manuscript he had brought along for his friends. But he said little. He listened and thought over the ideas and the pronouncements of the others.

He cut a different figure in the salon of Madame de Saint-Marceaux. There, elegant, superior, and remote, he would be found near the Érard piano, in the light of the gas lamps that illuminated the heavy gathered folds of the velvet curtains. Here the desire to shock, which Ricardo Viñes attributed to him, found ready listeners and was encouraged. When he spoke slightingly of timid, academic, or conservative critics, or if he declared roundly that Willy (who was probably in the next room) let others write his reviews for him and made use of any ideas he could pick up, one was reminded of old Brahms, who, taking his leave of a social gathering in Vienna, asked forgiveness if there were anyone in the room he had neglected to offend.

It is useful to describe the psychological climate that surrounded Ravel, the young composer. People gossipped a lot about his gifts, his knowledge, his elegance, and his cultivation. But at the same time indignation was not withheld at the overweening arrogance with which he made merry at the expense of authorities with well-earned and recognized positions. They were not disposed to forgive a second time what they had overlooked in the Conservatory student Claude Debussy ten years before. Mediocrity allied itself with bureaucracy in a formidable *entente cordiale*. Ravel encountered the prejudice of the powers that be at the very time when he could have benefited from their good will.

On a certain morning in 1904 a rehearsal was going

on in the Casino de Paris. The auditorium of the famous vaudeville theater was empty. In the arena a giant mechanism had been built, and on it workmen were still busy. A new, hazardous variety number was to be rehearsed. It was called *Tourbillon de la Mort* ("Whirlwind of Death"). Two onlookers made their way in—men with dark, full beards in the current style. The elder, discreetly dressed, was nervous; the younger man on his left, evidently his son, was a slight youth with an intelligent face and an exquisite, almost striking elegance: Ravel *père,* inventor of the unusual apparatus, and his composer son.

But there were also two other people in the huge theater. One, a man, was a double cripple with an undeveloped arm and a club foot. And yet one forgot this great bodily handicap when one looked into his face, a bearded, scholarly countenance with eyes eager for everything beautiful. On his arm, both supporting him and leading him, walked a blonde of youthful beauty. She wore a long, rather trailing gown of a heavy knitted silk material, very much in the current style. The Ravels entered into conversation with these strangers and discovered that the married couple were the Godebskis, Cyprian and Ida, both of Polish origin.

Meanwhile, the rehearsal had begun, and the "Whirlwind of Death" gave its first performance before spectators. In it an automobile rolled down a steep ramp, then hurled itself up off the incline, made a leap into the air in which it executed a complete somersault, and, by a miracle, came to a stop on its four wheels. The driver, swathed in thick cloths and leather coverings, stepped out smiling and unharmed.

Joseph Ravel beamed, thinking that this invention could possibly bring him more than the automobile he built and drove over the streets of Neuilly in 1868, even more than the two-stroke engine he patented. From the Casino de

61

Paris the "Whirlwind of Death" later made its perilous way around the circuses and variety stages of the world. Only the precision of a master engineer could have made this invention dependable. This circus act was a bravura piece of technical virtuosity, much in the same way as were many of Maurice Ravel's piano pieces.

Toulouse-Lautrec might have painted the scene of that morning, the deserted auditorium, two spotlights beamed at the ramp down which the death car rushed, in the stalls the three bearded men and the pretty blonde, occupied with looking after her crippled husband. It was a typical Toulouse-Lautrec setting: a touch of theater, of elegance, the faces of intellectuals, and the aura of feminine charm that emanated from a fashionable young woman. Actually, Cyprian Godebski had been a friend of the talented painter, who died far too early (1901). Toulouse-Lautrec had painted his portrait and frequented his house, one which had been visited by two generations of writers, painters, and musicians.

Cyprian Godebski, Cypa as his friends called him, was not a rich man. But to be admitted to the salon of this Polish couple was equivalent to a patent of nobility for anyone who had anything to say in the artistic life of Paris in the first two decades of the century.

Perhaps it is no coincidence that the deep and unbroken friendship between Maurice Ravel and the Godebskis began at this rehearsal in the Casino de Paris. That day saw a combination of the most extreme daring and the highest precision, a combination that had inspired Ravel's father to his creative accomplishments. The tiniest error in the engineering plan would have made catastrophe and ruin inevitable. A calculating intelligence was wedded here to daring and the exploring power of imagination, a bohemian disposition to which had been applied the science of engineering. Joseph Ravel was an artist at the drawing board and in the workshop.

Out of such elements was the music of Maurice Ravel created. At its best it displays the triumph of precision and the high polish of perfection. It serves as a reproof to impetuosity. No note is without its considered place and its special function in the structure of these thoroughly finished forms. One can well suppose that Ravel had studied technique as thoroughly as had his brother Edouard, with whom he had played four-hand piano pieces as a child and who was destined to survive him by more than two decades. His chord successions often resemble closely intermeshed cogwheels and differential gears; his polyphony at times has the fascination of mechanical toys, which Ravel, incidentally, always adored; and his rhythms possess the organization of beautiful machines.

Igor Stravinsky, who, when he first arrived in Paris, made the acquaintance of Ravel, as well as that of other musicians such as Debussy, Florent Schmitt, and Manuel de Falla, was devoted to Ravel and perceived this special quality in his music. For his older friend he coined the often-quoted expression, "a Swiss clockmaker." It was the tradition of industrious craftsmanship of the Swiss watchmaker, amounting almost to genius, that lived on in the blood of Joseph Ravel and of his son and enabled them to attain the summits of their productivity.

Cypa Godebski, too, who loved the arts as an amateur, had a feeling for the precise, the perfect, the completely calculated, as it were, scientific aspect of the fine arts. In addition, he became a member of the Apaches; he mingled with the others in the studios of the Sordes brothers, but, apart from that, maintained his own salon, his regular gatherings of artists in his home in the rue d'Athènes. Ravel soon became one of the most faithful members of the Godebski circle. Indeed, when he acquired his permanent home in Montfort-l'Amaury, he rented a permanent room in the Hôtel d'Athènes, quite near the Godebski residence, for his frequent visits to Paris.

PRIX DE ROME, 1905; *NOËL DES JOUETS*, 1905; *SONATINE*, 1905

Ravel had been leading a divided artistic existence ever since 1900, a sort of creative double life. He had rapidly become well known through his *Shéhérazade* Overture, and even more through the *Pavane pour une Infante Défunte*. Yet at the same time he continued to attend Gabriel Fauré's composition class at the Conservatory, in which he had matriculated as a student. Like every young composer at the Conservatory, he dreamt hopefully of the Prix de Rome. To become a laureate of the Institute was to achieve the highest honor one could win in this field.

The Prix de Rome, instituted in 1803 and awarded annually through a competition before a jury, carried with it a stipend for three years of living at the Villa Medici in Rome. To win it, one had to compose a cantata on a prescribed text, in complete seclusion, that is, under strict observation and without any direct contact with the outside world.

Ravel risked this adventure first in 1901. A photo taken during the period shows him surrounded by his fellow competitors. Ravel sits at the right, noticeably apart and in the foreground, on a stone parapet at the edge of the steps. He is wearing side-whiskers in the style then called *favoris,* and a moustache. The other four competitors in the picture—Bertelin, André Caplet, Aymé Kunc, and Gabriel Dupont—also wear beards. Ravel is dressed with excessive elegance, wearing a dark suit with a high-buttoned waistcoat. A white handkerchief peeps out of his left breastpocket, snow-white cuffs protrude from his sleeves, the high turned-down collar sets off a bright-patterned cravat. As his legs are crossed, the white shoes are distinctly visible, as are the foppishly patterned socks. The head is shielded from the June sun by a white straw boater. He holds a cigarette in his right hand; the left is half inserted into a trouser pocket. None of his rivals compares with him in looking so worldly; he is the dandy of the group.

The cantata chosen for that year was called *Myrrha;* the text by Ferdinand Beissier was of almost unbelievable banality. But when he dealt with an academic assignment, Ravel followed the rules very exactly. He knew how to solve the problems that his teachers put to him with incredible virtuosity and smoothness, without running off the rails into the personal and individual style his *Jeux d'Eau* had already demonstrated.

He wrote his friend Lucien Garban in a letter of July 26, 1901, about the outcome of this first effort for the Roman laurels:

Almost everybody present would have given me the prize, even Massenet who voted that way all the way through. I was told I have one unusual ability, and that is that I have a fountain of melody out of which music flows without the slightest effort. This graceful metaphor came from your respected teacher Xavier Leroux, who, like Vidal, expressed himself as very enthusiastic about me. I was even assured (*horresco referens*) that Lenepveu rated my cantata very highly, but of course not highly enough to prefer it to the one his own pupil submitted. You will ask "Why did they not award you the first prize?" Who would have thought it, but this low blow was dealt me by my orchestration. Although my composition was one of the first to be finished, I wound up in the rear and was left with very little time over for my orchestration, so that it was found to be somewhat thrown together. I just have to start afresh. That's all there is to it.

The pupil of Lenepveu who was given the first prize instead of Ravel was André Caplet, in fact a very gifted composer, an intimate friend of Debussy, and later highly regarded as a conductor of both classical and contemporary music in America as well as in Europe.

The next year, 1902, Ravel repeated his only half-successful effort, the same year that also brought him a significant success in the premiere performance of his *Jeux d'Eau* by Ricardo Viñes. But apparently his youthful mastery was not yet adequate for the Rome cantata, this time called *Alcyone*. This time Aymé Kunc, later the director of the Conservatory at Lyons, won the race, in which Ravel fell badly behind. At peace with himself and apparently unmoved by this mishap, he continued to work on the score of his string quartet and of the *Shéhérazade* songs. And again in 1903 he made a third try to conquer the laurels and the Villa Medici. That year the work chosen was called *Alyssa*. Again Ravel failed; the lucky winner was Raoul Laparra.

Now Ravel took a breather, but without actually abandoning the effort, for he felt he owed this confirmation of his talent to his parents, to whom he was attached by a deep love. In the year 1904 he held back. That was the year in which he struck up his firm friendship with Maurice Delage and the Godebskis. He was twenty-nine, so he had just one more year's time, as entrants over thirty were not admitted to the competition. Certainly Gabriel Fauré, who had been indignant over the negative vote in 1903, encouraged him to make one last attempt.

So in 1905 Ravel intended once more to take part in the competition, knowing it must be for the last time. And now the inconceivable happened, something that set half of Paris beside itself with excitement and indignation. The jury, of which Massenet was still a member, denied Ravel the right to take part. It caused a scandal of immense proportions. The newspapers printed such angry articles against the jury and all its members that finally Théodore Dubois resigned as director of the Conservatory and Gabriel Fauré was called in as his successor.

As a result of all this furor Ravel was, it is true, outwardly and brilliantly rehabilitated, but there was no possibility of ever again competing for the Prix de Rome. His thirtieth birthday was behind him, and with it he had crossed the age limit established by law, even though he had the satisfaction of knowing that everybody in France who felt a sense of justice stood on his side, even those who, like Romain Rolland, had always been his foes artistically. Rolland, then one of the leading personalities in France, both as a writer and as a musicologist, addressed a letter to Paul Léon, the Minister of Culture, in which he said:

I am no friend of Ravel. I can even say I have no sympathy personally for his delicate and polished style. But justice compels me to say that Ravel is more than a student of great promise. He is one of the best regarded masters of our school, of whom it has not many. I do not for a moment question the good faith of his judges. But then they have delivered a verdict of death on this jury for all time. It is a case that reminds us of that of Berlioz. Ravel entered the Prix de Rome test not as a student, but as a composer who had already passed his examinations. I am astonished at the composers who dared to judge him. Who will judge them in their turn?

Ravel uttered no word nor took any stand about the scandalous decision, but his lifelong abhorrence of official interference by the state, and especially the French state, in matters of art and artists had its origin here. He did not hesitate in 1920 to reject the offer of the decoration of Chevalier of the Legion of Honor, which had already been decided on and of which he was informed by the newspapers. His farewell to the Conservatory was made easy for him by this Prix de Rome affair. He took his revenge in creative style: he was content to publish two masterpieces in the very same year. One, the *Sonatine* for piano, was dedicated to M. and Mme Godebski; the other, the *Miroirs* for piano, opened the second period of his productivity.

But the year 1905 brought forth still another little work of art, one that gives a two-fold representation of Ravel's genius. It was his song *Noël des Jouets* (only published long after its completion) to a text he himself had written. He dedicated it to Madame Jeanne Cruppi, a lady sincerely devoted to him artistically, who later also interceded for him with the management of the Opéra Comique.

Ravel's special love of little things and childish toys found highly original expression in these five verses. The charm of the poem lies not only in the subject matter of its theme, but also to some extent in the polished play of rhymes and assonances, of which a translation can give no true conception.

NOËL DES JOUETS

Le troupeau verni des moutons
Roule en tumulte vers la crèche,
Les lapins tambours, brefs et rêches,
Couvrent leurs aigres mirlitons.

Vierge Marie, en crinoline,
Ses yeux d'émail sans cesse ouverts,
En attendant Bonhomme hiver,
Veille Jésus qui se dodine.

Car, près de là, sous un sapin,
Furtif, emmitouflé dans l'ombre,

Du bois, Belzébuth, le chien sombre,
Guette l'enfant de sucre peint.

Mais les beaux anges incassables
Suspendus par des fils d'archal
Du haut de l'arbuste hiémal
Assurent la paix des étables.

Et leur vol du clinquant vermeil
Qui cliquette en bruits symétriques
S'accorde au bétail mécanique
Dont la voix grêle bêle: "Noël."

THE CHRISTMAS MANGER

Sheep in shining varnish tinted
Crowd around the holy crib,
Tiny bunny drummers marching
Still their reed-pipes short and shrill.

Crinolined is Virgin Mary,
Eyes wide open to the scene,
Waiting frosty Father Winter,
Tending tenderly the Child.

And not far, under a pine-tree,
In the shadow lies in wait
Beelzebub, the hound of Satan,
For the Child of sugared mien.

But the angels safe from breakage
Hang by threads of golden brass
From the boughs of spreading yule-trees
Breathing peace upon the view.

In their flight their tinsel tinkle
Joins with the symmetric sound
When a cow with wheels inside her
Lifts her voice and moos "Noël."

Ravel gives the music to these words the rocking rhythm of old shepherd songs, pastorales, and sicilianos. Six equal running eighths rock in a dotted motif, the melody of which is the exact inversion of the old Christmas carol *Silent Night, Holy Night*. An even quieter middle section allows harmonic niceties, belonging unmistakably to Ravel's style, to come into the foreground. From its opening in B minor the piece moves to a close in B major. Together with a step-up in the tempo there is an increase in the number of small note values as well, and, in a kind of stretto, Ravel brings the piece to a closing climax in a resounding triple forte. The scene, in its passionate climax, has a dramatic effect. The limits of song are overstepped. Here Ravel prepares effects that he was able to master completely only at a much later stage of his creative development.

The style of the *Sonatine* emerges quite differently. Emotion and mechanics become compatible worlds in this piece. Just as clear and self-contained as are the three mood-impulses of the three clearly separated movements, equally astonishing is the unity achieved through the motivic kernel common to all of them. Preoccupied with analyzing the *String Quartet*, one has often neglected to observe that the *Sonatine* too is a monothematic, or more correctly, a monomotivic, cycle. The impulse of a single interval, the fourth, sets the themes of all three movements into motion: the theme of the first movement, marked *modéré;* that of the *Minuet* where falling fourths become rising fifths; and finally that of the *Toccata* where the fourth, now rising, again appears, only to return to its original descending form in a quiet secondary theme.

The work owes its existence to a quite external stimulus, a commission from a music magazine. Its spontaneous success is owed possibly more to its playability than to the marvel of its construction.

CRUISE WITH EDWARDS;
INTRODUCTION AND ALLEGRO, 1905

Cypa Godebski, Ravel's friend since the remarkable rehearsal of the "Whirlwind of Death" in the Casino de Paris, had a sister who far exceeded him in fame and social glamour. Misia Godebska, by reason of her beauty, wit, and musical gifts, led a colorful life that is mentioned in many memoirs of the turn of the century, some of which bear her Christian name in their titles. She was, as a young girl, admired by Mallarmé. Her portrait was painted by Pierre Bonnard and by Auguste Renoir. Her first husband, the wealthy Thaddeus Natanson, published the *Revue Blanche,* the leading literary journal of the period.

Misia left Natanson to marry the even richer millionaire Alfred Edwards, son of the physician to Abdul Hamid. As publisher of the newspaper *Le Matin,* Edwards was one of the most influential men in France. Later she left him to marry the penniless Spanish painter José Maria Sert.

Edwards used *Le Matin* as a forum in the battle for Ravel against the shocking judgment of the Prix de Rome jury. At the time this campaign was going on he bought his wife Misia a luxury yacht for inland waterway cruises through France and neighboring countries. It was christened *Aimée.* In June, 1905, it set out on one of its long trips, a cruise down the Aisne and the Meuse to Liège and to Amsterdam on the lower Rhine, then up the Rhine to Mainz, and from Mainz to Frankfurt, and then back to the coast of the North Sea, and from Dordrecht and Ostend to Le Havre. Ravel, who badly needed some diversion after his recent misfortune, was invited by the Edwards, as were also two painters they had befriended, Pierre Bonnard and Laprade, to accompany them and share the pleasures of the journey.

The adventure began with a race. Ravel had just received a hurried commission to write a work for harp for the Érard firm. He had worked on it for eight days and three sleepless nights. He had to delay his departure to finish the work and then had to catch up with the *Aimée* at Soissons. This journey took him first through twenty-nine canal locks in the Ardennes, then through Belgium and Holland, and at last to Germany. During the cruise Ravel seemed to show little interest in his traveling companions, even those who had made the cruise possible for him. He makes no mention in his letters of the Godebskis, the Edwards, or of the two painters. Therefore, his enthusiasm for the beauties of unfamiliar scenery and his rhapsodizing over machines and factories past which the route led him seem all the more striking. Ravel, a man who wrote only very irregularly to his friends, suddenly wrote letter after letter to Maurice Delage, his old Apache comrade and the composer of the gifted *Four Hindu Poems.*

In the first of the eleven letters he wrote from the yacht, beginning in June, 1905, he says: "The joy of this day, old boy! And that is only the beginning. The nightmare of recent days is forgotten." To be sure, he wished to preserve his contact with the outside world. He asked that mail be sent to him at Mézières and that Delage inform their common friend Sordes of his expectation for letters.

A second letter followed from Le Chesne on June 7:

The Ardennes. We have gone through twenty-nine locks, one after the other in one rainy morning. I never left the bridge. Wrapped in my raincoat, I watched the parklike meadows of reeds and yellow iris slipping past us. Then, after lunch, everything changed. The day a little clearer but still rather cloudy. They let the ship run free upstream through a Normandy of hills, quite the opposite to what one would expect.

Before, we were in the middle of Flanders. Now, a tiny harbor with a black church steeple and red houses.

Yesterday we got an amazing impression from the ship as it moved forward in the middle of a canal bordered by high, straight-standing and regular rows of trees. Looking ahead from the bridge where we stood, the effect was unusual and striking. It made me think of a French garden, of the beautiful ships of the eighteenth century, and also of some illustrations in the novels of Jules Verne.

All the time I thought I was dreaming. Maybe it was due to the thoughts that keep me from sleep. It is remarkable that I do not feel tired at all.

The associations of which Ravel speaks were characteristic of his personality. The French tradition, to which this professed modernist was so attached, points up the similar, sometimes contradictory aspects of his music. He dreamed of France in the baroque period, of the fantastic novels of Jules Verne, and of the lithographs and woodcuts of Gustave Doré.

Surprisingly, he did not mention Vincent Van Gogh, whom one might expect the impressions of this landscape would have suggested. Perhaps he had not then yet come to know his work, although Pierre Bonnard must have mentioned Van Gogh. Can one, therefore, not conclude from this that in those early days of the journey Ravel was completely withdrawn from his companions?

On June 11 another letter:

We are arriving at Liège. A positively wintry rain awaits us there, about like that in the rest of the country. Liège is very long and drawn out. I believe it looks very different on the other side. At the moment we are cruising through an industrial district. Black houses or brown bricks. Splendid and unusual factories, especially one that looks like a kind of romantic cast-iron cathedral under a protective cover of armor plate. Red smoke and tongues of flame shoot up from it. Just now the Exposition is open. It seems to be enjoying great success, so we shall not be bored for the two days we stay here. This day has not offered anything much worth mentioning beyond an astonishing glimpse of Huy, a little town very much in the style of Gustave Doré, at the foot of a fortified hill.

And on Monday morning he concluded:

After we had busied ourselves at the Exposition, we got back very late yesterday. We saw Senegalese villages, Russian seacoast villages, merry-go-rounds, etc. The city is very pretty, very lively. Magnificent sunshine. I am rushing to the post office to fetch our mail. We are happy to be alive.

René Chalupt, the publisher of some of Ravel's letters, connects "the romantic cast-iron cathedral" in spirit with the *Sunken Bell* of Gerhart Hauptmann, which much later, and for a long time, held the composer's imagination as a subject to set to music. But what is particularly striking in the letters is the sensitivity to colors, the optically keen sense for the recording of incidental and grotesque impressions. It is as though Ravel were concentrating his entire consciousness on the experiences that his eyes brought him, as though he had turned away intentionally from the world of the audible, which was his own world but which in the very same year had brought him such cruel disillusionment. Yet he was able to refer to the recent unpleasantness in a letter to Jean Marnold.

This interesting man, the critic of *Mercure Musical,* was a scion of the Napoleonic general Morland. He was the most passionate champion of Debussy and Ravel among the older music critics. He wrote about *The Case of Wagner,* translated Nietzsche's *The Birth of Tragedy* into French, and tried to apply mathematical thought processes to his musical analyses. Ravel considered him a close friend and also felt high regard for Marnold's daughter Georgette, who helped him with the furnishing of his villa at Montfort-l'Amaury several years later.

Dear Mr. Marnold: In the last few days before my departure I was terribly occupied with my work for harp commissioned by the Érard firm. Eight days of concentrated work and three sleepless nights made it possible for me to finish it for better or for worse. At the moment I am recovering on a fabulous trip. Every day I offer thanks to the gentlemen of the Institute. Your article in *Mercure* aroused enthusiasm among all of us on board.

A fortnight passed before the next letter. Dated Amsterdam, June 26, it is addressed again to Delage:

Back now from Haarlem. The pictures by Frans Hals are a revelation. Thanks for your card. Please write only on the back. Besides, in this land of the heathen it is impossible to get any news. I thank you for your good intentions about the quartet. However, I believe the second revision is at Luquin's, rue de Château, I mean d'Eau. Just now life on board is impossible. They are caulking the deck above me, repairing the keel below, hammering all over to their heart's content. See you soon.

You can hardly count on my return before a month. We are going up the Rhine as far as Cologne, I don't know where.

Three days later came the next letter:

We are in harbor in dry dock. They are working on the bridge. They are repairing something, I don't know what, looking ahead to more voyages. So we have been here three days, and I haven't yet been to the museum. There is so much to see. Amsterdam is entirely different from what I had imagined.

A collection of gaily colored houses with decorated gables, the palaces and modern buildings unusual in their colors as in their architecture.

Canals everywhere. The whole city is built on pilings,

which gives it an amazing character, but also a fishy smell. I had hardly arrived when I went off to the zoological gardens and the aquarium. I think I shall be returning there often.

Yesterday an excursion to Alkmaar, a cheese market with continual bell-ringing. On the way, one of the most magnificent views. A lake surrounded by windmills. On the fields, windmills to the horizon. Looking at this mechanized landscape, you believe yourself to be an automaton, too.

On July 5 they were already far away from Amsterdam. The letter to Delage is headed:

On the Rhine, near Düsseldorf. Since yesterday we have been in Germany, on the German Rhine. This is nothing like the Rhine as I had imagined it to be, tragic and legendary. There are no nixies, gnomes, or valkyries. It is not populated by castles or rocky peaks among fir trees. There is no Hugo, Wagner, or Gustave Doré. Perhaps it may be like that a bit further on in the neighborhood of Cologne. Just now everything is all right, maybe better.

What I saw yesterday will remain imprinted on my mind's eye, together with the harbor of Antwerp. After a muddy day, on a very broad river between gloomy flat banks without character, we discover a city of chimneys and of cupolas that spew out flames and blue or reddish rockets.

It is Haum, a gigantic foundry in which 24,000 men labor day and night. As Ruhrort was too far to go, we made a halt here. So much the better, otherwise we would not have seen this wonderful spectacle. As night fell we disembarked to go to the factories. How can I describe to you these castles of flowing metal, these fiery cathedrals, the wonderful symphony of transmissions, of whistles, of frightful hammer blows that envelops us? Over all a red, gloomy, burning sky.

A thunderstorm broke over us. We turned homeward thoroughly soaked, each of us variously affected by it. Ida wanted to weep from fear, but I from joy. How musical all this is! I have the firm intention to make use of it.

This morning we sailed off in rainy weather. A very

pale sun high in the sky. Blue patches are visible every other moment through the yellow mist. Then we glimpse something like great fairy-tale palaces. These are still more monumental factories, with which the region is overcrowded.

There was another letter the very next day:

This morning I saw the museum [at Cologne] where there are fine primitives and bad moderns. The Cathedral makes a wonderful impression from a distance and is still beautiful close up, although it has been excessively renovated. Thanks for all the pains you are taking over those miserable revisions. The ones you have will suffice [the quartet]. I entreat your attention to certain directions I have given regarding general and other tempi. I am delighted that you will be resting at Mary's. You will need to, after the enormous labor you performed on the harmony after I left. Once and for all, old chap, thanks for your letters. Have no doubt of the pleasure I feel when I see your handwriting at the General Delivery window at the Post Office. I had to tell you that. It would have been silly not to know how sincere I am aboout that. Write me in Cologne if you have any news for me. We shall be in Frankfurt in four or five days. Then we come back here.

Ravel's uneasiness about news has been explained to us by Chalupt. He was then counting on financial support from some wealthy sponsors and was awaiting good news from Delage, who, however, did not much believe there was anything to it. The next letter was written on July 12 from Frankfurt:

We got here last evening. Have already visited the museum. It contains an admirable Rembrandt, some Cranachs, and above all, a Velázquez! As to the old city, it is unique. It is so well preserved, you would think there is some trick to it. A flood of memories. The birthplace of Goethe, Rothschild, and Luther (!) The house where the peace treaty of 1870 (!) was signed. Breakfast in a magnificent garden. All in all, a day that could have been one of the loveliest if it had not been for worry over letters from you and Sordes.

Ravel had hopes of being sent to India on a cultural mission. This stirred his imagination greatly. He was attracted not only by the prospect of getting a well-paid post requiring little exertion or activity, but perhaps even more by the chance of living in one of the exotic lands of which he loved to dream. Nevertheless, the vehemence of his reactions, which extended even to annoyance with both of his well-meaning friends, is unusual.

With striking composure, Ravel had outwardly ended his discomfiture over the misfire of his efforts for the Prix de Rome. He thought he was through with the episode, but evidently he was not. His one-sided concentration on visible impressions during the yachting cruise betrayed, so to speak, the manner in which his spirit shrank into a corner where no shocks and injuries could be expected. He sometimes gave the impression all through these weeks of living in a sort of dream world. He had never been an absent-minded person, but it did happen that, shortly before his departure, he left behind at his haberdasher's the entire manuscript of the harp composition he was supposed to deliver to Érard without delay. This little oversight drew a whole chain of complications after it.

Three days later he apologized from Koblenz for his excitability:

Forgive me, old chap, for my abominable suspicions [he wrote to Delage]. I received your telegram on arrival in Koblenz. Now my friends see me in the ridiculous posture of a man who feels guilty. Let's assume the rumor is well founded. It makes it even worse that the moment was so lovely, so moving. Do you know I was actually quite ill all night after getting your letter? I didn't sleep much yesterday either and I am certain a third sleepless night is lying in wait for me. This wonderful trip! Everything that could happen did.

I really believe I should have had a secretary. Did you ever doubt it for an instant?

See you soon. Madame Ida Godebska is looking over my shoulder and worrying me because she is in a hurry to take off.

These *nuits blanches,* these sleepless nights were then a new and burdensome experience for Ravel. Later they became the rule. During at least the last ten years of his life he suffered from chronic insomnia. It forced him to stay awake half his nights, and the friends who were then his daily associates often found it difficult to avoid his occasionally very urgent demands for companionship and conversation.

His last letter was addressed to Delage on July 20:

In exactly one week we shall be together again, when we can discuss everything we have written each other and what we are thinking. Then we can be finished with it. I cannot conceal my joy at getting back. It is at its height in spite of my pleasure in this seductive journey, the memory of which I shall always cherish. The weather turned fine again for our departure from Holland. From Dordrecht to Veere a splendid crossing. We saw schools of seals again in the North Sea. A fast trip to Veere, a big, dead city, now a village showing the remains of former wealth. Middleburg properly winds up this series of noteworthy Dutch cities. It is one of the most typical, with a splendid town hall and, above all, an unforgettable church.

I don't need to tell you how happy I would be to see you on my arrival. Write me by return mail to Le Havre and send me your current address. I'll wire you the hour of our arrival. See you soon, my dear friend!

The ending of the letter betrays a warmth of feeling unusual for Ravel. This cynical soul, who always endeavored scrupulously to hide his sentiments, had obviously suffered from his separation from Delage but waited until the last possible moment to let him know it. In another way, also, the impact of his impressions from this voyage is unmistakable. A series of new worlds was revealed to him, above all an industrial world of weird, menacing nocturnal beauty, from whose gloomy darkness flames shot out, and whose silences were penetrated from time to time by piercing whistles and bursts of thunder.

Ravel was thirty. His school years were behind him. His future, without material security, was full of unknown menaces. One might describe what impressed him during these weeks of summer, and was constantly expressed in his letters, as the realization of the fantastic quality of reality, of that which gives the whole world a demonic face and form beneath its outward appearance. The dreams of his childhood recurred, dreams of the tales of seacoasts and seascapes his mother had recounted to him. But these dreams now were in altered, richer forms, often beyond understanding. Where now were his visions of the gentle Arcadian sunshine that was still mirrored in his *Menuet Antique?*

Ravel painted them for the last time in the harp work that preceded his voyage in the Edwards' luxury yacht with the Godebskis and the two painters. He called it *Introduction and Allegro*. He surrounded the harp sonorities with the colors of two wind instruments and a string quartet. Two thematic ideas govern the concise construction, which runs less than a quarter of an hour.

First there is a succession of fifths and fourths through which, starting from the third degree, B flat, the tonal center, G flat, is reached in a gradually descending sweep. Shortly the strings sound the falling and then rising scales of the second theme, which in turn provides the harp with a cue for a spacious rising, then descending, arpeggio

Left: Ravel (right) with his pianist friend and colleagues, Ricardo Viñes, 1905.

Below: Nijinsky and Ravel at the piano playing a score from *Daphnis and Chloe*, 1912.

View of Ravel's home, La Belvédère, in Montfort-l'Amaury, from the street.

Ravel used the traditional instrument, with its unique transposition technique and its diatonic basis, differently from the way Debussy did in 1904 in his two *Danses* for chromatic harp. The skill with which Ravel, the supreme artist of pianism, avoided being misled by pianistic forms and exploited every secret potentiality of mechanism and rapid pedaling in the harp is unique. The treatment of the virtuoso harp solo displays no less skill than does that for the winds and the strings.

The opening is specially governed by the stippled colors of the little staccatos in the flute and clarinet. The artistry of construction of the piece, which is confined to a sort of working out of the two main themes, rather steps into the background when compared with the skill of the instrumentation. Harmonically the piece compares unfavorably with the happy discoveries Ravel made in the three *Miroirs* or even in *Shéhérazade*. A concise cadenza for the solo harp leads to the close, which, in its adherence to conventional formulae, possibly betrays the pressure that compelled him to finish the composition while packing his trunk for the trip and being fitted at his tailors.

MIROIRS (ALBORADA DEL GRACIOSO), 1905

But now entirely new problems occupied Ravel's life and thoughts. The uncomplicated, shining world of his youth had disappeared. It is as though weird apparitions had taken possession of his imagination. However, these very specters seemed to bring wings to his new creativity. Then years of tireless and fruitful labor, years of lofty aspiration, caused it to soar even higher. Astonishingly, the piano *Sonatine* belongs in this period of dramatic expansion. It appears as a transfigured recollection of the composer's past, for quite different dreams led up to it and continued during its birth.

The new period produced five piano pieces. These are dedicated to his best-loved companions among the Apaches: Léon-Paul Fargue the poet, Ricardo Viñes the pianist, Paul Sordes the painter, Calvocoressi the critic, and Maurice Delage. The album was given the name *Miroirs,* a name less suggestive of impressionism than of program music. In his autobiography Ravel said of it:

The *Miroirs* of 1905 are a collection of piano pieces which mark a decided turn in the development of my harmony, so that musicians had to revise the views they had previously been accustomed to hold about my style. The first written and, in my view, the most typical in the collection, is the second piece in the album, *Oiseaux Tristes.* These are birds lost in the mazes of an extremely dark forest during the hottest hours of summer.

In his reminiscences of Ravel, Vlado Perlemuter said the composer wished to hear this arabesque played, not in strict tempo, but with certain diminutions, that the marking *"lent"* before the cadence applied only to the chord over which it is written, and, finally, that the chord in the last four measures must consistently dominate the moving voices.

The piece is one of the gloomiest and most depressing of Ravel's youth. It cannot be compared with any of the earlier works with respect to the skill with which the pedal is used as a veil. It is also much more eccentric harmonically and much more difficult to relate to a tonal center than is usually the case in Ravel's compositions.

The theme consists of a repeated note, B flat, following which there is a rapid ornament to be played rubato. This rubato ornament has great descriptive power. It is apparently intended to copy a birdcall, probably that of a blackbird. For the first time in Ravel's output his love of animal life can be seen, as can his precise and almost inventive observation of nature, which enabled so confirmed a town-bred individual to achieve a significant extension of language. In this connection one remembers his visits in Amsterdam to the zoological gardens and to the aquarium, the joy he experienced at seeing a school of seals in the North Sea. This text will later re-emphasize what an important and stimulating part the animal kingdom played in Ravel's life and work.

A similar gloomy mood is created by the first piece in the album. Ravel named it *Noctuelles (Night Moths)*. Consequently he dedicated it to the big-city enthusiast Fargue! Admittedly, this is not the night of romance, or the perpetual darkness of the *Nocturnes* of Chopin, or the night filled with passion and drama of *Tristan and Isolde*. In Ravel's night, to which Paul Verlaine's *Un grand sommeil noir* had introduced him ten years before, weird companions reel and dance. The piece is prophetic of several later compositions. Here again, according to Perlemuter's testimony, Ravel wanted a tempo rubato and strong accents in the left hand.

The third piece, *Une Barque sur l'Océan,* surpasses the purely pianistic content of the others. It contains performance directions that point to orchestral models. Harp and wind sonorities are evoked by every means at the disposal of a compositional technique indebted to Liszt but well versed in the most modern chemistry of sound.

The fourth work in the *Miroirs* collection is the famed *Alborada del Gracioso*. Except for the *Habanera* this is the first time Ravel used a title actually Spanish.

Alborada, literally the "Song of the Dawn," is a form of serenade of North Spanish origin from the mountain region of Galicia. The word is etymologically cognate to the

French *aube* and the Italian *alba*. Ravel may also have been thinking of the old troubadour songs with which the knights parted from their ladies at the break of day. The *Gracioso*, however, is the jester in Spanish comedy, the fool in the household of a Spanish nobleman, as Calderón and Lope de Vega liked to portray him in their plays. His morning serenade would necessarily be different in quality from the parting lyrics of the minnesingers or the songs that were sung to awaken princely personages in the seventeenth and eighteenth centuries.

If disconnectedness and the lumping together of incompatible ideas can be considered part of the picture of modern music, then Ravel has provided a copybook example with this piece. Orchestral colors seem to have hovered before his eyes, as in the *Barque sur l'Océan*. In fact, he did orchestrate the *Alborada* soon after he composed it, and in that version it is almost more famous than the original piano piece itself. The fascination of this music, apart from its atmospheric magic, is that it makes the line between serious thought and its parody difficult to discern. In creating it, Ravel, presumably entirely by intuition, becomes the painter of a psychopathological state of fluctuation in which the state of normal awareness and that of illusion merge, then separate. To this end, tonal ambiguity and chords containing three chromatically neighboring tones play important roles. Pianistically, besides the flutelike gossamer staccato and martellato, the *Alborada* uses the effect of a double glissando, for which Ravel's hands, with their very short thumbs, must have been specially suited. A Spanish flavor is clearly imparted by a certain dryness in the piano idiom, reminiscent of a strummed guitar.

The last piece in the album is again a piece of program music, It is *La Vallée des Cloches*. In this valley we hear the bells that five years earlier Debussy's *Sunken Cathe-*

dral had anticipated. The composition may have been suggested by the title of Gerhart Hauptmann's play of 1896. It is, in fact, a tone painting in three sound-colors, which, both symbolically and realistically give the effect of distant tolling. It is a new use of the piano. One is at once prepared to attribute to it some poetic idea, without being certain what it is. Quite different from the *Alborada,* the bell piece has an astonishingly unified character, as though it were cast in one continuous pour.

Even the F minor middle section, with the striking performance direction—*largement chanté*—is organically consistent with the opening and the close. The role played by the interval of a fourth is remarkable and characteristic, not only in the motif of the second bell, in which B–E and G sharp–C sharp follow each other, but also toward the close, where two fourths are placed above each other.

The similarity of the last measures to the coronation scene in Moussorgksy's *Boris Godunov,* to which Hélène Jourdan-Morhange thought it relevant to call attention, is in keeping with the style French and Russian music had been following for some decades.

The entire album occupies a special place in the music of the period. In contrast, Debussy's *Images* of the same year is traditional, almost academic. Ravel's palette of colors is staggeringly new and bold. To discover a parallel to the coloristic inventions of this musical speech, one can think only of the orchestra Richard Strauss called for in *Salome.* But it is certain that Ravel evolved his sounds without any outside influence. His interest in the musical developments of the day, beyond what was alluded to in his own Parisian circle, was at that time far narrower than it became some years later. The contact with his Apache friends explains why during those years questions of modern painting and literature excited him more than those of his own specialty. One senses this in his letters, which set forth the views of a man only visually oriented, whose casual verbal mannerisms stem from the affected literary idiom of the period.

HAUPTMANN; MAETERLINCK, 1906

Political and religious discussions hardly touched the thirty-year-old Ravel. Otherwise we would certainly find some echo in his correspondence of the issues that at that time were dominating the world's attention, such as the complete separation between church and state in France or the unsuccessful Russian Revolution of 1905–1906.

At the end of the nineteenth century Paris stood at a critical point in the art of the theater. On the literary side, symbolism and naturalism had, by the power of their momentum for change, driven the scenic arts into a movement that was directed against the traditions of the Comédie Française. Outstanding stage personalities like Sarah Bernhardt and Eleanora Duse (who was idolized in Paris) were bringing new types of expression into the theater. Ravel was passionately interested in all of this. His creative and artistic interests were steadily expanding through his association with his circle. While the esthetic dandy of 1895 did not entirely turn his back on the effects of symbolism, nor on his esoteric hostility to the masses, yet his instinctive appreciation of beauty was growing wider, deeper, and less restricted.

Ravel was a conscious and active participant in the life of the theater, in a society in which every premiere was discussed with animation. It followed the opening and the appearance of theater novelties with avid enthusiasm, while it showed little interest in the growing renaissance of ancient music instigated by the followers of the Schola Cantorum, or in the founding of the Paris Bach Society, or in the performance of Claudio Monteverdi's *Orfeo*. We do not know to what extent Ravel had actual detailed knowledge of the modern drama. It would be exciting to suppose that August Strindberg, who lived quite a long time in Paris at the turn of the century, had met the young French musician. We do know, from Strindberg's diaries, that the circles in which Strindberg moved touched on Ravel's. However, such a meeting has never been documented. On the other hand, we do know of a theatrical event that did move Ravel greatly.

The great, epoch-making event of those years was Gerhart Hauptmann's drama *The Sunken Bell,* the play that, after its German success, had conquered France in the brilliant translation by Ferdinand Hérold. The tragic play about the bell founder Heinrich and Rautendelein, the "elfin creature," electrified Ravel with its union of Christian and heathen philosophies, of Eros and mythos, of mighty iron forging and gentle lyricism. It was an unusual example of the very essence of operatic material, halfway between reality and symbol, and it was exactly what Ravel had long dreamed of.

A reference to it appears for the first time in his correspondence in 1906. On July 1 he wrote to Ida Godebska, who was making the same cruise for a second time with the Edwards on board the *Aimée:*

Here life is going along peacefully again. We feel easier about my father's health. The doctor allows him little trips in the car. Apart from that, we shall have to leave for Switzerland in a few days. This time it will be on account of my mother. She has to do something about her feet. We provide a masseuse for her every day. If I wanted to follow up all the invitations I get, my *Sunken Bell* would remain corked up in its bottle for a long time.

Ravel was working on *The Sunken Bell!* What a subject for the conjurer of bizarre moods of nature, for the engineer of the most delicate movements of feeling, for the musician to whom, more than to anyone else, the perception of reality had become a sensation in sound.

The libretto was written for him by Ferdinand Hérold, who gradually became his close friend as the work progressed. A *conte lyrique,* a lyric fable, grew out of the German "fable-drama," and a veritable creative intoxication took possession of Ravel during its creation. He revealed the details in his letters to Maurice Delage.

He stayed in Levallois from 1906 on and worked like mad. In summer the little family, on doctor's orders, moved to Switzerland for a few weeks. They found a house in Hermance, not far from Geneva, on the shore of the Lake. In a letter to Delage, August 20, Ravel said:

Now, old chap, I am installed in Switzerland and, lord knows, I weep no tears for the sea. While it isn't the same, yet it's pretty good. Sometimes the Lake reminds me surprisingly of the Mediterranean. The shore is not at all gray. Intensive and unexpected colors, false values. And then these boats with sails in dazzling colors, in odd shapes. Above all, the soft air of astonishing purity. My father feels cheered up by it. He assures us he has almost no more headaches now. The people, too, are very unusual. A cousin of mine, who was once a watchmaker, is now the first violin at the Geneva Theater.

I am waiting for a piano so I can get back to work on my *Bell.* I was temporarily interrupted. I had a wound on my finger that was causing me terrible pain. I hope it will not hinder my work. I couldn't bear that.

Just imagine. Apart from all I have finished on the first act, I have a good part of the second ready. (You wish to have an opera in five acts? . . . . You will have one in a week!)

And on August 24:

I have got my piano. This morning, without delay, I began to work on the *Bell* as soon as I came back out of the water. These baths in the Lake are a delightful sensation! We shall doubtless stay here until September 10. You ought to come over here if you leave Brittany. Then you will see for yourself how well one can work in this climate. The hotel cooking is pretty good. They don't know anything here about comfort, but you don't stay in your rooms much. We are assured that there are still fine days to come in September. Think of the tiresome time you had in Paris and write me when you plan to arrive. I'll fetch you from Geneva.

Ravel worked on the score of this opera for years. At last he got so far that on January 15, 1909, a contract was signed with the publishers Durand in Paris. It bears the signatures of Ravel, Hérold, and Gerhart Hauptmann. It provides that the income from the opera, now a work in four acts, should go two-thirds to the composer and one-sixth each to the poet and the French translator. This contract was relatively favorable to the composer if one remembers that negotiations with the publisher S. Fischer for setting to music Gerhart Hauptmann's *And Pippa Dances* were broken off because of the poet's higher demands. An operatic setting of *And Pippa Dances* was also contemplated and sketched by Arnold Schönberg in 1906–1907, but the plan was never carried out.

Ravel had to abandon his work on *The Bell* in 1914 when the outbreak of World War I made it seem impossible, at least for the foreseeable future, for him, as a Frenchman, to collaborate with a German dramatist. Roland-Manuel, Ravel's pupil and, later, biographer, testifies that many years later, in 1924, elements of *The Sunken Bell* were incorporated into the second act of *L'Enfant et les Sortilèges*. The words by the poetess Colette were used with the *Bell* music instead. The theme of the tree and the chorus of frogs come from the prewar fragment. Nickelmann's *"Quax, brekekex,"* yielded to the French phraseology of Colette.

It is difficult to imagine how *The Sunken Bell* could have worked out as a Ravel type of opera. There are differences that cannot be ascribed solely to the discrepancy in substance between two dissimilar worlds, between the fairy world of Gerhart Hauptmann with the floating contours of his backgrounds, so rich in fantasy, and Ravel's fairy realm with its boundaries always so clearly and rationally drawn. To reconcile these might have been a fascinating project, as were the cases of Maeterlinck and Debussy, or of Oscar Wilde and Richard Strauss. On the other hand, the interposition of fate that prevented the completion of the collaboration may have been a blessing in disguise.

There is no doubt that Colette's beguiling charm, so much closer to reality in spite of being so animated by her imagination, was much closer to the essential nature of Ravel's art. Hauptmann's drama also lacks one element that became more and more indispensable for Ravel in bringing out his esthetic creativity. For him the protagonist, as leading character, must not occupy the foreground so completely as to camouflage entirely the greater force behind it—the real protagonist both psychologically and artistically.

At almost the same time that Ravel began to work on *The Sunken Bell* he became fascinated with another play, as possible material for an opera, and it captivated him almost as completely. It was a work of entirely different character, a brief, succinct, strange playlet of realism, far from all myth and magic, but penetrating deep into the human soul, personifying the contrasts between bright day and dark night. This one-act drama is by Maurice Maeterlinck, the same Maeterlinck whose *Pelléas et Mélisande* had been set to music by Debussy. It is called *Interior*.

It tells of a little family sitting happy and unsuspecting in a lighted room awaiting the return home of a daughter. You see two men standing outside in the dim darkness of the garden. They feel unable to come in and break the sad news of the daughter's suicide to the cheerful family. Then a mourning procession draws near. The grieving of the crowd becomes audible. The garden door of the room swings open of itself, and one sees the impact of the frightful blow on the family.

But this Maeterlinck project was never carried out either. Was it because Ravel was not able to enter into such tragic situations, such inconsolable sentiments, as those chosen by Hauptmann and Maeterlinck? We do not know. We do know only that eventually it was more cheerful material that brought him to the theater and for which, at last, he composed musical settings.

Ravel was not a heroic figure. Epic themes contradicted the dandy in him, contradicted his whole approach to life as they did his esthetically elegant convictions. The depiction of a pathos contrary to the heroic, which Claude Debussy had wrested from his own sensibility, could not engross the creator of the *Sonatine*. Nevertheless, heroic materials exerted a remarkable attraction on him from time to time. Even the legend of Joan of Arc captivated him for a while as a possibility for dramatic representation, although, admittedly, it was not Schiller's *Maid of Orleans* with her youthfully brave and shining courage. By the time Bernard Shaw's *Saint Joan* came out after World War I, Ravel's imagination had long been diverted into channels other than those of irony and derision. The heroic Maid appealed to him in the thoughtful and realistic version of the novelist Joseph Delteil, which appeared at almost the same time as Shaw's interpretation of history. The painter Luc-Albert Moreau went so far as to sketch costumes for the projected opera. Such temporary states of fascination were not infrequent with Ravel. The little library he left behind gives curious confirmation of this.

One can suppose that Ravel's genius, that many-sided creative sensitivity, with a thousand antennae reaching out and picking up reactions from reality and from art, might have evolved the ability to cope with materials of great tragedy if it had ever been trained to submit to discipline and develop endurance.

The story of Maeterlinck's *Interior* is like one of those dreams filled with anxiety that occasionally attack life itself. It is a psychological drama that increases gradually in tension until the inevitable explosion at its close, a close that advances mercilessly like the Greek *moira,* another "Whirlwind of Death" that stabs the most sensitive region of the psyche.

Psychology is the driving force behind all the dramatic, as well as all the lyric, products of Ravel's imagination. With his very personal and sardonic outlook, he recognizes common attributes in the souls of all living creatures, the human qualities in animals, the animal in humans.

Were not the anxiety and sorrow of the birds in the dark forest, as portrayed in the second of the *Miroirs,* actually a reflection of human anxiety? As a creator Ravel held himself aloof, like an emotionally motivated animal, from such deep subjects as fate, tragedy, and death. The reactions typical of an undersized human being worked themselves directly into the nature of the works of art he produced.

HISTOIRES NATURELLES, 1906; MA MÈRE L'OYE, 1908

In the autumn of 1906 the mail brought a postcard to Ida Godebska. Ravel wrote to her:

Please hurry back. The Autumn Salon will close very soon and you will miss the Gaugins. I am finishing the orchestration of *Barque sur l'Océan,* working on the *Histoires Naturelles,* and shall soon take up the *Bell* again.

What does the reference to the *Histoires Naturelles* signify? More than ten years before, in 1894, Paris had discovered a new poet, Jules Renard, who, with his brief impressionistic descriptions, was striving to accomplish about the same thing Peter Altenberg was trying to do in Vienna. The language of his *Poil de Carotte* had so enchanted Hugo von Hofmannsthal that he had published his work in German under the name of *Fuchs* in the *Insel.* In 1904 Renard delighted his French readers with a tiny volume of poems in which animals were observed with the eye of a poet and described in human relationships. The formula is as old as the philosophy concealed behind it. But Jules Renard gave his metamorphoses a charm that was not even approached by any of his literary predecessors.

In German, as in French, literature such a representation of animals goes back to the Middle Ages. Even Goethe took satisfaction in the embodiment of the *Reynard the Fox* legends. However, Renard's animals are entirely different creatures—mostly monkeys, frogs, and hares, such as one admires on old Japanese scrolls, all tangled up with human sentiments. Ravel, in his own description, says of the poems:

Jules Renard's clear and direct speech, the deep, concealed imagery of his verses, have long charmed me. His text forced on me a special kind of declamatory line, clearly tied to the accents and stresses of French pronunciation. The premiere of the *Histoires Naturelles* at the Société Nationale de Musique called forth a veritable scandal. This was followed by vigorous debates in the musical press of the day.

The poet Jules Renard did not wish to know anything about his animal poems being set to music. He felt they were actually prose pieces. Thaddeus Natanson, the divorced husband of Misia Edwards, undertook to try to bring the two authors together for an understanding. In fact, the composer paid a call on Renard in January, 1907, but did not succeed in convincing the poet that his words needed any musical enrichment. Shortly after this unsuccessful peace mission, a performance took place. It ended in a row. Friends of Vincent d'Indy were in the majority in the audience. Jane Bathori could have sung like a goddess and not have had any effect on these defenders of petrified tradition. Ravel had done only what was very natural to him and appropriate to the essence of these barnyard animal dramas. He allowed the prose of Jules Renard to be delivered in the diction of ordinary daily life, without the traditional affected French sounding of the silent ultimate syllables. He did exactly what Richard Strauss once demanded that French music should do. He broke with a formalistic tradition that had become useless. But the effect of this was so revolutionary that hardly anyone asked about the sense of the words or the music. Well, they screamed, does he mean wantonly to annihilate our sanctified traditions? That we will not tolerate.

Charles Koechlin described the situation in a letter to Nicholas Slonimsky:

The Société Nationale has been useful to French art, but since about 1900 it has come under the influence of Vincent d'Indy. While pieces by mediocre students of the Schola Cantorum were being performed in the Society's concerts, they often refused to consider works of real merit by others. Ravel was received with suspicion. In his first performance the entire ring of the Schola was rude to the point of discourtesy.

Since their choice spirits could not agree about the work, the Schola Cantorum spread the word about that it was nothing but an artistic jest, so one need not take this "café music plus ninths" seriously. A leader among the younger critics who came to Ravel's defense was Émile Vuillermoz. It was just these songs that he studied thoroughly. He pointed out two important modern tendencies they exhibit. First, that Ravel had taken to heart Verlaine's wise counsel and sought to wring the neck of elocutionary diction and high-flown language. Second, that the songs must be regarded as governed by the new esthetic of the motion picture, with its rapid sequences and sudden changes in lighting. Debussy, however, rejected them as tricks of a fake magician.

What do these sins against a national tradition really look like? They are five songs for a middle-range voice and piano. They sing of the peacock, the cricket, the swan, the kingfisher, and the guinea fowl. Ravel dedicated each to a different friend. Some of these dedications conceal mischievous subtle digs.

The "Peacock" is for Jane Bathori, the singer who had inspired the creation of the whole cycle. The story is sketched as if by a gifted draftsman: The peacock's bride has kept him waiting. She pays no attention to his loud passionate call, his "diabolic" cry. He calls out, "Léon, Léon!" Finally he struts up the steps in resignation. The wedding is postponed until tomorrow. As he doesn't know what to do with himself the rest of the day, he spreads the fan of his tail out proudly, but he is unobserved by the hens, who are bored with admiring him.

The opening in both F and C is a very early instance of bitonality. It is followed in the middle section by a whole chain of harmonic hazards, including Ravel's pet idea from his *Habanera*, the friction among three neighboring half tones. Above all, the pompousness of the peacock's tread and the royal and exotic gesture of spreading his tail are masterfully portrayed. "Without haste and with dignity" is the direction given for this slow, courtly march, the tempo of which at the end is majestically broadened.

The second song, devoted to the cricket, is much quieter. The little insect is putting his home in order. He is winding up his cricket watch slowly and with care, until evening falls outside and the poplars point to the moon like long fingers. What was it Ravel wrote to his friend Maurice Delage from Holland? "You think you are getting to be an automaton yourself." Jules Renard's picture of the little winged creature keeping his tiny watch going clearly must have delighted Ravel. An animal that behaves like a person, and with it a machine that is an integral part of its life—this whole fanciful view of reality served him as a stimulus to creativity, recalling the feeling he had among the windmill sails at Alkmaar.

Again he allows the half tones lying close to each other to grate in the high octaves. This time it is the watch key that arrogates to itself the dissonant sound picture. The singing voice is treated almost entirely in declamatory fashion, with a tendency in the melodic line to rise constantly, working its way upward step by step within the octave range, then always recommencing from below, just as a watch's key winds up its coils. Only at the end, when evening has come, does the melodic line, now falling, run out.

The dedication of the third song reads: "For Madame Alfred Edwards, born Godebska." It tells of the swan that glides across the pond just as the luxury yacht *Aimée* did through the canals of northern France and Belgium. The white bird looks as though it aspires only to the most exalted ideals. Its glance follows the clouds as though it would love to fly among them. Then, the next moment, it plunges its beautiful head down into the "sobering pure water," like the swans in Hölderlin's poem *Die Hälfte des Lebens,* and fattens on the worms it scoops up from below. The moral is cutting enough. This swan is akin to the dying swan in Saint-Saëns' *Carnival of the Animals,* but the fable goes far beyond that in its skeptical derision of mankind. Musically as well, the spirit of Saint-Saëns is invoked: slow, rustling divided chords persuade the listener that the new impressionistic piano idiom is not too far removed from the salon style of the period after Chopin and Liszt.

This animal picture of Renard's also merges with impressions from the world of humans. Thus, when the swan's neck emerges from the water, it is "as if a woman's arm is freeing itself from a sleeve it is pulling away." The song takes on the melodic character of a cantilena most strongly. The declamation retires modestly behind the melody. Rising fourths, sometimes also their falling inversion, are the dominant intervals.

Now follows a decided contrast after so much questionable beauty, so much wearisome and wry laughter that ends in frowns. It is the only one of these songs that pictures a colorful creature quite peacefully and directly, and the animal is the kingfisher. There is no satire, only a full measure of harmonic invention, in which the gnashing and splitting neighboring half tones of the *Habanera* and the cricket song play their parts. "As slowly as possible" is the direction for this song. It begins with a chromatically descending series of seventh chords, after which the opening words of the lyric, *"Ça n'a pas mordu ce soir"* ("The fish haven't been biting this evening") , awaken at once a feeling of cheerfulness in the listener. The song is a truly impressionistic sketch in which not one note is superfluous or inadequate. Renard's language is used to present a picture of the bird he admires, which he compares to a big blue flower on the end of a stalk.

The dramatic scene that closes the album of *Histoires Naturelles* follows the lyric peace of "The Kingfisher" in animated tempo and high dynamics. It is introduced by chords a tritone apart, coupled bitonally. One of Ravel's classmates at the Conservatory was Jean Roger-Ducasse. In 1902 he had won the second Prix de Rome with his cantata *Alcyon* when Ravel's work, similarly titled and on the same text, had lost out in competition against it. The last song, "The Guinea Fowl," is dedicated to this fellow student.

This hunchback of the poultry run flings herself in blind rage upon the tail of the peacock, whose strut annoys her. She is quarrelsome without reason, perhaps because she feels she is being ridiculed because of her figure and her bald head. She gives vent to endless ear-splitting shrieks that stab the air like daggers. Sometimes she rushes out of the barnyard, disappears, then returns more excited than ever, throws herself to the ground and rolls in the dust after she has laid her egg secretly far out in the field.

The scene is full of glaring lights and glittering colors, as restless in tempo as the unpredictable creature it pictures, with grace notes and percussive martellato figures that are reminiscent of Moussorgksy and of Ravel's own *Scarbo*. In this album Ravel applied in virtuoso style his love of animals, his satire, his critical sense, and his dramatically realistic skill of representation.

He would still often seek to capture the soul of animals in his music, first in the kindergarten suite *Ma Mère l'Oye*, later in the opera to the text Colette wrote, *L'Enfant et les Sortilèges*. And Ravel succeeded again and again, as perhaps no one else has but the Danish poet Hans Christian Andersen, in finding the rare language of fairy tales to build insubstantial bridges of fantasy between reality and imagina-

tion and in understanding how to reconcile the highly sophisticated with the most naïve.

Above all else, Ravel loved children, possibly because they were even smaller humans than he. It often happened that when he was invited out in company he would
disappear from the adult gathering and would finally be
found in the nursery, deep in a game with the little ones. As
a frequent guest of the Godebskis he was also a friend of
their two children, Jean and Marie. As early as 1905 he
wrote, in a letter to Ida Godebska: "Please tell Jean I am
making him some astonishing tiny paper chickens. Kiss my
bride's tender little fingers for me." Ravel's "bride" was
Marie, then five years old. She was called Mimi. Later she
became a follower of Jacques-Dalcroze and his rhythmic gym-
nastics. Both children played piano well. As a surprise, Ravel
made them a gift of a composition. He himself wrote of it:

Ma Mère l'Oye, children's pieces for piano four hands,
date from the year 1908. My intention of awaking the poetry of
childhood in these pieces naturally led me to simplify my style
and thin out my writing. I made a ballet of this work, which
was performed in the Théâtre des Arts. I wrote the work in
Valvins for my young friends Mimi and Jean Godebski.

Two children, six and seven years old, played the
pieces at the premiere in Paris in 1910. It was at the first
concert given by the Société Musicale Indépendante, which
was founded as a protest against the Nationale. The suite is
in five movements, as is the *Histoires Naturelles* set of
songs.

It begins with the "Pavane of the Sleeping Beauty,"
composed in the Aeolian church mode. The second movement is "Tom Thumb," written in archaic style in C minor,
in which successions of sixth chords bring to mind the *faux
bourdon* style of the fifteenth century. The third movement

is the "Ugly Empress of the Pagodas." It evokes the Chinese pentatonic scale, using mainly the black keys on the keyboard. In the fourth, one hears "The Conversation Between Beauty and the Beast," between the beautiful princess and the monster who later reveals himself as a prince who had been bewitched. Musically it is a slow waltz, in which the bass voice imitates the dark grunting of the beast until, gliding over a glissando, it is transformed back into its original beautiful form. The little suite closes with the "Fairy Garden." Ravel paints its picture with freely combined notes of the C major scale, gently rocking on the white keys in every combination of chords one can imagine. In choosing these subjects Ravel went back partly to Perrault's *Fairy Tales,* partly to Spanish and oriental stories. "Beauty and the Beast" is one of the treasures among old French fairy tales, and has even been used by Jean Cocteau as material for a film.

Ravel orchestrated these children's pieces for the ballet performance in the Théâtre des Arts in January, 1912. He added a "Prelude" and a "Dance of the Spinning Wheel" to it and enlarged the interludes. The new version, in which changes in the sequence are permitted, is markedly more extended than the original. It cannot be compared with the original in childlike charm and consistency, however. Again, in spite of Ravel's mastery of orchestration, the thin, horizontal linearity of the original score loses its musical sense when transferred to so large an instrument as the orchestra.

LEVALLOIS, 1906; *L'HEURE ESPAGNOLE*, 1907

Levallois is not an attractive section of Paris—it certainly cannot be called elegant or comfortable—although it lies, like the more distinguished Neuilly, in the big bend formed by the Seine toward the west. At the beginning of the century it was still a somewhat rural neighborhood, not much built up, typical of the outskirts of a big city where new industries can get established because they can buy land more cheaply for their factories and dwellings than they can inside the city. When the engineer Pierre-Joseph Ravel moved to Paris in 1875 from the Basque coast one could only live in Levallois if one worked there, since travel into the city was so time-consuming and conveyances were so rare. Every visit to a theater, or shopping trip to the Grands Boulevards, meant a whole day's excursion, and so it was necessary to stay in a hotel overnight. Although at that time the Ravels made their home in the center, Father Ravel knew the neighborhood well, for it was not far from Levallois that he had set rolling toward Neuilly the vehicle that was driven by the motor he had invented and patented.

After 1900, Paris began to undergo changes that revolutionized the whole traffic system and gradually drew together the enormous complex of settlements previously divided into many municipal districts. Paris acquired its famous underground railway, the Métropolitain, or, as people soon called it for short, the Métro. During this quarter century the Ravel family had frequently moved its dwelling place. To some extent their unstable way of life was in their blood. They had to be very thrifty, but they set great store by a certain amount of comfort. Besides, there was much music-making in the family. Even though Maurice Ravel had long ago laid to rest his youthful dream of making a career as a pianist, he played the piano regularly, and, of course, his own pieces, that is to say, a kind of music that sounded extraordinarily dissonant and modern by then current concepts. Such tenants do not have it easy with landlords.

Sometime after Levallois came within a quarter hour's ride from the city center by Métro, a large comfortable house became available at the corner of the rue Chevalier (now called rue Louis Rouquier). That was in 1905. The little family moved out into the district, which at that time was still airy and rural. In the neighboring streets a variety of workshops had been established, including factories for producing machine tools and machine accessories. Edouard Ravel, the younger of the two sons, found work there as a machinist in the Bonnet family's plant.

Maurice was on his way to becoming a renowned, even a somewhat notorious composer. But the desire to stay together was so strong in the Ravel family that the son could not make up his mind to move away from his parents and live alone. He clung to them with the ardent devotion and filial affection that only a French son can feel for his father, even if the father is actually a Swiss. He had, also, good reason to be concerned about his father, who became seriously ill for the first time in his life in 1906. He barely recovered in his Swiss homeland, where he had been sent to recuperate, but the attacks and spells of weakness could not be arrested. This was all the more reason that the two sons felt they had to see to it that their parents were relieved of burdens.

At this time Maurice Ravel was involved in a variety of stage projects. He was planning the composition of operas, possibly also of a ballet. Gerhart Hauptmann's tragedy *The Sunken Bell* and Maurice Maeterlinck's *Interior,* as we know, filled his creative imagination. In the midst of

102

these serious, high-flown, and tragedy-laden ideas, a very gay one-act play, Franc-Nohain's *L'Heure Espagnole,* crept up on him almost unawares.

Franc-Nohain took his first literary steps in an illustrious environment. He wrote for the *Revue Blanche* of Thaddeus Natanson, the first husband of Misia Edwards. He rapidly became famous for his articles. The little comedy, so remote in a way from the style of this exalted and aristocratic periodical, had been performed in the Théâtre de l'Odéon with wholly unprecedented and superlative success. The piece—which remained in the repertory for a long time—in spite of its being a situation comedy with no suggestion of any problems, has a certain colloquial literary charm and, more than that, the merit of perfect form and a story free from dramatic gaps.

All this was most engaging to Ravel's artistic inclinations, as was the Spanish atmosphere, which always attracted him and was so congenial for him, especially in that year of 1907. So he decided spontaneously to set the comedy to music, without the slightest alteration, just as Debussy had done with Maeterlinck's *Pélleas et Mélisande* and Richard Strauss with Oscar Wilde's *Salome.*

In the short autobiography that Roland-Manuel published after Ravel's death, the composer, in a keen analysis of his own personality, makes it clear that *Histoires Naturelles,* the anthropomorphic portrait of animals by Jules Renard, had prepared him for his work on this comedy in music. But among the notes Jean Godebski left to the writer René Chalupt for the preparation of his book on Ravel, there were some far more informative statements by the composer about this first and most successful work for the stage. Ravel writes:

What I tried to accomplish was rather ambitious, that is, to reanimate the Italian *opera buffa,* at least in principle. In its final form this work does not follow the lines of its older model, its only ancestor, Moussorgsky's *The Wedding,* his faithful setting of the story by Gogol. *L'Heure Espagnole* is a comedy in music. There are no alterations in Franc-Nohain's text, except for a few phrases. It is only the final quintet that, in its general style, its vocalizing, its atmospheric effects, is reminiscent of the ensembles of the script. Apart from the quintet, the music is more ordinary declamation than vocal line.

French pronunciation, like every other, has its own accents, its musical profile. I do not see why one should not make use of these properties to try to create a true prosody. The spirit of the work is unfeignedly humorous. I wanted to express satire, above all through the music itself, through its harmony, its rhythm, and my orchestration, not, as in an operetta, through the arbitrary and comical piling on of words. The modern orchestra seems to me exactly appropriate for underscoring and exaggerating comic actions. When I read Franc-Nohain's *L'Heure Espagnole* I realized that this amusing fantasy was well suited to my basic idea.

Many things in the work tempted me, the mixture of self-confident entertainment and intentionally laughable lyricism, the background of unaccustomed and amusing sounds that envelopes the personages in this clockmaker's shop. Finally, the advantage that I could draw from the picturesque rhythms of Spanish music.

Yet it seems rather, indeed it must be presumed, that there was still another motive persuading Ravel to set this comedy to music, a motive that, admittedly, he would be the last to recognize, and, if he recognized it, the first to suppress. *L'Heure Espagnole* is a gay song in praise of the perfect male body, of simple, strong, and inexhaustibly potent masculinity. Beyond that, it is a burlesque of a sexually unsatisfied woman who has in her own home every desirable thing that a man could provide except the one thing she desires most.

First, there is her honest but very dull husband, completely consumed with the inner workings of his mechanical clocks, an excellent artisan, highly regarded by most people. It is his duty each week to wind up all the clocks of the city churches and clock towers. This task obliges him, without taking precautions, to leave his wife Concepcion, who is hungry for attention, alone for quite long periods. Next, there is the poetic dreamer Gonsalve, a youth of much musical talent, whose addiction to love is nevertheless so literary that he is better at wooing verse forms than a lady. Lastly, there is the elderly banker Don Inigo Gomez, to whose shortcomings, for all his wealth, the young wife cannot blind herself.

Maurice Ravel was thirty-two when he composed *L'Heure Espagnole.* We know from the testimony of his friends that he was gregarious, circulating with equal confidence and composure in artistic circles and in the international society of Paris. We also know that he was sensitive and much addicted to culinary pleasures, especially to the kind of food he had been accustomed to in his mother's home. If one does not measure the man by his music, he hardly appears to have been an ascetic and monastic personality. One cannot suppose that he was otherwise in matters relating to love, yet there is no visible evidence in his life of any amatory ties or any intimate relationships either with women, or, as has sometimes been conjectured, with men. All his oldest and most trusted friends, both masculine and feminine, have confirmed this, some with regret. Only the friend of his youth, Inghelbrecht, asserted in a conversation with this writer that Ravel had occasional encounters with prostitutes.

We must then imagine that this man, small of frame, suffered from his bodily inadequacy, his lack of masculine perfection, just as, we think, he endeavored to cover up by a showy elegance of dress what nature had failed to provide him. The jockey-like appearance, the variety of beard styles during his early years, the graceful swagger stick, the big trunk stuffed full of haberdashery, all this is the mark of a narcissistic assertion of self.

Sigmund Freud has outlined the concept of over-compensation. This is an aspect of certain neurotic conditions, when an existing shortcoming is balanced to the point of excess by a powerful urge toward the expression of its opposite. If we set Ravel's type before us, and beside it the chief masculine character of *L'Heure Espagnole,* it is difficult not to believe that we are witnessing an unconscious act of overcompensation. The muleteer Ramiro, who drops in at the clockmaker's house at the very moment when the master of the house is obliged to leave his pretty young wife alone in order to carry out the weekly duty of his office, is the ideal of a simple and complete man. He possesses neither the settled appearance of the husband, nor the lyric dreams of the young poet, nor the banker's riches. He has nothing at all, but he is something. He is a specimen of uncomplicated nature, an embodiment of strength, health, and the capacity for love. And this muleteer, after unwittingly carrying up and down the stairs an unwelcome suitor concealed in a gigantic grandfather clock, is the one who will make Concepcion happy.

It is a gay piece of buffoonery, entirely in the spirit of the French farces of cuckoldry and the Italian *ex tempore commedia dell' arte.* But if it were merely primitive and unworthy of Ravel it would not have been graced by a counterpoint of very curious animation. For, along with the humans and their little failings, and along with the pair of perfect lovers, the stage of *L'Heure Espagnole* is populated by the chimes, the ticking, and the little pantomimes of the many musical clocks in Torquemada's workshop. Stravinsky called Ravel, whom he admired and respected as a friend, "a Swiss clockmaker." In fact the skill with which the striking of the hours and the little melodious presentations of the numerous musical clocks are coordinated in the overture is itself a piece of masterful clockmaking. Ravel must have inherited this Swiss fine artisanry from his father, the engineer.

At the beginning of the work he spreads out, as it were, a carpet of quiet, slowly moving quarter notes, holding the meter flexible with alternating measures in 5/4 and 3/4 time. And now bizarre automatons step forward on this carpet. First, there is the bell in the soprano register, then a very high tune on a carillon, and at the end a melody on somewhat lower bells. Fourth, there now follows a trumpeter who blows a broken B major triad, and, as a fifth, a pair of music-box figurines who dance a gavotte. The sixth is a little cockerel crowing fortissimo. The seventh is a twittering and trilling canary. With all this, the pendulums of dozens of clocks, which Torquemada does not seem to notice, are ticking away. He is seated at a table, with his back to the audience, working at something that is not visible. This variegated and apparently disorderly background of sounds provides the frame for the muleteer's entrance.

What was it that Ravel wrote from the cruise on the luxury yacht of his friends Misia and Alfred Edwards when he was made restless by the friendly windmill sails of the Dutch landscape? "You think you are becoming an automaton yourself." *L'Heure Espagnole* exhibits automata as people and people as automata, one a lyric poet far from reality, another the wealthy man-about-town, the third a duty-bound artisan and merchant. Only the two principal characters, the woman and the muleteer, act normally, like opposite poles drawn together by the magnetism of love. It is precisely they who are the personification of Ravel's unsatisfied amatory wishes, one in Concepcion's man-madness, the other in Ramiro's naïve, primitive strength.

In every note and every measure the score of this

little comedy in music is a model example of the perfection-ism that for long had hovered before Ravel's eyes. It was composed in a single creative rush in the spring and summer of 1907, while he was living with his parents in Levallois, therefore surrounded by the hundred workshops of a remote industrial district entirely lacking in poetry. There the com-poser could see automobiles being driven about, these auto-matic creatures, the sight of which at that time still excited the children and adults of the metropolis as something fan-tastic, novel, and strange. The dreams and tentative experi-ments of the father had become a mechanical essential of modern life, the growth of which Maurice Ravel had ob-served with the technological curiosity of "a Swiss clock-maker."

One Saturday at the beginning of July, Albert Carré, a former operetta actor, man-about-town, and, since 1898, the very successful director of the Opéra Comique, al-lowed Ravel to bring him the new piece and play it for him. Ravel wrote to Ida Godebska on July 11:

Carré began by finding the text indecent. That should not surprise you, in view of the Director's strict ideas of moral-ity. But then he came to the business in hand. He thought the treatment at the beginning drags a bit and should be altered somewhat. Naturally, I agreed, but I am determined to do noth-ing about it. When I have finished it I shall look him up again. On many sides I am assured that this gives me reason to hope. Evidently Sévérac got more definite promises, but, thinking over the result, I really believe I can expect something better after this hesitancy.

Ravel was too optimistic. It is true that Carré ac-cepted the work for first performance and even announced advance news of it on his billboards. But year after year went by without the premiere taking place. Déodat de Sévérac, Ravel's friend for many years, evidently had better luck. His comic opera *Le Coeur du Moulin* was presented in Carré's theater in 1909, but it could not be held in the repertory.

Before its public premiere Ravel's *L'Heure Espagnole* had a memorable private showing in a studio in Montmartre for an audience of twenty. Jane Bathori, Ravel's friend since youth and the tireless prophetess of his music, sang the role of Concepcion. The orchestra score was played on piano four hands by Maurice Ravel himself and a younger pianist of Catalan origin, Philipp Jarnach, then already renowned in Paris as an accompanist. He was later to become an intimate friend of Ferruccio Busoni.

Only on May 19, 1911, did the work finally reach the stage of the Opéra Comique. From there it traveled to the lyric theaters of the entire world.

This little opera was not Ravel's only indulgence in hispanicism. Twelve years earlier he had produced his *Habanera,* the piano piece with the chords that found a much slandered echo in Debussy's work. From the *Habanera* came the *Rapsodie Espagnole* in the same year, 1907, with the motive of four notes running through it like an *idée fixe,* with its yearning overture to the night, its emotional malaguena, and the furious "feria" finale.

GASPARD DE LA NUIT, 1908

During the period of suspense between his Spanish year and the premiere of the opera, Ravel was subject, in heaping measure, to a variety of both internal and external experiences. He had not forgotten the phantoms that had disturbed his nights ever since the episode of the Prix de Rome. Worry over his grievously ill father magnified these into fantastic shapes. At last they drove him into an effort of creative significance.

Soon after he had completed the score of the little opera, he got to know a book by Aloysius Bertrand with the curious title *Gaspard de la Nuit*. It had been recommended to him by the well-read Ricardo Viñes, his friend from early youth.

Ghost stories are as rare in modern French as they are in the literature of the classic period. And yet the example of E.T.A. Hoffmann left a very deep impression on literary style in France. In that land, noted for clarity, there was a remarkable and unexpected readiness to learn the language of horror. Possibly this may have been an aftermath of the terrors of the Revolution.

Even before Erckmann and Chatrian had published their grisly tales from the shores of the Rhine, Aloysius Bertrand, an eccentric character of Italian descent who died in Paris at an early age, had explored in a novel form the area of spectral entertainment. He wrote a kind of lyric prose marked by exquisite refinement of verbal sounds. Many writers in the succeeding generation imitated Bertrand's prose poems; certainly Théophile Gautier and Charles Baudelaire learned from him.

In addition, the title *Gaspard de la Nuit* can be traced back directly to Hoffmann, whose music-intoxicated fantasies in the manner of Callot had appeared in 1815. Bertrand, in fact, called his collection of tales *Fantasies in the style of Rembrandt and Callot*. Both Hoffmann and Bertrand were therefore influenced by the grotesque etchings of Jacques Callot, a baroque forerunner of Francisco Goya, a bold visionary who pictured the horrors of war and of death.

The expert polish and perfect virtuosity of these fantasies by this "goldsmith in verse," as Sainte-Beuve called Aloysius Bertrand, must have enchanted Ravel. The jewel-like finish of the poems may also have led to the unusual title *Gaspard de la Nuit,* as Bertrand was, no doubt, aware that the Persian name Kaspar means nothing other than "keeper of the treasure." Certainly, these were ornaments of most superior craftsmanship.

During the labor of composition, which kept Ravel chained to his writing desk in the house at Levallois all through the three months of the summer of 1908, he wrote another of his letters to his friend Ida Godebska. In this one, of July 17, he said:

Dear Friend: Soon I shall be able to escape; not, however, into the green, as the grass has already been mown, but into the blue, if not that of the Seine, then into that more intense blue of happiness among friends.

At the moment, inspiration seems to have quickened. After all too many months of pregnancy, *Gaspard de la Nuit* will perceive the light of day. As soon as these three pieces are finished, I shall do the corrections on my *L'Heure Espagnole* and complete the orchestration. As for *Gaspard,* the devil has had a hand in it. No wonder, for the devil himself is indeed the author of the poems. Now I can work in peace. Practically no one is left in Paris. The Delages have gone off on a long auto trip. They won't stop until they reach the end of the world.

Yes, it was true that the devil himself had written the poems. Bertrand lets the reader read between the lines to see the devil's uncanny hand. But it was not only the diabolic elements that Ravel chose in the studied and tasteful selection he made out of the whole body of the verses. *Ondine* attracted him just as certainly as did the lugubrious aspect of the gibbet, or the infernal dwarf *Scarbo*—Ondine, whose cool, glittering mermaid's body had also inspired E.T.A. Hoffmann, Albert Lortzing, Aleksandr Dargomyzhski, and Antonín Dvořák to write works for the lyric stage, and Jean Giraudoux to create one of his loveliest plays.

Aloysius Bertrand ends his tale of *Ondine* with this sentence:

And when I replied that I was mortal, she, pouting and sulky, wept two tears, then, with a brief burst of laughter, disappeared in a shower of foamy spray that trickled down white on the blue of my window.

Here the sculptor in sound and tone color associates himself with the jeweler in words. In his *Ondine* Ravel perfected, with extreme virtuosity, the arpeggio technique that he invented for his *Barque sur l'Océan* in his *Miroirs* of 1905, and with which he had projected the methods of Franz Liszt into the modern world of sound.

We know from Vlado Perlemuter that Ravel did not wish his *Ondine* to be played too slowly. It was meant to be songful, tender, and expressive, yet never dragging or played with an affected ritardando. A few years later, Debussy published a piano piece of the same name in his second volume of *Préludes*. It has no similarity whatever to Ravel's. In a detailed comparison of the two pieces, Jules van Ackere calls attention to the firm melodic line and crystalline clarity of Ravel's *Ondine,* beside which Debussy's appears blurred, fragile, and elusive.

This observation would apply not only in this specific instance, but in general to the relation between the work of these two composers. Even the leaning toward the spectral and cryptic is completely foreign to Debussy. He would never have been able to treat musically a subject like the gallows, the second piece in the *Gaspard de la Nuit* cycle. This *Gibet* is an unusual study of the utmost weirdness and horrible, deathly fascination, in which heaven and hell appear to have made a paradoxical rendezvous with each other.

The piece, from beginning to end, is built up on an obsessively repeated note, such as Ravel had first employed in his earlier *Habanera,* repeated in the "Cricket

Song" in his *Histoires Naturelles,* and would drive to its peak in the ostinato rhythm of *Bolero.* But here, in this picture from inferno, which reminds one of a scene in Verdi's *Masked Ball,* the ostinato is the death knell, the bell which, in Bertrand's own words, "sounds on the horizon, at the city walls, while the corpse of one who has been hanged is reddened by the setting sun."

The scene has a dreadful fascination. It has the gothic, medieval character of the ominous bell that tolls the dreaded hour of execution, with its oppressive suspense, which Ravel, with chromatic cunning, has made the central theme of this tone poem.

He dedicated it to his old friend, the critic Jean Marnold, at the same time hinting, in friendly maliciousness, that this would be the only one of the three pieces he would be able to play. In fact, it is less of a virtuoso work in its writing than the other two. It serves as the slow movement in the three-part sonata-like cycle. However, this makes all the greater its demands on the skill of the performer in rendering and distinguishing the tone colors of *Le Gibet,* especially if he obeys Ravel's direction to keep time with absolute strictness. The work is written in several layers of color. By contrast with the other two, it uses an almost orchestral palette.

The third of these pieces is in the form of a swift scherzo. The mood reproduced is of the purest Hoffmann-esque spirit. *Scarbo* is the name of the devilish imp who appears at night in the room of a sleeper in the rays of the silver moon under a sparkling sky. He whirls about like a top bewitched, suddenly springs to the peak of a tower like a figure on a Gothic cathedral, then tumbles in a heap like a spent rocket.

Ravel himself wrote of *Scarbo* that he wanted to compose something that would be even more difficult than

Mili Balakirev's much-feared *Islamey* fantasy. This grotesque piece, with its witchlike speed and richness of tonal excitement, provides an effective contrast to the almost deliberate pace of the gallows movement.

When the pianist Perlemuter studied the *Gaspard de la Nuit* cycle with him, Ravel told him he planned the *Scarbo* as a caricature of romanticism but that (and here his voice sank to a whisper) perhaps he had let himself be captivated by it. The vehement, driving seventh, under which Ravel wrote the words *quelle horreur,* is closer to true romantic feeling than to any caricature of it. Pianistically, this *Scarbo* is the most difficult work Ravel ever composed. Obviously, the famous passages in seconds were written for the remarkably stubby thumbs of his own hands.

The entire cycle is the acme of shrewdly perfected pianism. In it the ideal of technical perfection, which Ravel, as the first musician of the new era to do so, had raised to artistic preeminence, is almost attained. Yet he never expressed himself more laconically about any of his works: "*Gaspard de la Nuit,* pieces for piano after Aloysius Bertrand, are three romantic poems of transcendent virtuosity." The premiere performance, January 9, 1909, in the Salle Érard, at a concert of the Société Nationale, was played by the unwaveringly faithful Ricardo Viñes. Even the witchcraft of *Scarbo* could not terrify him.

But reality soon forced these specters and death-intoxicated apparitions into the background. To recover from the tour de force of composing *Gaspard,* Ravel allowed himself only three weeks in the Godebski country house at Valvins, not far from Versailles. Even here the phantoms gathered around him, for he read the exciting novel *Doctor Lerne* by Maurice (not Jules) Renard. In this a demon biologist first mates plants with animals by grafting them together, then carries his process further with animals and people, and finally consummates a union, condemned by God, between himself and his automobile, of which the offspring is a robot of terrifying strength and intelligence.

How could this book not have fascinated Ravel, who loved automatons, who had sung the beauty of clock-works, and who aspired to give his music the perfection of a beautiful machine?

But there were also friendlier creatures at Valvins. Jean and Mimi Godebski, whom Ravel adored, had to stay at home with their English governess while their parents and Misia Edwards were making a tour of Spain. During these happy weeks new hope arose for the premiere of *L'Heure Espagnole*. It was announced in the program of the Opéra Comique, as was Déodat de Sévérac's *Coeur du Moulin*. But Ravel had still longer to wait, longer than the more fortunate Sévérac.

At the end of September the idyll came to a close. Ravel was called back to Paris. His father's illness had rapidly become worse. The engineer Joseph Ravel died October 13, after years of suffering, partly by the same unendurable headaches that later beclouded the life of his son. Grief over this loss appears to have stricken the son fearfully. It took months before he found the strength to resume his work and two years before the completion of his next major composition.

RUSSIAN AND GREEK INFLUENCES; *MÉLODIES POPULAIRES GRECQUES*, 1907; *DAPHNIS AND CHLOË*, 1912

In these years Ravel took refuge in the company of many who, later became indispensable to him. He received visits from the young composer Edgar Varèse, who was full of revolutionary ideas; he circulated among the Sordes and the Godebskis, and could be met in Misia Edwards' salon, where all the celebrities of the century met each other; he attended concerts and the theater. His critical sense was being shaped by his own desire for perfection. A concert of the Société Nationale called forth acid criticism from him. He expressed it in a letter to Cypa Godebski:

Dear old chap: You can thank your attack of mumps that it kept you from hearing the concert at the Nationale. Oh, those filthy musicians! They don't know how to orchestrate. They fill up your ears with Turkish music. Fugal interludes replace handiwork. Themes out of *Pelléas* amplify their ideas. And what a noise all this makes! Tam-tam, Basque drums, snare drum, glockenspiel and cymbals, anything that occurs to them. One of them breaks the record by adding xylophone and Chinese wood blocks. With just a little music added it might be lovely.

In all this Schmitt sounds like an intruder: ample inspiration and melody, a splendid and capable orchestra, everything that is missing in the others. Finally, one can tell the difference in quality, in spite of deplorable performances and a singer without a voice.

Cheerful footnote: *Aegina*. The composer, Mlle Z., left in the lurch by a cautious soloist, sang her composition herself. I would not have done that. She has a voice like mine, only louder. First the audience thought it was sitting in on a painful birth, then it settled down and accepted the situation with the greatest cheerfulness in the world. Then there was a little scherzetto that ran about thirty-five minutes to close out the evening. I hid at the exit so as not to run into the composers, and I ran to the bar. A lemonade and three glasses of water, nothing to get me excited.

Give me some sign of life as soon as you are better. At the moment my father's doctor has expressly forbidden me to see you, although it seems not to be infectious. I am finishing the *Heure*. Durand will get the ending of the score tomorrow.

This letter was written March 14, 1909. It was a year full of achievements in the arts in Europe. In Germany there were clashes over the premiere of Richard Strauss's *Elektra*. In Vienna, Schönberg had written his first atonal songs and piano pieces. F. T. Marinetti, the Italian futurist, had published his manifesto in *Figaro*. Painting and sculpture had produced the first works of analytical cubism. All these were, sooner or later, discovered and discussed by Ravel. Certainly, his feeling for tradition was much too strong to allow him to become a partisan of the latest innovations. But the attraction of these many and varied experiments in art was felt. It is true that Ravel did not collect modern paintings, but the domestic environment that he created for himself noticeably reflected the influence of futuristic, cubistic, and impressionistic works of art.

In the summer of 1909, Paris experienced, in addition, an artistic sensation with the first guest engagements of the Ballet Russe and the great premieres of Sergei Diaghilev. Misia Edwards was one of the enthusiastic admirers of this new, colorful, and exotic art of the theater, which was to be seen on the stage of the Théâtre du Châtelet. She financed Diaghilev, introduced him to society, and brought him into contact with important French artists. Jean Cocteau, then just seventeen, the painter Pablo Picasso, then already on the threshold of fame, Debussy, Ravel, the rising star Stravinsky—all became regular attendants at her salon where, along with French, Spanish and Russian became the principal languages spoken.

The Russian craze, which must have encouraged Diaghilev's success, was in keeping with the interests of modern composers. Just as Debussy was influenced by Moussorgsky, so Ravel was spiritually guided by Borodin. There is no doubt that, in addition to Diaghilev's ballet productions, the modern intellectual audience was transported by the new settings of *Boris Godunov* and *Prince Igor*.

In May, 1909, Ravel began to write as a music critic. His comments, though not very extensive, were often original and, for his artistic attitude, always significant. The journal *La Grande Revue,* which, among other features, ran serialized novels, including Gabriele D'Annunzio's *Forse che Sì, Forse che No,* asked a few modern French composers to state their opinions of Wagner. Florent Schmitt declined. Ravel was cautious and wrote: "First one must acknowledge that Wagner, before everything else, was a splendid musician." It seemed to him too late to pass judgment, after all that had been written by Nietzsche, Catulle Mendès, and Péladan.

Naturally, Ravel also took part in the Russophile movement, although he himself had by that time outgrown the influence of Slavic romanticism. It could not satisfy his ever growing obsession with perfection. The credo of musicians like Moussorgsky and Borodin, members of the group of The Five, was anti-academic and anti-Western. They all believed in some naïve and primeval instinct that was not to be adulterated by technique or skill. It was only in their desire for instrumental virtuosity, in which only the well-schooled Balakirev had matured, that Ravel felt himself at one with them.

Diaghilev, too, adored the ideal of technically perfect production by the totally disciplined body, as later Stanislavski's theater demanded, the summing-up of all the methods through which the dancer becomes a vehicle of artistic expression. At about the same time (1909) he discovered two composers whose orchestral sound and whose rhythmic sense were congenial to his esthetic world. One, twenty-seven years old and little known, lived in St. Petersburg and was called Igor Fëdorovitch Stravinsky. The other, already surrounded by the aura of a new reputation, was Maurice Ravel. Everybody knew that the composer of *His-*

toires Naturelles was passionately fond of the theater and that he was working on operas based on Gerhart Hauptmann's *Sunken Bell* and Maeterlinck's *Interior*. That was how the relationship between Diaghilev and Ravel began, one that was extremely variable but lasted for twenty years. The composer has written very little about it. What he did say relates only to the one work that he composed expressly for Diaghilev:

> *Daphnis and Chloë,* a choreographic symphony in three movements, was commissioned from me by Mr. Sergei Diaghilev, the director of the Ballet Russe. The story is by Michael Fokine, then the choreographer of the famous troupe. It was my intention, when I wrote it, to compose a large fresco painting, less in keeping with antiquity than with the Greece of my dreams, which was more closely related to a Greece such as French artists had portrayed at the end of the eighteenth century. The work is constructed symphonically, on a very strict tonal plan, based on a small number of motifs, the full development of which is assured by the symphonic unity of the whole.

This immense score, uniquely expressing Ravel's genius, was not completed until 1912. Meanwhile he had other encounters that stimulated and enabled him to test the scope of his versatility. The hundredth anniversary of the death of Haydn was to be celebrated in Paris. Among other works composed in homage to him by French composers and appearing in the Review of the International Music Society, there is a little minuet constructed by Ravel on five notes, some of which are the letters in the name Haydn (leaving out y and n). The name symbol is used five times in the piece, once in retrograde motion and once in retrograde inversion. It was evident that Ravel had not in the slightest degree outgrown the contrapuntal skill André Gédalge had taught him and that this playing with the letter names of the notes did not hinder him from introducing, at the conclusion of the middle section, a series of chromatically altered chords over an organ-point B (H in German), the initial of Haydn's name. It is more than likely that this Haydn celebration in Paris focused the attention of French composers on Haydn as never before. During the period of neoclassicism after 1909, they fixed their admiration on him and constantly acknowledged him as the musician who perfected the sonata form. But it was a folkloristic source that stimulated Ravel in that year of 1909. Through his friend Michel Calvocoressi, the important Greek musicologist, he learned of a collection of Greek folk songs from the Island of Chios. He wrote harmonic settings for some of them with piano accompaniment. Another, *Tripatos,* is a dance with sung words that tell the story of a sickly girl. Her fear of death is assuaged by her father with these words: "Be still, my child, do not fear. You are lovely as a queen and you will marry." Ravel followed the mood of the song harmonically with a few delicate strokes. He captured the elements of the soothing melody with a vocalise that adorns it gracefully. *Tripatos,* composed in 1909, was not published until thirty years later in a special issue of *Revue Musicale* in memory of Ravel after his death.

In 1910 there followed a collection of four folk songs, one each of Spanish, French, Italian, and Hebrew origin. Ravel was no folklorist in the serious sense Bartók was, or the young Stravinsky. If he made use of a folk tune, it was by reason of the same esthetics that influenced him to adopt other sources, the choice of which clarifies the development of his entire outlook and output.

The simplicity of folk songs was for him only a mask. He gladly availed himself of it in order to conceal behind it the countenance of his own modern, high-strung, many-sided and multicolored tonal speech, always to be recognized by the knowledgeable. So he never conceived "in the manner of" folk song or in a nationalistic spirit. He made use of bits of motives and phrases out of a folk tune and hung these before his own style like a visor. This procedure has no analogy in the work of other composers. It gives Ravel's folk-song treatment, so to speak, a paradoxical magic, because simplicity remains in a constant state of tension with sophistication. This tension aroused the playful instinct of the composer.

Ravel obviously had many discussions with Calvocoressi about his work on Greek folk songs, and these undoubtedly left influences on his general musical thinking. The history of the origins of the *Mélodies Populaires Grecques* goes further back than Ravel's biographers have hitherto noticed. Calvocoressi, whose testimony on this point is the most competent, alluded to it in 1939 in the *Revue Musicale*. He states that in February, 1904, he called Ravel's attention to Greek folk songs. The occasion was a lecture, entitled *Songs of the Oppressed* and treating of Greek and Armenian folklore, that Pierre Aubry had to prepare on short notice. The singer Louise Thomasset was persuaded to collaborate, but she made it a condition that the songs be accompanied by piano. Calvocoressi turned to Ravel and with him selected four Greek songs that had appeared in a collection in Constantinople in 1883 and another, *Les Cueilleuses de lentisques,* out of a Pernot collection. In thirty-six hours Ravel composed a piano accompaniment. The performance took place February 20 in the School of Advanced Social Studies.

In the 1905–1906 season Marguerite Babajan sang three more out of the Pernot collection. These and *Quel Galant* out of an older collection issued by Matsa, together with the *Cueilleuses*, were printed in 1907. *Tripatos* was later added as a sixth song. Ravel himself held back three others: *A vous, oiseaux des plaines, Chanson de pâtre épi-rote,* and *Mon mouchoir, hélas, est perdu.*

In his pastoral romance *Daphnis and Chloë,* Longus, the Greek poet of the epoch in which Christianity was spreading in the Occident and the Orient, portrays a bucolic Hellas the serenity of which is disturbed by a band of pirates. They subdue maidens who have sought shelter in the sanctuary of Pan, among them Chloë, the beloved of Daphnis. At the victory celebration of the invaders, while Chloë is dancing at the behest of the robber chief Byraxis, the great god Pan sends satyrs, creatures of fable, and consuming flames, into the ravine of the pirate lair. The miscreants flee, leaving Chloë behind. She returns home to her beloved.

The scenario is by the choreographer Michel Fokine. Even before his collaboration with Diaghilev, Fokine had submitted plans to him in St. Petersburg for a ballet using this material. His notes included a program for the art of the dance that dispensed with entrances and set numbers and combined in one unity music, painting, and the plastic arts. This was only much later realized by the Ballet Russe.

The same pastoral Mediterranean spirit colors the romance of Longus and Fokine's scenario as pervades the timeless Hellenic folk songs, and yet what a difference in style there is between the piano accompaniments of 1904–1909 and the score that was begun in 1910 and completed April 5, 1912! Ravel wrote it for the sound of the richest orchestra he ever would recruit. The colors of the woodwinds are prismatically differentiated as though a continuum of timbres were floating before him: piccolo, two flutes, an alto flute in G, two oboes and English horn, E flat clarinet, two B flat clarinets and a bass clarinet in B flat, three bassoons and contrabassoon, four horns and trumpets, three trombones and a bass tuba, and two harps. The busily occupied, often subdivided, string quintet has the deep C string of the double bass as an added underpinning. Then in percussion: tympani, bass drum, cymbals, triangle, drum, Basque drum, side drum, castanets, celeste, and glockenspiel. The chorus is wordless, used in chromatically gliding vocalises, and coordinated with the instrumental palette.

As for the premiere performance, which took place in the Théâtre du Châtelet on June 8, 1912, it was full of incident. It was not only that the unaccustomed character of the music demanded extra care of the dancers in their preparation, but that Ravel himself procrastinated in completing the score, which took him over three years to finish. Before it was completed, the first Suite, made up of portions of the ballet, was extracted for concert performance. Gabriel Pierné conducted its premiere in Paris on April 2, 1911, at the Concerts Colonne. Ravel heard a rehearsal, March 23, with which, he wrote Cypa Godebski, he was content. His letter, dated from La Grangette, describes the spring: "Many still clumsy little birds are preparing their concerts."

The premiere of the *Daphnis and Chloë* Suite caused confusion in the press. The reaction was a mixture of respect and shock. Even a progressive musician like Alfred Bruneau, who wrote scores to Émile Zola's libretti, thought the freedom of form and orchestration overstepped every boundary, that anarchy reigned in the harmony and polyphony. The artists in Diaghilev's immediate circle did not feel very differently. Ravel's closest coworkers in the realization of the piece were far removed stylistically from the Hellenistic vision of this music. One was the painter Léon Bakst, the gifted Russian scene designer, who deified ancient Greek culture. He also loved barbaric bright colors and therefore was able to realize incomparably Rimski-Korsakov's *Schéhérazade,* but he had no relation whatever to the eighteenth century, to the Grecian mood Ravel felt so completely. Michel Fokine, on the other hand, had a much more modern concept of dance for his scenario.

In spite of all doubts and difficulties, Diaghilev, who wished to proceed with certainty, concluded contracts with the young solo dancers in his company, Tamara Karsavina and Anna Pavlova. They were to alternate in the part of Chloë in the 1910 spring season, while Waslaw Nijinsky would undertake the role of Daphnis.

Then one deadline after another was missed. The premiere of the work, which was condemned as undanceable, was constantly being postponed. Finally, only a few months before the premiere in 1912, Diaghilev himself had doubts. He tried to get out of his contract, by which he had bound himself to stage *Daphnis and Chloë,* with the publisher Durand. Durand pacified and persuaded him, nevertheless, to carry out his obligation, a task that seemed so impossible.

But during the stage rehearsals in the Théâtre du Châtelet, there was constant friction between the choreographer Fokine and Nijinsky. Diaghilev, who intervened in the quarrel, antagonized Fokine, so that after the premiere there came a break between them. The corps de ballet also experienced great musical difficulties, hard to believe of the company that only a year later did Stravinsky's *Sacre du Printemps.* For instance, the 5/4 time in the finale of the *Danse Générale* simply would not impress itself on the dancers. Finally they found a solution. They kept repeating the five syllables *Ser-gei Dia-ghi-lev.* Today such a rhythm appears quite harmless, although this finale has lost nothing of its fresh musical charm for us. It is not, by the way, uninfluenced by Rimski-Korsakov's *Schéhérazade.*

Because of the friction between the troupe and its artistic leadership, the premiere performances were not up to expectations. The principal success of the evening was not

Ravel's with his *Daphnis and Chloë,* but Nijinsky's with his highly daring narcissistic interpretation of Debussy's *Prélude à l'Après-midi d'un Faune.*

It is no wonder that relations between Ravel and Diaghilev cooled off somewhat after that. Ravel was, in any case, much less dependent on success than was the moody Russian Apollo with the monocle. Ravel sat through his own premieres cool and composed, as though the whole affair were of no concern to him. About a year before the premiere of *Daphnis and Chloë,* the long delayed premiere of *L'Heure Espagnole* had taken place at the Opéra Comique (August 19, 1911). It was an evening of great social glamour. Before the house lights went down, Ravel said to his friend Maurice Delage that they were the only two in the house who were wearing black evening clothes instead of the midnight blue that had recently become the fashion. In such matters, too, he was a perfectionist, entirely willing to submit to the laws of change in fashion, though he might choose, in perverse rebellion, to violate them.

Despite the tensions of their relationship Ravel's work for Diaghilev was not entirely brought to a close. Ravel's few orchestral works had demonstrated his powerful understanding of the sound of modern music. There are colors in his early *Shéhérazade* score that, from the soloistic use of the winds, especially the woodwinds, produce effects of remarkable sonority. The *Rapsodie Espagnole* expands the area of these new sounds even more consciously.

But one cannot compare Ravel's style of orchestration with that of either Debussy or even Richard Strauss. In Debussy there is almost always present a soft orchestral mist from which the colors emerge, shining gently like the contours of a landscape in a dim dusk. In Strauss there is a preference for massive orchestral sonority, derived from Wagner, out of which orchestral solos emerge only occasionally, and then always with a definite illustrative intention. If Debussy's orchestral sound covers and intentionally veils its textual associations, Strauss's brings them all too close to the listener, like an overassertive advertisement.

On the other hand Ravel's concept of orchestral sound is often closer to that of Gustave Mahler. Both composers make use of soloistic colors with a recklessness and boldness such as had hardly been done since the writing of concerted music in the seventeenth century. At the same time both also indulge in the effect of grouping together whole choirs of instruments. But this choral type of instrumentation is itself, in a way, a concentration of the soloistic principle.

When, in *Daphnis and Chloë*, daybreak is portrayed with the unforgettable harp arpeggio and the alternating doubled flutes and A clarinets, there is a color combination, a specifically orchestral one, that takes for granted the presence of a multiplicity of players. And yet the domination by harp, flute, and clarinet is such that you believe you are listening to masterfully extended and sublimated chamber music. Still, Ravel does not content himself with these three colors. The first chord, over which arpeggios and glissandos are executed, has a complex timbre basis. Muted subdivided violins and violas without mutes perform a pianissimo pattern of which the tonal center, A, is intoned by partly muted, partly unmuted celli and contrabasses. This A is the point of departure for a chromatic gliding figure in the bass which steps down to F sharp, then later to D sharp, finally to D. It is thus a variant of a harp glissando, made rhythmic and stretched over a much wider time span, but for this reason reduced to the much narrower spread of the fourth, A to D. Here the deep strings supply a kind of sonorous background, out of which flutes and harps lift their voices in splashes of striking color. The horns, muted, make their appearance simultaneously with the clarinets, playing the tritone B flat–E.

In the fifth measure the celeste introduces a new timbre. This tone portrait, done, as it were, in a half-light, brightens up gradually as the strings, stand by stand, from the concertmaster on down, remove their mutes. In the eighth measure (No. 156 in the score) all the strings play without mutes. Ravel wrote in the score: "Gradually day breaks" and, one measure later, "One hears birdsong." With these voices of nature, instrumental solos come forward, first the piccolo, then the flute; and with these a theme finds entrance, rising gradually out of the double bass region, which portrays the rising sun. It is an original theme, consisting of a fourth, a minor third, and a whole tone, that takes on ever higher dynamic values as it occupies higher octave positions, but without actually leaving the piano region of sound. It acquires the character, first of a tender, then later, an ardent, song of praise when it is taken up by the woodwind choir and is developed by clarinets and the bass clarinet.

Though this Ravel orchestra evokes dark and quiet tints, one feels one is in a landscape to which bright sun belongs. Even in the nocturnal shadings one does not hear either the twilight mist of Debussy's coloristic thought or, at other times, the massive and sometimes brutal energy of Strauss's orchestra. Ravel's coloring is always bordered and delimited by exact contours. It is laid on with a most sharply pointed brush, which makes for a penetrating sound impression.

To do this, Ravel does not favor the more characteristic or striking colors of the instruments. He requires the services of performers who are capable of playing in pure colors. The main roles in his orchestral sound are assigned to the winds, especially the woodwinds, and to the percussion, where Spanish or exotic elements are favored. Thus, he does not hesitate to enliven ancient Greece with the voices of castanets and Basque drums. As with many French musicians (and, after Ravel, above all with Darius Milhaud), there is evident here the unconscious vision of a unifying Mediterranean feeling that pays little attention to any differences between the eastern and the western shores of that sea. Ravel's exoticism is Mediterranean. If his Spain embodies more the Moorish-Arab of the Andalusian than the chivalric West Gothic of the Castilian culture, so also his Greece is not that of white marble statues but that of the gaily garbed shepherd peoples. We know today what Ravel's contemporaries did not know, that his music, especially the orchestral, has many ties to a non-European culture.

VI 1912–1914

STRAVINSKY; SCHÖNBERG;
THREE MALLARMÉ SONGS, 1913

Diaghilev, with the full intensity of his feeling for artistic expression, which was out of the ordinary and always looking to the future, had recognized the unusual charm of Ravel's orchestral writing. In 1912 a plan was ripening in his mind to stage in Paris Moussorgsky's unfinished and partly unorchestrated opera *Khovanshchina*. As he did not agree with Rimski-Korsakov's approach, he looked for a composer who could bring Moussorgsky's sketches to completion. Igor Stravinsky, to whom he turned for this purpose, was in the midst of his work on *Le Sacre du Printemps*, but he proposed to Diaghilev that he should undertake this task together with Ravel. Ravel visited Stravinsky at Clarens on Lake Geneva, where it was agreed that Stravinsky should orchestrate two sections and the closing chorus of the opera, for which Moussorgsky had written down only a theme of a Russian folk song, and that the rest of the work of orchestration should fall to Ravel.

So Ravel migrated to Clarens for a few weeks in the beginning of spring, 1913. He settled at the Hôtel des Crêtes near the Hôtel du Mont Blanc, where Stravinsky was staying. The months of March and April were taken up with the work of orchestration. Unfortunately, it did not go very well. Stravinsky in his autobiography speaks of it as a mixture that fell apart even more readily than Rimski-Korsakov's conception. Ravel's orchestration remained unpublished, but it served as preparation for his work on *Pictures at an Exhibition* nine years later.

Nevertheless, the time he spent with Stravinsky had creative consequences. The Russian friend spent a few weeks in the autumn of 1912 in Berlin where Diaghilev was fulfilling a guest engagement with his Ballet Russe, and where he gave *Petrouchka* a German performance. At that time, the beginning of October, Arnold Schönberg, in the Choralion Hall, was rehearsing the premiere of his *Pierrot Lunaire* with the actress Albertine Zehme. The work is written to a poem by Albert Giraud and is scored for an exactly notated speaking voice and an ensemble of five instruments. The dress rehearsal took place October 9 before an invited audience of critics and the general public. Stravinsky, who was present, was both fascinated and repelled. The ambivalent impression was extremely strong. He could not put it out of his mind, and its aftereffect is found not only in the harmonies of *Le Sacre du Printemps* but equally in the chamber opera he wrote five years later in Switzerland, *L'Histoire du Soldat.*

As the score of *Pierrot Lunaire* appeared only in 1914, Ravel could not have seen it at Stravinsky's in Clarens. However, Stravinsky must have given his friend a faithful description of the work, probably even played parts of it for him from memory. Ravel seems to have been captivated by it no less than Stravinsky. And so something occurred that neither of the two could possibly have foreseen. In the midst of straining to meet Diaghilev's deadline for the delivery of the completed orchestration, the two musicians composed some songs with an accompaniment very similar to the ensemble for which Schönberg had composed *Pierrot Lunaire:* piano, string quartet, two flutes, and two clarinets. Stravinsky made use of some Japanese poems, while Ravel set the *Soupir* of Stéphane Mallarmé, whose poem *Sainte* had already been the text of one of his earlier songs in 1896. Almost at the same time, in 1913, Claude Debussy had set Mallarmé's *Soupir* to music with piano accompaniment. Ravel's settings were dedicated to Stravinsky, and, in return, the latter dedicated to his French friend the last of his Japanese songs, *Tsaraiuki*.

In 1911 Ravel had become a close friend of the Italian composer and pianist Alfredo Casella (eight years his junior) and his wife Hélène Kahn-Casella, who were then living in Paris. On April 2, 1913, Ravel announced to Hélène Casella from Clarens:

> I wanted to write you at once, but I was in a pitiable state. With me composition takes the form of a serious illness. I suffer from fever, sleeplessness, loss of appetite. Out of this for three days there emerged a song to a text by Mallarmé. . . .
>
> What I speak of on the next page is not for you. Not that the subject is unsuitable, in and of itself, but it relates to our sacred Independent Music Society. I have some plans and suggestions for it that may interest our worthy colleagues.
>
> To the Committee of the IMS
> An admirable plan for a Concert to stir up a Row.
> Pieces for (a) Speaker, (b) and (c) Voice and Piano.
> String Quartet, two flutes, and two clarinets.
> (a) Pierrot Lunaire (21 passages, 40 minutes) by Schönberg
> (b) Japanese Songs (4 passages, 10 minutes) by Stravinsky
> (c) Two Mallarmé Songs by Maurice Ravel.

At that time Ravel's plan for this concert did not come to fruition. It was carried out fifty years later by Pierre Boulez in Paris at the Théâtre Marigny. The second Mallarmé song of which Ravel speaks is *Placet futile;* in August, 1913, he added to them a third, *Surgi de la Croupe et du Bond*. It was finished August 27 in Saint-Jean-de-Luz and is the most interesting of all.

The close relationship of the three cycles, Schönberg's, Stravinsky's, and Ravel's, is evident if one substitutes mentally a singing voice for the speaking voice in *Pierrot*

Lunaire. In his Japanese songs Stravinsky applied the same freedom in chord progressions with which Schönberg had liquidated tonality, as well as the same timbre-polyphony in which the instruments demonstrate their most striking registers. Ravel went even further than Stravinsky harmonically. Here, too, he strove to realize his ideal of perfection, and he succeeded, especially in the last of the three pieces.

In the Mallarmé songs he attained the high point of his unfettered harmonic imagination. They anticipate prophetically what a generation of French musicians after World War II first made use of as a point of departure for experiments in sound. The step from Ravel's Mallarmé songs to Pierre Boulez and his Mallarmé songs with orchestral accompaniment is not too great, yet in these extreme experiments Ravel managed to remain true to his ideal of natural French prosody.

RAVEL AS MUSIC CRITIC, 1912–1913

In 1912 *Comoedia Illustré* persuaded Ravel to join it as a music critic. The works he reviewed have, for the most part, since been forgotten, but the way he reported them frequently reveals something about the writer and is always highly informative as to the state of musical life at that time in France.

After the premiere of Camille Erlanger's *La Sorcière* at the Opéra Comique he wrote some ironic and malicious remarks about the libretto:

The eminently philosophic content of the book is evident to us. Zoraya, the Moorish maidservant, delivers herself of some Voltairean commonplaces about the inconsistency between the Gospels and the sufferings of the virtuous.

And about the music he said:

> The writing for the singing voices, on the other hand, was extraordinarily uneven. This shortcoming is not peculiar to this work alone. One finds it in practically all contemporary music for the voice. We can thank the fateful example of Wagner for the special disrespect most of our modern composers pay to the most expressive instrument of all. In Mr. Erlanger this approach reaches its most extreme level. . . . All this is well suited for moving declamation and the heavily marked accents of the German language, most of all for the Wagnerian type of expression. But when applied to French it is paradoxical. In the theater it is essential to understand the words of the text, and this suffers.

On the other hand, he wrote of the third act of Mozart's *Idomeneo:*

> We must be grateful to Mr. Rouché for the deep study he gave these lustrous fragments. They have a sublimity to which nothing in our art can be compared, a sublimity in which sheer tragedy alone is expressed in the musical phrase. In this all the artifices that Gluck applied in his music drama fall short. Their uselessness has become apparent to his successors.

Then there was a revival performance of Moussorgsky's *Boris Godunov.* Ravel began his discussion by referring to his recollection of the preview in 1908:

> Only three weeks earlier we were afraid it would be dropped. Mr. Sergei Diaghilev was apprehensive about doing the snow scene. We can thank the perseverance of Mr. M. D. Calvocoressi, the producer, that it was not. They also had the courage to request Rimski-Korsakov to restore certain passages he had deleted because of musical "impurities!" When the scenery arrived, all seemed to be lost again. The unaccustomed splendor of the boldly painted pictures antagonized the opera management, though it finally became accustomed to them. Gradually even the least important workers were won over, first

to having confidence and then to showing enthusiasm. And it was a triumph! The audience approved everything: impurities, scenery, interpreters, chorus, and extras. At one stroke all the dilettantes concluded that Claude Debussy had never invented anything and that Rimski-Korsakov was nothing but a mischievous fool. But a week later both these victims won back their due place in the honorable regard of their contemporaries.

Those epic times are now far behind us. Moussorgsky's work has since lost none of its glamour. But it no longer belongs to us. Even before we recognized the originality of its author's conception, it was enrolled in the ranks of the masterpieces. Now it needed only the final confirmation of a lashing by *Le Temps*. At last it has had a taste of that too.

Now the production has even run into the fearful obstacle of a "tradition." Once and for all, Mr. Chaliapin is the greatest opera singer of our day. I have ample reason to admire his handling of recitative. He almost speaks it while still adhering faithfully to the melodic line. But he is beginning to abuse this technique. There are expressly lyrical passages in *Boris Godunov* where melody is indispensable and the time quantities indicated by the composer must be observed. Nothing justifies the insertion of scornful laughter and deep sighs, the effect of which is so obvious and so very unmusical. Surely this is not the true Moussorgsky that is being offered us. Would it be too much to ask if we wish for the restoration of the parts of the true *Boris Godunov* we have lost? Mr. Diaghilev intends to produce the inn scene for us, never before shown in France. Why not have the courage to dare a little more? Why not restore the omitted passage in the fifth scene, where the parrot escapes and there is the vision of the tolling bells? Otherwise the musical commentary to this scene is unintelligible. Why has he deleted the short yet significant role of the Jesuit Rangoni? Why does he continue to destroy the dramatic sense of the work, the populace as a principle actor, by inverting the sequence of the last two scenes?

When shall we get to see this inspired work in its original form at last? Must we wait until it has fallen into the public domain? Or until the copyrights of all these masterpieces are

taken away from shrewd but ignorant publishers who have acquired them by devious methods?

Ravel's observations and opinions were confirmed
point by point during the succeeding decade. The repetition
of Moussorgsky's masterpiece, in both versions for which
Moussorgsky himself is responsible, the first form and the
final "original" form, has since been frequently undertaken
with great success both in Russia and in other countries. By
the same token, Rimski-Korsakov's version has proved to be
artistically inferior, not only in details of the orchestration,
but also dramatically. The criticism of Chaliapin will also be
confirmed by anyone who ever witnessed the terrifying willfulness of this great singer and actor on the opera
stage or in the concert hall. Ravel's discussion constantly
harks back to the impression made by the Russian production in 1908. He rates it superior to the French performance
even in the choreographic direction of the choruses.

On the whole he yearns for "the barbaric greatness
and the bold simplicity" of 1908. From his esthetic point of
view, his discussion of *Boris* is no less characteristic than the
brief reference in which he compares the third act of Mozart's *Idomeneo* to Gluck. To him Gluck is a sort of predecessor of Wagner, a battler for the dramatic principle at the
expense of the musical. Ravel's taking this position is basically his declaration of war against recitative and a declaration of love for melody. It is worthy of note that it was just
Mozart's *Idomeneo,* this extreme example of opera seria,
that gave Ravel the occasion to do so. Mozart himself, in
spite of its not very successful text, loved this opera of his
with great tenderness. The melodic forms in the score re-
appear frequently in his music, not only in *Don Giovanni*
and *The Magic Flute* but also in his instrumental compositions.

However much the dramatic setting of a story

might interest him, or he might judge the content of the treatment by his own life experiences, Ravel showed himself in this question of esthetics quite clearly the defender of the purely musical principle. He set it above all the other arts of the theater. Even though he himself might constantly make use of newly developing forms of speech-song in French prosody, yet the singable melody was the highest aim of his operatic aspiration.

This is also the explanation of the stand he took as reviewer of Vincent d'Indy's opera *Fervaal*. The work has the subtitle "Musical Narrative in Three Acts and a Prologue." He reported the revival of the work, which had had its premiere fifteen years before (1897) in Brussels, by first of all setting himself apart from any mere charge of Wagnerism:

It is an undeniable fact that in every age capable artists have been influenced by other original masters even to the suppression of their own personality. Thus we have Debussy-like works and we shall have more of them. If we look back we can assert that we have had completely Wagnerian works. Among these *Fervaal* is the most noteworthy.

This "Musical Narrative" is essentially Wagnerian in its music, its dramatic structure, its philosophy, and its staging, in the symbolism of its personages and in their misty speech. The musical prosody sometimes reminds us unpleasantly of that which the French translators of Wagner felt obliged to import. In fact, the verbal accent, which in our language is pretty weak, is set here with such stress that its effect is all the more painful because it often misses the mark. The sentences are interrupted by pauses without good reason, which, in spite of their brevity, suffice to remind us of the declamatory fits and starts of the heroes in *Tristan*, the *Tetralogy*, and *Parsifal* in the translation of Wilder and Ernst.

It is only because Wagner's philosophy is no more original than that of M. d'Indy that the evil of complete similarity is no greater than it is. One can only deplore the fact that the same measures are used to bring this philosophy out onto the stage as are applied in Wagner's masterpieces of primitive Teutonism. Both express their essence more through words than by action, even in situations in which the symbolic content is repeatedly expounded with Teutonic thoroughness, by similar characters, and in the same gloomy and childish dialogue. The recollection of Mime and Siegfried and of Wotan and Erda is constantly awakened.

The music, entirely apart from the libretto, is not less influenced by Wagner. First of all, one is conscious of Wagner's principle of structure. Not only are the leading motives developed and modified according to Wagner's principles, but their character, their melodic and rhythmic relationship, and the basic coloration (though less luxuriant) of their harmony stem from this system, or rather from this inspiration.

Wagner's work is a typical example of wide-ranging assimilation. In so far as he welded together the most variegated materials, this giant built himself a glittering and original palace, the dimensions of which are in harmony with its form. M. d'Indy has installed himself in this handsome structure and carefully locked up all the doors and windows. The burning sun which the master builder let into his house has been replaced by candles that are extraordinarily bright but throw off little warmth. In this artificial light the subjects of the narrative get gloomier and gloomier and finally are ready for death. The metaphor is more meaningful than the creator of *Fervaal* intended, for this hero assures the victory of life and of love, while he carries the corpse of a woman up to the heights.

We see how intensely Ravel occupied himself with the question of Wagner's influence on French music. He himself never succumbed to this influence. And it is precisely this that differentiated him from Debussy. Debussy not only made the pilgrimage to Bayreuth; he surrendered to Wagner in the *Proses Lyriques* both textually and musically.

Ravel, whose writings bear the stamp of extreme subjectivity, is full of contradictions in his points of view and in his conclusions. It is only when one knows how to penetrate these generalizations that one recognizes their essential unity.

In 1912 he published, in addition to his criticisms, a fuller essay on Wagner, Brahms, and the school of César Franck. It is a kind of profession of artistic faith:

In art it is not possible to practice mere craftsmanship in the strict sense of the word. Inspiration plays an unlimited part in the elegance of construction of the well-marked divisions of a work. Mere determination to produce something is necessarily fruitless. This is most clearly demonstrated in most of the work of Brahms. This can be confirmed by the *D major Symphony* recently played at the Lamoureux concerts. The thoughts are those of intimate and tender musicality. While the melodic contours and the rhythms are very individual, they are closely related to those of Schubert and Schumann. They hardly appear before their pace becomes heavy and laborious. It seems as though the composer is ceaselessly plagued by the desire to do as Beethoven did. But the charming essence of his inspiration is not compatible with that of those broad, fiery, almost disorderly developments that spring directly from Beethoven's themes, or, more properly, gush forth from his inspiration. Brahms acquired his craft by study, something his predecessor Schubert lacked by nature. He did not merely discover it in himself.

Must one ascribe the disillusion one feels at each rehearing of César Franck's *Symphony* to similar causes? There is no doubt of it, even though the two symphonies are very dissimilar in their thematic values and in their embodiment. Yet their shortcomings have the same sources, the same disproportion between ideas and execution. In Brahms: clear and direct inspiration, sometimes lively, sometimes melancholy, scholarly broad speech, difficult and well-developed workingout of an idea. In Franck: melody of a cultivated and cheerful spirit, daring

138

harmonies of especial richness, but a devastating poverty in form.

The construction of the German master is skillful, but one is too aware of artificiality in it. With the composer of Liège there is, at best, an attempt at construction. He makes poor use of clumsy, outdated school-book forms. One point in which the superiority of Brahms is evident is in his technique of orchestration. It is most brilliant. On the other hand, with Franck the errors of instrumentation pile up. Here the double basses drag clumsily, there crashing trumpets double the fiddles. Where the inspiration is greatest, one is disturbed by the noise of a country fair.

It is no wonder that in Germany, as in France, use has been made of these two composers in the struggle against Wagnerian influence, because their imperfections arouse an impression of coldness and tedium. The overpowering spontaneity of the man who summed up the entire treasury of sentiment of the nineteenth century must have alarmed those very musicians who were the first to succumb to his powerful magic. Even today, when we hear the Venusberg music, which is one of the most typical works of Wagnerian art, one grasps, after this explosion of passionate joys and pains, after this wild inundation of heathen vitality, how necessary a peaceful and even determined retreat had become.

Here we find that remarkable word "retreat." It has great significance, but this can easily be misunderstood. But behind it lies one of the most justifiable aspirations of nearly all important artists at the beginning of the twentieth century. It does not imply a turning back in a historical sense, nor a reversion of technique and style to the level of long or recently past eras. In Richard Strauss this reversion was, in a higher sense of artistic ethics, only a clarification, a kind of permissible compromise with the tastes of a comfortable and rather backward audience, when he took flight from the complex and advanced harmony of his *Salome* and *Elektra* to the Mozart-like sounds and cadences of his *Der Rosenkavalier*. This restraint never for a moment bore the character of a retreat. Many of his later works, such as the *Die Frau ohne Schatten* or *Die Ägyptische Helena* prove that the riches acquired earlier were not thrown overboard as ballast, but were only stored away for other enterprises.

But restraint was to become the distinguishing mark of Ravel's simplifications. In *Daphnis and Chloë* he had elevated orchestral sound to a disturbing level of voluptuous beauty and richness as, previously, in *Gaspard de la Nuit,* he had conjured up a maximum of contrasting effects from the palette of the piano. He abandoned this esthetic of the extreme, with the result that the later works are documents of a new determination of restraint, of the lean and "stripped down" style, as it had been exemplified and embodied in such an epoch-making manner by Erik Satie. Indeed, had not Ravel dedicated some of his revolutionary Mallarmé songs to the cynical Satie, the old goat-bearded master of Arceuil, the friend of Debussy, the former Rosicrucian and companion of that peculiar Wagnerian and poet, Joseph Péladan, to the Satie who, in persistent self-denial of material possessions, led a life of poverty and Socratic wisdom? And was not the *Surgi de la Croupe et du Bond* precisely the most radical and austere-sounding symbolic vision of a vase with flowers?

On the other hand, Ravel is a tenacious and persevering defender of new scenic forms and ideas. If an unusual combination of pieces like Chabrier's *Éducation Manquée,* Rameau's *Theseus,* and Fauré's *Dolly* was presented at the Théâtre des Arts, he used the opportunity to comment on the backwardness of the French theater:

Today, when in all countries, especially in Germany and Russia, comprehensive experiments of the greatest artistic interest are taking place, which have no lesser aim than to renew the art of scenic design from the ground up, we address every effort to the perfection of stereoscopy in colors, to improving on a repetitive skill in staging, and expending gigantic exertions of strength on a diminutive stage. In this excessively narrow space we combine dramatic and lyric gifts of the most varied and highly prized character. Perhaps French taste, weary of nothing but the pictures and stupid banalities that are ceaselessly put before it, this taste, which in matters theatrical has long been somnolent, will at last awaken and require the directors of our great theaters to satisfy it.

Again and again the critical consciousness of this musician, misjudged as one-sided, turns to subjects that, while intimately related to his true artistic calling, that is, the life in music, cross the threshold of other arts. His concern for the creation of a new prosody for the conquest of a traditional musical declamation in direct contradiction to colloquial speech legitimates him as a musician in words. His reference to the necessity for reforming the French operatic stage is evidence of his desire to participate in the modern development of the graphic arts and of the effect on him of the teachings of Diaghilev and Maeterlinck, and perhaps also of the German naturalistic and art theater movements.

Despite all the character traits recognizable as either of Basque or Swiss origin, Ravel exhibited all his life an uncommonly French quality that was the source of creative consequences. He was *novarum rerum cupidus,* "eager for new things," as the ancient Roman wrote about the Gauls.

The "new things" might be of ancient origins, or, in other instances, might belong to cultures geographically far removed. But the charms they exercised were discernible to Ravel and became fruitful in him. The *nouveau frisson,* the latest thrill, which the esthetic of the late nineteenth century liked so much to offer, retained its stimulating power for him. With the sensitivity of a seismograph, this overcivilized and elegant little man reacted to the fading of one type of charm and to the rise of another that would succeed it. However, he was too much aware of tradition and also too much the conscientious craftsman not to find the lessons of the past fruitful.

VALSES NOBLES ET SENTIMENTALES, 1911

In 1911 a kind of riddle or quiz concert series was started by the Société Independante, which had split off from the more conservative Société Nationale. Works on the programs, partly premieres, were played without naming the composers. One, from Ravel's pen, bore the handsome but perplexing title *Valses Nobles et Sentimentales.* He wrote:

The title *Valses Nobles et Sentimentales* sufficiently indicates my intention of writing a cycle of waltzes after the example of Schubert. Following on the virtuosity that is the basis for *Gaspard de la Nuit* I use here a distinctly clearer style of writing. This makes the harmony more concrete and causes the profile of the music to stand out. The *Valses Nobles et Sentimentales* was given its premiere at one of the concerts of the S.M.I., where the composers are not named, in the midst of protests and catcalls. The audience voted the authorship of each piece. By a small majority the paternity of the waltzes was ascribed to me. The seventh strikes me as most characteristic.

The seventh of the eight waltzes in the album is also the broadest dramatically and the richest harmonically. The concept of chord-timbre, as distinct from the chord itself, characterizes Ravel's entire lifework and creates in these *Valses,* in a magical way, a harmonic world of chromatic neighbor-tones.

It is an artful, sophisticated device of Ravel's to remain aware always of the gravitational pull of the tonal center, and yet to place it in question in every measure, in every chord, and almost in every note. Ravel's separate chord combinations are of a daring abstraction not at all far removed from the discoveries in the area of atonality that Arnold Schönberg was making during the same period and that kept his school busily occupied for years. But with Ravel these innovations are always related to a basic tonality, the legitimacy of which is never for a moment questioned or disturbed, so that the listener is cunningly and artfully persuaded to accept as simple what in fact is very complicated.

The enigmatic harmonic osmosis that unifies the sounds in Schönberg's *Stefan Georg Songs* of 1908–1909 is also present in this work. This is seen very clearly in the fourth waltz, with its fusion, at the very beginning, of two keys, E major and C sharp major. Out of this arose a new world of sound that both disturbed and captivated a whole series of composers, for example Richard Strauss in his *Elektra,* Debussy in his prelude *Feuilles Mortes,* and Alban Berg in his *Songs,* opus 2.

Also characteristic of the very sensitive feeling for dissonance that prevails in these pieces is the beginning of the first waltz with the "notes beside the notes," for instance the E sharp, which is, so to speak, to be understood as the leading tone to the leading tone F sharp, or the D in the tenor line which draws attention to and splits the interval of a second in the chord F sharp–A sharp–C sharp–D sharp that lies above it. The augmented triad appears in these pieces constantly, often in chromatic progressions gliding upwards and downwards as in the second and the seventh waltzes; the chromatic change always has the effect of an alteration, that is, it lets the key or chord of departure shine through.

Certain closing cadences build a very enchanting contrast to this most highly refined and chromatic dissonance treatment. Through these, to be sure, Ravel's love for old, modal harmonies is verified, as when, for instance, he avoids the leading tone in leading to the tonic at the end of the first waltz. The cadence in the seventeenth to twentieth measures, closing the first part of the piece, already prepares the way for this final progression.

Both times Ravel permits the closes (here on the dominant, there on the tonic) to be preceded by chords that unite all, or nearly all, the notes of the key in pandiatonic layers of thirds, which invoke the tonal center by first gathering around it all its tonal spans. The resolution in the tonic triad then has the same psychological effect as the snapping back of an overstretched rubber band to its original relaxed state.

The suggestion in the title points back to Schubert, who indeed wrote not only dozens of waltzes and German dances, but also thirty-four *Valses Sentimentales* and twelve *Valses Nobles,* presumably all between 1823 and 1825. What may have delighted Ravel in them is the technique of the gliding middle voices and the melodic suspensions, so unusual and extraordinary in Schubert, as, for example, in the thirteenth of the *Valses Sentimentales.* Ravel's fourth waltz is so close in mood and key to the third of Schubert's *Valses Nobles* that one can play the two pieces after one another without doing violence to them stylistically.

Ravel dedicated this collection of waltzes to Louis Aubert, whom he knew when they were fellow students at the Conservatory, and who had himself written symphonic dances, of which the *Pièces en Forme de Mazurka* especially pleased Ravel. Along with the dedication the manuscript carries as motto a quotation from Henri de Regnier that is typical of Ravel: *le plaisir delicieux et toujours nouveau d'une occupation inutile* (the delightful and always new

Above: Ravel's balcony overlooking **his garde**n at La Belvédère in Montfort-l'Amaury. *Below:* Ravel's piano **in his study** at Montfort-l'Amoury.

Above: Ravel at Lyons-la-Forêt in **1923, with** his pupil and friend Roland-Manuel. *Below:* Lyons-la-Forêt, 1923. From left: Ravel, Maurice Delage, Mme. Delage, Mme. Suzanne Roland Manuel.

pleasure of a useless occupation). This coy recognition of uselessness, or "art for art's sake," typifies the attitude of many artists in the years just before World War I. It is a part of the musical and intellectual dandyism that Ravel embodies so distinctly.

It did not take long for the dancer Natasha Trouhanova to discover these noble and sentimental dances as music suitable for ballet. She used them to accompany a choreographic story of an amorous nature and taking place in the house of a Parisian courtesan of the Restoration period, therefore during the epoch in which Schubert wrote his dances. Ravel orchestrated the dances in fourteen days. In that form the work later also passed into the repertory of symphony orchestras. The dance recital of Trouhanova, April 22, 1912, was an outstanding event. Four different composers conducted their own works: Paul Dukas, his *La Peri;* Vincent d'Indy, his *Istar;* Florent Schmitt, his *Tragédie de Salomé;* and Maurice Ravel, his waltzes.

Free as the *Valses Nobles et Sentimentales* are of any intention of achieving virtuoso effects, they are also sophisticated in their blending of chordal and polyphonic thinking. They are works of complete transparency as well as great uncompromising harmonic daring. It would be some years before Ravel would return creatively to this first elaboration of the spirit of the Viennese waltz. But before that would happen, a period of painful trials and great spiritual transformations had to be gone through, not only by him but by the whole European cultural community.

SAINT-JEAN-DE-LUZ; *PIANO TRIO,* 1914

After the death in 1908 of his deeply loved father, Maurice Ravel altered greatly, both inwardly and outwardly.

He shaved off his beard, combed his hair back without parting it, and more and more lost the rather arrogant and haughty air that had irritated so many on meeting him when he was younger. He appeared kindlier and occasionally even a little saddened. On the whole, his appearance took on a vaguely Spanish cast, which was the way such a keen observer as the painter Jacques-Émile Blanche described it.

Ravel bore successes and failures with equal indifference, and his self-control generally managed to conceal his sentiments and feelings. This was carried so far that even to his intimate friends he affected a certain coolness and occasionally indicated that feelings were rather unnecessary and inartistic. He said once to Maurice Delage: "One must have a head and have guts, but never a heart."

This sounds much like one of Friedrich Nietzsche's later paradoxes. It certainly springs from sources of intellectual dandyism, affirmation of the supremacy of mere outward sensation and the cult of reason at the expense of the deeper emotions. It may have expressed a Mediterranean ideal, but it certainly did not correspond to the romantic venturesomeness of his music.

Ravel liked to pass the summer months in his Basque homeland. For many years Saint-Jean-de-Luz, just across the cove from his birthplace, Ciboure, was his customary summering place. The view delighted him. In July, 1911, he wrote to Ida Godebska:

Won't you come back soon to these unique pine forests? You could get here so easily, where the sea is rimmed with acacias! And these gentle green hills up and down which the little oaks, trimmed into round balls in the Basque manner, do somersaults. And over everything the Pyrenees with their fabulous rosy tints. And then the light! This is not the harsh brilliance of the rest of the South. Here the sun has a gentle softness. The people react to it. They are lively but elegant. Their fun is not vulgar. Their dances are nimble and joyous, but not exaggerated. Even their religion, though they observe it faithfully, is mixed with a grain of skepticism

And in later letters as well, these praises of the Basque country keep recurring. Certainly there were no more of his mother's relatives, Deluartes or Delouarts who came from that neighborhood, still living, but there were still a number of friends of his youth.

There were the Gaudins, a well-to-do middle-class family with two sons, Pierre and Pascal, and two daughters. One of the latter, Marie Gaudin, four years younger than Ravel, had been a childhood playmate. Sometimes during his summer sojourns the composer lived at the Gaudins in the old crooked rue Gambetta near the Cathedral. The brothers, Pierre and Pascal, were good friends of Ravel's, nothing more. But he was inseparable from Marie. She was enthusiastic about him, in honest admiration of his genius. She waited on him and took care of all his little comforts. Ravel, who had a deep but purely friendly feeling for the young girl, accepted all this quite naturally. He sent her on all kinds of errands, sometimes having her run five times in a morning from the beach to the house and back to the beach when he forgot his lighter, his cigarettes, his pencil, or anything else.

There were children, too, in the Gaudin household. He loved these graceful little beings as sincerely as they did him. A little niece of the Gaudins demanded that he play her to sleep every evening. Ravel did this with touching patience and even saw to it that the piano was pushed into the nursery. His repertory for this purpose was limited, so sometimes he extended it by playing variations and free improvisations on the familiar pieces the child always asked for. She would notice such changes, protest against them at once, and he would meekly obey, playing them the way the little one was accustomed to hear them.

In the summer of 1913 Ravel stayed on in Saint-Jean-de-Luz longer than usual. The year had been fruitful. He had worked with Stravinsky on the score of *Khovan-schchina,* written two Mallarmé songs, a piano prelude, two parodies "in the manner of" Borodin and Chabrier, and completed a couple of musicological essays. At the end of May he had taken part in the battle over the premiere of Stravinsky's *Le Sacre du Printemps* in Paris' newly opened Théâtre des Champs Élysées. On that occasion he had to submit to abuse from an indignant upper-class lady because he told her to stop her shouts of disapproval. Then he traveled to the Basque coast so he could find peace to finish various works he had in mind. While there he wrote a third song in the Mallarmé cycle.

He could not tear himself away from his summer surroundings, and in the middle of October he was still in Saint-Jean-de-Luz. He wrote in great haste to his friend Cypa Godebski:

Old chap, I beg you to try to see Diaghilev immediately after you get this letter if he is in Paris, or your sister, or I don't know whom, but relieve me of a terrible apprehension. I have just received a newspaper clipping in which, for what it's worth—but the source is reliable—it reports that Stravinsky is confined to a mental institution in Petersburg. I am coming home at the end of the week, but you can understand that I cannot wait that long for news. Please answer by return mail, or, better, wire me. The article undoubtedly appeared in *Comoedia.* It is signed "The Prompter."

One notes from this cry for help that this enemy of sentiment forgets all his strict principles when they relate to children or friends. The report about Stravinsky was fabricated. It was true that after the hapless premiere of *Le Sacre du Printemps* he had taken refuge in a sanatarium in Neuilly for a couple of weeks, but the reason was typhoid.

Mentally he was entirely sound. From there he had gone to his summer place, Ustilug, in Volhynia, and by autumn he was resting again quietly in Clarens on Lake Geneva working on his opera *The Nightingale*.

That year Ravel seemed to be weary of the big city. He remained in Paris only a short time. February, 1914, saw him again in Saint-Jean-de-Luz where, after a while, he attacked a work of pure chamber music, his first for ten years since the *String Quartet* of 1903. This time it was a piano trio, something he had planned for years. He had often spoken of this intention. Once when Maurice Delage asked about it, he answered: "My *Trio* is finished. I only need the themes for it." This was a remarkably noteworthy comment, and the best argument against the assertions of his opponents that Ravel's music was only the result of his intoxication with sound and with an impressionistic succession of melodic, harmonic, and rhythmic notions.

The truth of his preoccupation with the overall plan of a work, the layout and the buildup of its structure, is, incidentally, to be gleaned not so much from this paradoxical and humorous retort as from many passages in his letters and his comments about his own music and that of others. Admittedly, he did not subscribe to a purely architectonic procedure in his composing. For him the alpha and omega of creation was an inspired idea, without which there could be no logical modulation and no stability in the musical structure. The relationship of the various parts, the proper proportion between the inspiration and the detailed work of development, was always the first essential to him as a measure of quality.

We have observed as identification marks of Ravel's simplifications his philosophy of self-restraint and his habit of complete identification with his material. These are also the qualities that identify the *Piano Trio* on which he labored so tenaciously in Saint-Jean-de-Luz. The coordination of piano, violin, and cello within the sonorities that modern French music had developed was itself a challenge. In spite of the occasionally almost orchestral effects, which surge up in the *Trio* because Ravel spreads the construction over the many different registers of the three instruments, one is still conscious of the emotional restraint he imposed on himself in this labor. It reaches its high point in the slow and solemn passacaglia of the third movement. Here the domination of line over color, of melody over harmony, is frankly emphasized. This is symbolically acknowledged in the dedication to his old counterpoint teacher André Gédalge, who brought up his Conservatory pupils in the school of pure melodic thinking. For example, he told Darius Milhaud that to compose music that is neither literature nor painting you must first learn to write eight bars of unaccompanied melody. His preachment of pure music was very convincing to Ravel. This showed especially in Ravel's later years.

(Gédalge gathered up what he had learned in his long career of teaching counterpoint in a book he called *Music Teaching Through Methodical Ear Training.*)

The first of the four movements of the *Trio* introduces a new kind of meter, eight eighths with asymmetric distribution of the accents, three plus three plus two, although, it is true, only in the upper voice, which carries the melody. The bass adheres to the normal accentuation of four quarters. Rhythms of this type are known to us from southeast European folk music (Béla Bartók made fruitful use of them in his own compositions). However, they are also close to certain Basque dance rhythms, as in the *zortziko* with its dotted five-eighth meter.

Ravel combines this striking rhythmic element with parallel fifths that give the movement an archaic tinge, even though chromatic alterations soon lead away from the initially Dorian melodic idea. Of the three instruments the violin is given especially virtuoso treatment.

The second movement is named "Pantoum." The name comes from the terminology of Malayan poetry. There it signifies a poem in quatrains, in which the second and fourth lines of the first verse are repeated as the first and the third lines of the second verse. Victor Hugo made use of this verse form. So have Théodore de Banville and Charles Baudelaire. But it is still an enigma why Ravel gave the movement this name. In the composition this movement serves as the scherzo. The rapid 3/4 tempo of the principal section is marked by virtuoso writing for the violin, especially in the alternation between pizzicato and bowed notes.

The tempo changes in the trio section. The piano develops a chorale-like melody in a solemn 3/4 tempo with broad chords, while the strings carry on the motif and meter of the principal theme. This creates a fascinating bi-rhythmic metric picture, with accents shifting within each measure. Perhaps by this device Ravel wished to suggest the association of the deferred repetition in the Pantoum verse form. But it is also just as possible that he was charmed by the strange exotic word itself, as he had been by the assonance of syllables when he chose the name *Pavane pour une Infante Défunte*. Leading one astray like that was in line with his predilection toward irony and jest, even when the subject was a work of art of such high quality and polished workmanship as this *Trio*.

The third movement is a passacaglia. It is elaborated exactly in the Bachian manner, with an eight-measure theme in the bass in 3/2 time, an ostinato repetition of the theme three times, with the accompaniment varying, during which it appears an octave higher each time. In the third repetition the contours of the theme itself are changed, but the succession of durations remains the same, in isorhythmic fashion. The fourth, fifth, and sixth variations are free. From number seven on, the original form of the theme is approached once more. This is attained in numbers eight, nine, and ten.

The plan of a continuous rise from the bass to the treble, and of a retreat after reaching the high point, is carried through consistently. Apart from that, it is linked with an intensification of the dynamics, which also reaches its high point exactly in the middle of the movement. By this means the effect of a ceaselessly increasing tension and its equally regular relaxation is created. It is a very simple but an uncommonly meaningful format, here realized through the well-known medium of variation over an ostinato.

The unusually brilliant finale is written in free rondo form. Measures in 5/4 and in 7/4 time establish the swinging rhythm of this movement, in which Ravel conjures up, by means of tremolo chords in the cello and wide-sweeping arpeggios in the violin, orchestral effects from a group of three instruments. Problems of form and rhythm occupy the foreground. As by-products of their solution we get new types of combinations between the piano and the strings.

Here the monothematic base of the *String Quartet* and of the piano *Sonatine* is abandoned. Nevertheless the four movements of the *Piano Trio* have a strong inner coherence. This arises in part out of the floating meter, partly out of the unusually clear contouring of the melodic lines. Both may be traced back to the influence of André Gédalge. As to tonality, the four movements describe a circle that leads from A minor (C major) through A major, Aeolian C sharp minor, to A major. The intimate blending of church modes with free chromaticism is paralleled by the mixture of simple and compound, of symmetric and asymmetric meters.

In the letters he wrote during the period of composing the *Trio* Ravel refers constantly to how this work took complete possession of him: "I have never worked with more insane, more heroic intensity," as he put it in a letter to Cypa Godebski on August 3. "Yes, I am working with the assurance and the clarity of a madman," he wrote a few days later to Maurice Delage.

VII 1914–1917

The years just before World War I were filled with intellectual, scientific, artistic, and economic events that laid the foundation for a new epoch. People were hardly aware of them. Advances in technology, such as the conquest of the air by flying machines and dirigibles, ever swifter racing cars, the linking up by telephone and telegraph of ever more distant lands, and then general electrification, altered life and made new materials as well as new subject matter available to the arts. The Italian futurists intoxicated themselves with the beauty of machinery. Automobiles, aircraft, and telephones entered into the lyrics of popular songs. Nevertheless, this technical age, in which progressive poets reveled, was still nothing but a phase. Real life itself looked beyond this progress and accepted it as something only temporarily sensational. In the same years in which electric street railways and underground transit lines introduced new forms of mass transportation, women's fashions dictated dresses and hats in which they could hardly enter into such vehicles.

It seemed that every technical advance released a conservative countermovement in circles of conservative middle-class society. The result was that radical and reactionary ideas were constantly marching side by side and becoming ever more antagonistic and irreconcilable. In the same feminine society that created for itself styles that were exemplified by long, sweeping frocks and wide, drooping feathers on hats, revolutionary ideas were spreading, such as the right of women to vote and the barefoot dancing and free love associated with Isadora Duncan. In Vienna the new artistic and technical developments went parallel with Sigmund Freud and the growth of the still experimental science of investigating the psyche itself.

Ravel came from a family in which problems of modern technology and questions of the latest fashion were eagerly argued. The engineering mind of his father had been occupied with the development of the automobile long before this vehicle became king and developed from the queer look of the horseless carriage into the long-nosed silhouette of the racing car. Pierre Joseph himself did not live to see the first triumphs of Wright and Blériot, but his sons were witnesses to the fever with which mankind reacted to these accomplishments. Edouard, Maurice's younger brother, became an engineer and so carried on their father's tradition without, however, becoming outstanding creatively. Ravel's mother, as a young woman, was connected with the high fashion industry. As a model for one of its largest houses, she had made the journey to Spain on which she met the engineer Ravel.

In Maurice Ravel's mind, which he dedicated almost exclusively to the "ever new satisfaction with useless activity," the propensity for things technical was sublimated along with his instinct for fashion. His esthetic philosophy undoubtedly had a close affinity with the precision workmanship that reaches its peak in Swiss watchmaking. His interest in the outwardly changing forms of contemporary creativity stood in constantly exciting contradiction to his loyalty to tradition. Nevertheless his inborn Latin instinct for preserving balance and avoiding extremes protected him. It was also characteristic of his disposition to think through to the end any subject he considered, whether of technique, form, or esthetics.

It is true that ever since his early compositions he had been regarded by conservatives as belonging to the ranks of composers to be feared because they represented the dangerous new spirit of the age. Nevertheless, the intention of joining any esthetic group of extreme radicals was far from his mind. He was not disposed to be the founder of any school. Whenever anyone tried to pin him down to expound the theory behind the work he had already completed, he drew back behind the protecting wall of the study he gave to any completely new and very contradictory problem with which he happened to be engaged. But his artistic concepts were always completely clear. They always preceded the creation of a new work, as can be seen from his retort about his *Piano Trio,* that it was finished and all he needed for it were the themes.

There is no doubt that Ravel kept himself fully informed about musical events and the graphic arts in other countries. Marinetti's manifesto of 1909 was as well known to him as was the music of Arnold Schönberg or of Aleksandr Scriabin. He was acquainted with the new phenomena in literature and knew the modern theater, from Maeterlinck's symbolism to Hauptmann's naturalism, as well as the modern ballet, for which Diaghilev had made Paris a center.

Nevertheless, his life as an independent esthete was financially restricted. His parents were able to offer him security only to a modest extent. His own efforts to achieve independence had not yet had any permanent effect. Even stage works such as *L'Heure Espagnole* and *Daphnis and Chloë* had not made Ravel economically secure during the years before World War I. Arthur Honegger, in his book *Je suis compositeur,* includes some touching statistics about the distribution of some of Debussy's and Ravel's published works. Ravel's *Histoires Naturelles,* of which five hundred copies were printed in 1907, was not sold out until 1913. The piano suite *Ma Mère l'Oye* for four hands did somewhat better, but the edition of five hundred copies printed in 1910 was not yet completely sold out in 1912. One can calculate how much material success this signifies.

Still, there was a wealthy Parisian *haute bourgeoisie* that was avid for culture and that made much of outstanding talents. Ravel's need for freedom and independence was so pronounced that he subordinated to it all attainable material necessities. Nor did he ever set himself up as a teacher or even aspire to be one. As a famous man he was overrun by composers hoping he would accept them in a master class. He declined all such offers, some of them very alluring, such as one from George Gershwin, who by that time was quite wealthy. In the modern world, whose technological innovations he put to use when he chose, he stood alone in solitary composure. His ties with others were limited to the narrow circle of his family and a few friends to whom he remained faithful all his life.

Ravel seems to have remained as unmoved by the social and political upheavals in the world about him as he was free of purely nationalistic prejudice. In this he was quite different from Marcel Proust, who eagerly crossed the line between the middle and upper classes and felt most at home in aristocratic society. Ravel remained indifferent to the social environment in which he circulated. Although the salons of the nobility were as open to him as the homes of the merchant millionaires, it made little difference to him whether he spent the evening among his Apache friends, in the bohemia of the intellectuals, or in the company of a duchess. The world of his interests was entirely esthetic and creative.

Necessarily, having this attitude, he was also a good European and a citizen of the world. His most intimate friends were either of Polish origin or, like Roland-Manuel, belonged to the prosperous Jewish class. If occasionally he asserted he was a Basque, he meant it more as a conscious exaggeration of his maternal strain.

Yet, in spite of his wide European horizon, Ravel had learned little before 1914 of the world outside his native France. The short voyage he made in 1905 as a guest on Misia Edwards' yacht acquainted him, in passing, with some Belgian, Dutch, and German landscapes between Amsterdam and Frankfort. In 1908 he spent several weeks on Lake Geneva with his father, then in his last illness. Five years later Ravel visited Stravinsky there in Clarens.

While Ravel was still in Saint-Jean-de-Luz working on his *Trio* he got the news of the outbreak of war. It shook him profoundly. It was as though an abyss had suddenly opened up before him, for up to that moment he had not had the slightest inkling of its imminence.

Two letters describe his distress, his inner sense of desolation. The first, dated August 3, 1914, is addressed to Cypa Godebski:

Heaven only knows, old chap, if this will reach you. I hope it will, for it seems to make it easier if I can write to a friend. Since the day before yesterday this sounding of alarms, these weeping women, and, above all, this terrible enthusiasm of the young people and of all the friends who have had to go and of whom I have no news. I cannot bear it any longer. The nightmare is too horrible. I think that at any moment I shall go mad or lose my mind. I have never worked so hard, with such insane, heroic rage. Yes, old man, you cannot imagine how badly I need this kind of heroism in order to combat the other, which is probably the more instinctive feeling. Just think, old man, of the horror of this conflict. It never stops for an instant. What good will it all do?

This sounds like the outcry of a helpless tortured heart. They are tones of passion and despair one was unprepared to hear from the cynical Ravel. The world of the esthete, of the intellectual dandy, seemed to be coming apart. The next day, in almost greater despair, he turned to his old friend Maurice Delage:

> Please write to me as soon as you get this, so I can feel the presence of a friend. There are lots of people here for whom I feel great sympathy. But that isn't it. If only you knew how I suffer. From morning on, without a break, the same frightful cruel thought, . . . to leave my poor old mother would certainly mean to kill her. . . . And then, the fatherland is not waiting for me to save it. But all this is only an effort to be logical, when from hour to hour I see distinctly it falls apart. I just keep working so as not to hear anything. Yes, I am working with the persistence and concentration of a fool. But suddenly the hypocrisy of this conduct overwhelms me and I begin to sob over my notepaper. When I go downstairs and my mother sees me, naturally I have to show a serene and, if possible, a smiling face. Shall I be able to keep this up? It has lasted four days already since the alarm gongs began.

Ravel battled with the decision that he must report as a volunteer. He realized that with his small stature and his delicate health he would not be conscripted. All these feelings were complicated by the compulsion to finish his self-imposed task first. At last, toward the last days of August, the composition of the *Trio* was ended. At the beginning of September Ravel traveled to Bayonne, the nearest garrison town, to offer himself as a soldier. His younger, stronger brother Edouard had already joined the troops as a driver. Ravel was rejected but took up voluntary orderly work in a hospital. (The reason for his rejection was grotesque: he was four pounds underweight.) He had to conceal this step from his mother. He kept from her also his concern for his friends, among whom Paul Sordes had been immediately shipped to the Eastern Front. Delage had been called up with his automobile.

In a letter of September 8 to Ida Godebska he eased his heart and described the situation in Saint-Jean-de-Luz, where he was living with his mother at 23 rue Sopite:

A Jewish banker has given the city 10,000 francs to care for the wounded. Then he collected a lot of ladies, young girls, and very young men in the Casino who have nothing to do since the golf links have been closed off. They come in to play games with the wounded, cause confusion everywhere, and discourage the best intentions of all. Fortunately very few badly wounded cases have been sent here. Besides they are making every effort in Bayonne to rid themselves of all the many Red Cross ladies who have given money contributions to be allowed to disturb the hospitals and are annoyed because they have to wash the feet of the wounded, hide behind their ignorance to avoid being asked to bandage up wounds, and grumble because a tearoom has not been installed for them.

One of his friends of the prewar years, Alfredo Casella, had been studying composition in Paris since the 1890's in, among other classes, the composition class of Gabriel Fauré. Casella had caused much discussion in Paris as a composer, especially at the concert he gave on April 23, 1910, in the Salle Gaveau, when he conducted his own works. Ravel and Casella were almost neighbors for a time and saw each other nearly every day. Hélène Kahn-Casella, the Italian composer's first wife, had been a close friend of Ravel's since 1911. He wrote her September 21, still from Saint-Jean-de-Luz:

I am two kilos too light to get mixed up in this magnificent fight. I have only one hope, that I pass the next examination and they succumb to the charm of my anatomy. My brother has done better. He is a driver in the 19th Motor Detachment. He has a fine uniform and a bright new Panhard car. I know that Florent Schmitt is bored in Toul, sitting there staring at the planes flying too far overhead and that Delage is furious to find himself in Bordeaux in the company of Madame de Noailles, Le Bargy, Maurice Rostand, and a lot of the other members of Paris society. No news of Stravinsky of any kind. So far, Switzerland is a faraway country.

I haven't the courage to set to work again, all the less since the two works I had begun and that kept me in harness since the *Trio* are not appropriate to the demands of the times: (1) *The Sunken Bell* in collaboration with Gerhart Hauptmann; and (2) a symphonic poem that had started very well, *Vienna!!!* and now it would be impossible to call it *Petrograd.*

The symphonic poem of which Ravel speaks here later got another name when it was finished after the end of the war. Ravel called it *La Valse.* The war, therefore, added a compulsory restraint to that which, for some years, he had imposed on himself voluntarily. The project of making an opera out of *The Sunken Bell* was abandoned. Among other external things he had to renounce because of the war with Germany and Austria were two journeys. He had previously been invited to Prague and to Berlin.

In a letter to Roland-Manuel he also mentioned, in addition to all these matters, a work for piano, which he first, in some uncertainty, called a *Suite.* Roland-Manuel, the former pupil who had become a friend, probably had the deepest insight into the private artistic life of the composer that Ravel, on the whole, had ever permitted any person to have. He informs us of the ceaseless, sometimes desperate, efforts Ravel made to be accepted for military service. In pursuing these, there was no introduction, no angle, no relationship he would not try to use. Finally, he even approached the cabinet minister Paul Painlevé, who had become a friend, with the absurd proposal that he be taken into the Air Force for the very reason that he was underweight for the ground forces. Indeed, he dedicated to this influential person one of the three *a cappella* choruses he wrote in 1915.

At last Maurice Ravel, like his brother, became a driver in a military convoy, but with much less success. It is true that in a photo taken in 1916 he looks like a dangerous warrior in his enormous fur jacket. But he could not help it that the truck, to which he was not accustomed, was constantly suffering breakdowns and blowouts. On the whole he bore his military life stoically. For him it lasted from November, 1915, to March, 1917. In those nearly eighteen months he was unusually communicative. He wrote to every possible friend, wishing to maintain contact with all. One of the first letters he sent was to Jean Marnold, a great-grandson of the Napoleonic General Morland and the critic who had battled so energetically for him in the controversy over the Prix de Rome. He wrote:

Driver Ravel, Automobile Convoy, Section T.M. 171 via B.C.M. Paris.

Dear Friend: Now I have been "at the front" for a week. I am still far from the actual front, but even further from Paris. Inwardly you feel it is quite close. The planes overhead, the troop convoys, the route-marking arrows, everything around here points to a gigantic battle in the making.

Every evening we have the sirens at the railway station and at the factory giving zeppelin warnings. When the neighborhood is under direct attack, the horns blow alert signals.

In spite of the rigors of war service, the absence of comfort, not to mention worse, in the barracks, I am not too unhappy. The food is good, and I make abundant use of it. I was almost immediately assigned to a fat Aries truck, which ran on only three legs and which they took away from me the very next day. The lieutenant, who knew my name, offered to let me drive our personnel car, but I modestly declined. They are going to assign me to a small truck, as this is what I am qualified to drive on these roads. He has promised to assign some interesting missions to me.

Meanwhile Ravel's creative imagination had gone off in a very singular direction. At first nothing came of the *Suite* he had previously announced, but as his thoughts had been stimulated by the idea of writing a work in suite form, which meant turning toward a forgotten courtly era, the first work he wrote during his year at war, after he had finished the *Trio,* was an excursion into a remote and splendid period. In doing so he became like the poet who himself wrote the texts for his own madrigals. These were three pieces written in the terse expressive French of the time of Rabelais, masterful in following sixteenth century poetic inflection and syntax, without sacrificing an underlying touch of irony.

Psychologically Ravel had good grounds for this turn to archaism. He was oppressed by the seriousness and the constant menace of the present, by its sham heroics. He turned toward a flight from the times, a flight from himself, a retreat to a better, a gayer world, a past that, to be sure, had also known the horrors of war. But this past epoch became an artistic dugout, a protective shelter against the daily routine of a war that made no sense.

There were three of these poems. The first, *Nicolette,* tells in terse phrases the tale of the lovely maiden who, among all her suitors, chose the old, stout, evil-smelling cripple because he had the most money. The second is more serious and realistic. *Three Beautiful Birds of Paradise* speaks of the men who must go to war, who go swaggering through the town in their beautiful gay uniforms. The third, *Ronde,* is addressed to maidens, in baroque flourishes, replete with puns and rows of odd expressions, warning them to avoid the Forest of Ormonde, where satyrs, centaurs, and wicked magicians lie in wait for them.

These verses, so far removed in tone from the time in which they were written, so far from touching on warlike themes, were set to music by Ravel with the strictness and the harmonic fantasy of an Italian or an English madrigalist. They are set for mixed chorus *a cappella* with a bow to the treasury of the old church modes, concisely written, stripped of every superfluous note, music of pseudoarchaic restraint, yet full of modern musical feeling.

Ravel sometimes took pleasure in wearing the mask of another period or of another folk. He had an innate gift for mimicry, and he loved to practice little deceptions on his friends, or even on strangers visiting him. His talent for musical parody had been manifest since 1913 when he wrote his two piano pieces "in the manner of . . . ." These are brilliant imitations of Chabrier and Borodin.

Sometimes he would identify himself completely with his self-chosen mask. Then a symbiosis between the model and his own work of art would result. This is seen in the hispanic idiom in some of his early works and in the Viennese dances in his *Valses Nobles et Sentimentales*. Mature civilizations like the French of the late nineteenth and early twentieth centuries rather enjoyed looking back satirically, and many times the irony drops away.

A group movement like neoclassicism, which had been proclaimed by Erik Satie as early as before the turn of the century, and which, after the end of World War I, swept all of the French moderns, began early to manifest itself in Ravel's very individual forms. In this respect the *Trois Chansons* for mixed chorus are a key composition.

Ravel took his military career, halfway between home and the front, very seriously. But this did not hinder him from taking a lively part in the artistic life of the nation. For him national sentiment was not a narrow-minded and jealous keeping watch over the national arts as it was for many others. In 1916 a highly prominent group of stay-at-home writers and musicians in Paris formed a League for the Defense of French Music. It was a typical creation of shortsighted nationalism, to which at that time all the warring countries were resorting. There were German writers, even of the highest rank, such as Thomas Mann and Gerhart Hauptmann, not to mention Richard Dehmel and Ernst Lissauer, who sinned in this regard. Ravel read the bylaws of the League and was beside himself over the limitations they contained. He addressed to them the following letter, which will stand for all time to the credit of his artistic integrity:

An enforced rest at last enables me to reply to the enclosure by you of your bylaws. I fully approve the wish for action which inspired the founding of the League. This wish was so active in me that it led me to give up civilian life without having been forced to do so.

But I do not believe that "the defense of our national artistic inheritance" makes it necessary to "prohibit the performance of contemporary German and Austrian works." It would actually be damaging to French composers to ignore the output of their foreign colleagues and thus to create a kind of nationalistic clan. Our art of music, being so rich, would soon degenerate and restrict itself to obsolete formulas.

To me it signifies little that, for example, Mr. Schönberg is an Austrian national. He is none the less a musician of great value, whose highly interesting explorations have a valuable influence on certain allied musicans, and have had on us.

In Germany, outside of Richard Strauss, we find only second-class composers, of whom we can find many without having to step over our own boundaries. But it is possible that young artists may soon emerge there, whom it would be interesting for us to know.

On the other hand, I do not consider it necessary that all French music, regardless of its worth, must be made to prevail and be propagandized abroad.

So you see, gentlemen, that my opinion differs from yours on many points, so I must deny myself the honor of joining with you. Nevertheless, I hope to continue to act like a Frenchman.

An answer was not long in coming. From it Ravel learned once more how dangerous it can be not to share the views of the majority. The League included many in high position, for instance Camille Saint-Saëns and Vincent d'Indy. But the chairman, one Tenroc, whose name today cannot be found in even the most comprehensive reference books, replied to Ravel:

I am delighted to learn how highly you treasure the worth of the musician Schönberg and the taste of Bartók, Kodály, and their pupils. The National League will be prepared at the right time, to caution your admiration in advance of a possible sacrifice, to find that your own music may be too painful for our public to hear.

Ravel was powerless to do anything against this shocking threat, because, as a soldier, he did not have the privilege of entering any public controversy. He had to be content to act as a Frenchman, as he had so pointedly expressed himself in his letter addressed to these stay-at-homes. And that is what he did, gallantly and modestly, in his own soldierly way.

Claude Debussy reacted much more nationalistically to the catastrophe of the World War. But he wrote in a letter to his publisher Durand: "To strut like a hero, while one stays safely at home, protected from the shells, seems to me ridiculous."

Four years later when the League was long forgotten and the war victoriously ended, Ravel gave additional and even more convincing evidence of his nonconformity and complete animosity to official and nationalistic meddling in artistic matters. Leo Bérard, the Minister of Public Instruction, had nominated him for the Legion of Honor, and this proposal, naturally, was approved. Only one formality was neglected. They had not asked the approval of the nominee himself. Ravel found out about the whole plan only after the news had already become public. He read about it on January 16, 1920, while on a visit to the country place of Ferdinand Hérold, the translator of Gerhart Hauptmann. He was disturbed by this news just as he was in the midst of his work on the score of the choreographic poem *La Valse*. He telegraphed his friend Roland-Manuel at once and followed that with a letter:

I have spent the day reading the telegrams, but I have sent no answer because the rights of the author of *La Valse* come first. What a ridiculous business! Who could have played this joke on me? I have written to Vuillermoz to check the announcements and wire me if he can do something about it. And I have to finish *La Valse* before the end of the month. Otherwise I would set off this evening.

The day after he finished the seventy-six-page score, he described his situation and the effect of the publicity to Jean Marnold's daughter. The undated letter must have been written at the end of February, 1920: "It was a success as a discreet rejection. I have a wheelbarrow full of newspaper clippings, which Argus and other services have sent me in the last three days. How they revile me!"

Satie, too, commented on the case. In Cocteau's short-lived avant-garde newspaper *Le Coq* he wrote: "Ravel declines the Legion of Honor, but all his music accepts it."

At that time, in the year 1920, Ravel struck and wounded French citizenry in its national self-esteem exactly as he had done four years earlier when he saw in German and Austrian composers not enemies but colleagues, men whom one should not kill or even boycott, but from whom one simply could learn. Charles Baudelaire, Theodor Fontane, and many other great personalities had felt as he did about the question of accepting public distinctions. And how could the ribbon of an order interest him when he was in the midst of the sublime high tension of his labor over the orchestral waltzes that recreate the Vienna of 1814 and 1815?

But the soldier at the wheel of a little convoy truck in 1916 had other thoughts than those of luxurious backgrounds and waltzes, even though Ravel's first inkling of the choreographic tone poem went back to a time before the outbreak of the Great War. Then he was simply performing his duty as a soldier. At the end of September, 1916, however, he was sent to hospital with dysentery. He lay in Châlons-sur-Marne for two weeks and was operated on. He spent the time reading and writing, including the following letter to Jean Marnold on October 7:

I have been in hospital now more than a fortnight. I was operated on a week ago. I have written to lots of people, even to some who are indifferent. It is only you to whom I have not given even a single sign of life. Yet you are one of the first to whom I wanted to send news of myself. This is because of a secret I shall never be able to clear up. When you saw Mama, I am sure you knew nothing. I hid it from her when I was sent to hospital. Now I send her only hints that I am still a bit tired, am taking a rest, etc.

It all went very well. All the fellow-sufferers among my comrades predicted unimaginable Chinese tortures and a miserable death. I must certainly be like the Spartan boy, because I found it quite bearable. I even hold the record for taking chloroform without gas pains, headache, or sickness. On the contrary, when I woke I wanted a cigarette as I was dying of hunger.

Now I must just wait here patiently for my recovery, in about two weeks. Meanwhile I am reading with enthusiasm. It is unbelievable what I can devour in books of every kind and level, down to Paul Bourget's *Sens de la Mort*.

They tell me that Saint-Saëns announces to the fascinated crowd that during the war he has composed theater music, songs, an elegy, and a piece for trumpets. If, instead, he had been servicing howitzers, his music might have profited by it.

Meanwhile the great world had not forgotten the sick hospital patient. In Rome he was soon made a member of the Academy of Saint Cecilia, and in Paris the Opéra Comique planned a ballet adaptation of his children's piece, *Ma Mère l'Oye.*

His furious reading seems to have been indiscriminate, as it had been before at certain times in his life. But among the books he raced through as a convalescent was one he could not put out of his mind. It was a splendid book, one that told of youth, love, longing, and death, of unusual and ghostly children's masked balls: *Le Grand Meaulnes* by Alain Fournier. It is one of the great French works of art concerned with renunciation and with an idealized existence. It moved the sensitive Ravel so greatly that he wanted at once to write music about it, a work for violoncello and piano, but nothing came of it. Nevertheless, something of the inspired, serene power of Fournier's prose did pass over into Ravel's next composition, one he had planned as a suite more than a year before and that soon took form in *Le Tombeau de Couperin.* Even later, *La Valse* reflected the influence of *Le Grand Meaulnes.*

LE TOMBEAU DE COUPERIN, 1917

In December, 1916, his hospital stay came to an end. Ravel returned happily and all unsuspecting to Paris. He hurried to his home in Levallois to find a dying woman. His brother Edouard had also arrived on leave. The two sons saw their beloved mother pass away. For both it was so terrible a blow that there seemed to be no possible consolation.

Edouard had to return to his unit; Maurice, too, had to be back in Châlons-sur-Marne within five days. From there he wrote to his "war godmother" (in France well-disposed ladies adopted soldiers as "war godchildren") , Madame Fernand Dreyfus, his friend Roland-Manuel's stepmother:

> Spiritually it is frightful. I had written her just a short while ago and received her pitiful letters that gladdened me so, . . . and yet they gave me such great joy. I was still happy at that moment, in spite of the unutterable apprehension in my heart. I had no idea it would happen so soon. Now I am left in this dreadful despair, this anxiety in my thoughts. It is not good for me that I am so far away from my dear Edouard. I am even more isolated here than anywhere else, surrounded by these worthy, gay comrades, who yet are so far from me at such a time.

Ravel suffered not only in morale, but even more, physically. The abnormally Siberian cold of the 1916–1917 winter set him back badly. His feet became frostbitten so that he had to be hospitalized again, but later he was discharged and sent home. That was in the spring of 1917.

He felt orphaned and alone, his brother still in the service, the home in Levallois cold and empty. He felt himself to be at the low point of his existence, even though now he was free, able to work again, something he yearned to do.

At this critical moment came the invitation from his war godmother Madame Dreyfus to her country place in the peaceful countryside of Normandy. He accepted this offer of hospitality and on June 20 moved out to Frêne, near Lyons-la-Forêt, where he was provided with everything he needed or could wish for. Here he felt like a man whose life had been saved.

But now a new and fundamental change was to be noticed in Ravel. He, the elegant one, the master of irony, the twister of paradox, who was accustomed to ignore and suppress his feelings, was moved to the depths of his being by his experiences in the war and, possibly even more, by the loss of his mother. The psychological blows to which life had subjected him took their toll. Grief, loneliness, war memories, terror of death and of life suddenly overcame him. His previous voluntarily chosen esthetic self-restraint, which had also brought with it a degree of renunciation in the sphere of human love, was altered by the realities of life, as a cruel fate forcibly dictated and imposed upon him an irreparable loss. He had seen friends dying around him in the bloom of their youth; and he had been obliged to bury her who embodied for him home, his origins, and his earliest musical impressions. But the shock to his capacity for feeling caused by the war years was not limited to his private life. Ravel was a different man. The change demanded a creative offering. His next work was a monumental epitaph, a collection of idealized obituaries. He named the work *Le Tombeau de Couperin*.

It is, in form, a suite, a set of dances in baroque and classic style: a forlane, a rigaudon and a minuet, introduced by a prelude and a fugue, and rounded off with a toccata.

When he began the work, Ravel wrote his friend Garban, of the Durand publishing house, that he would like to have a couple of pieces by Liszt sent him, including the *Études d'Exécution Transcendante*. This request is striking for its evidence of an interest entirely apart from the baroque and classic content of the *Tombeau*. Apparently, Ravel wished to test out the piano style he had already developed to so high a pitch by comparing it with one of the most difficult virtuoso works of the nineteenth century. However, the Liszt studies did not, by any means, serve as a model for this piano suite, as possibly did Balakirev's *Islamey* for his *Scarbo* or Schubert for the *Valses Nobles et Sentimentales*.

Actually, the toccata, the most difficult portion of the Ravel suite, is easy if measured against the superlative difficulty of Liszt's piano study. In any case, the writing of this closing movement has a finish that Ravel himself compared with that of Saint-Saëns, as Hélène Jourdan-Morhange, his violinist friend, has disclosed to us.

Ravel himself drew the illustration for the title page of Durand's edition of *Le Tombeau de Couperin*. It shows, standing on a raised pedestal bordered with flowing drapery, an urn-shaped vase of baroque outline, out of which trails a delicate sprig of laurel. Under the words *Le Tombeau de Couperin* stands Ravel's familiar monogram, in which the block letters M and R are run together.

Tombeau, the French word for "tomb," has been used in French literature and music since the seventeenth century to signify "homage to the dead." The musical *tombeaux* were associated, in sense and style, with the laments and plaints that, especially in France and Italy, had been the custom ever since Monteverdi's *Plaint of Ariadne* and Froberger's mourning pieces. François Couperin had himself recognized this convention with his musical obituaries for Lully and Corelli. Even before him, his uncle Louis Couperin had honored the memory of his teacher Chambonnières with a *tombeau*.

Which Couperin did Ravel intend to celebrate with this monument? He leaves it to us to surmise, as he liked so much to do about the historical periods of his other subjects. Later he did let it be known that his aim was simply to pay tribute to French music of the eighteenth century in general. Perhaps this explanation was also meant to be ironic, but it was probably more accurate than it pretended to be. In fact, only one of the famous Couperins survived into the eighteenth century; that was François le Grand.

Wanda Landowska, the harpsichordist, stated that his *Arlequine* was Ravel's favorite piece.

There is a deep, painful, even tragic emotion concealed beneath the bright, playful movement of these dances and their artful imitation of harpsichord speech. Each of the six movements is dedicated to a man who lost his life in the World War.

The inexpressibly mournful *Minuet* is dedicated to Jean Dreyfus, the son of his wartime godmother, to whom he had addressed his *Menuet Antique* and the second movement of his *Sonatine*. The *Toccata* is for Captain Joseph de Marliave, whose wife was the distinguished pianist Marguerite Long, to whom contemporary French music is so greatly in debt (she played the premieres not only of the *Tombeau,* but also in 1932, of the *Piano Concerto in G,* which Ravel dedicated to her). The *Rigaudon* is in memory of the brothers Pierre and Pascal Gaudin of Saint-Jean-de-Luz, whose sister Marie had been Ravel's friend since his early youth. "Rigaudon"—Marie Gaudin: the assonance of the middle syllables may have unconsciously dictated the choice of this dedication.

It is one of Ravel's most characteristic gestures that he should clothe in dance form these deepest emotions of his life, the double reaction to the war and to the loss of his mother. The whole work breathes farewell. Ravel, so to speak, has stepped forth from the world of childhood and youth into that of serious maturity. The creative expression of this transformation is a species of withdrawal, a veiling and concealment of the depths of discovery behind a bright, almost elegant disguise. Suddenly the tough, dandified motto, of which he delivered himself to Maurice Delage— "One must have a head and have guts, but never a heart"— takes on entirely new meaning. Feelings are transient. Even the tragedies of antiquity and the great historic myths owe their immortality, not to the depth of emotions they express, but to the form in which the artistic instinct and understanding of their creators clothed them. Indeed, the emotional depth of Ravel's six-movement epitaph was concealed behind its hard, sculptured, and classically ordered form.

But restraint is not necessarily synonymous with retreat. Ravel, the radical modernist, was not trying to make his peace with a comfortable majority of his audience when he wrote these dances. The *Tombeau de Couperin* is no *Rosenkavalier*. One must examine the harmonies of these pieces with care to perceive with what ingenuity and well-planned skill that which he began in *Valses Nobles et Sentimentales* is carried further. Ravel's paradoxical esthetic of concealment is expressed, as is the indirect reflection of his purpose, when he pours his deepest sentiments into forms that before him were used to serve only occasions of sociability and flirtation.

The *forlane* is based on the oldest of the dance forms represented in the suite. The forlana comes from the north of Italy, out of Friuli, where it borders on Slavic regions to the east. In form it is related to the livelier *gigue* and the *passamezzo*.

The rigaudon is of ancient French and Provençal ancestry. Rameau loved it, Henry Purcell treasured it, and Johann Sebastian Bach made use of it in suites. But Ravel was not content merely to copy older models. He changed their forms and bathed them in a new light, harmonically, melodically, and sometimes rhythmically.

Let us look at the *forlane*. It is in the key of E minor, or more precisely, in an imaginary church mode, as is demonstrated by its avoiding the leading tone at the cadences. But the tonic is also circumvented and evaded. The very first chord brings to the initial melody tone (E), not only the fifth (B) and the minor third (G), but, at the same time, also the chromatic neighboring degree (D sharp), which here functions not as a leading tone but becomes, so to speak, a dissonant component and a psychological darkening of the tonic chord.

And in an exactly analogous manner, the dominant (B), when it appears in the melody immediately after the opening note, is accompanied by its neighboring A sharp as if by a shadow, a mysterious companion pointing away from it. And yet in the very first measure the opening dissonance returns, except that the note D sharp now lies in the upper voice and rubs against the E in the accompanying chord, where it also encounters the tones G sharp and B sharp.

The melodic curve, which all too fast and, as it were, unexpectedly, has led to the most remote note of the key, now rolls back. The B sharp, which earlier was introduced as a chord component, now, in conjunction with the fifth of the subdominant (A–E in the bass), is converted into a C natural, and thereby becomes the third of an A minor triad as if in a process of unmasking.

This same note (whether considered as B sharp or C natural) on its return meets with a new dissonant chord (A–C sharp–E sharp), then slides down to B natural, then makes a drop of a seventh through to C sharp, an interval which is immediately repeated. Surprisingly, it then reaches the major third on G sharp, but steers stepwise over F sharp toward the tonic and, after an oscillating detour upwards and then downwards to the lower neighboring tone (D), finally affirms the objective it has attained.

If, together with this particular melodic progression, we also examine the chords in the accompaniment, we find a most striking avoidance of the repetition of tones. It is, so to speak, a complementary procedure, which brings together the greatest possible number of different tones in chords before any of them reappears. The first three chords are augmented triads (B–D sharp–G, G sharp–B sharp–C, A–C sharp–E sharp). They have no note in common and contain every step in the chromatic scale except D, F sharp, and A sharp. But the process goes further. The harmony goes on to make use of a series of minor thirds (E sharp–G sharp, A–B sharp, G–A sharp, F sharp–A). Therein, two tones which were omitted at the beginning are used (A sharp and F sharp), and they have hardly sounded when there also appears the last missing tone, D, now in the even more striking role of a penultimate tone, as a substitute for a leading tone.

All of this is, at the same time, both primeval and modern, archaic and most novel; that is, archaic in its insistent adherence to modal forms and modern in pressing together the entire chromatic scale into such a narrow compass.

No less interesting than the harmony is the periodic structure of this little introductory segment. The melody is in four- or possibly eight-bar phrases. But its inner asymmetry makes it seem otherwise. How is this accomplished? Again, by a mixture of very simple and very sophisticated devices. The *forlane* is based on a quietly rocking theme in 6/8 time. Ravel adds to this a dotting of the first eighth. This produces a lightly skipping rhythmic effect. In the first bar this takes place in the first half of the measure while the second half remains steady. In the second bar both halves of the measure are marked by the skipping motion. But in the third bar Ravel postpones the skip until the second half of the measure and repeats this treatment in the fourth bar. So we have here a fully asymmetric rhythmic phrasing within a four-bar melody. This creates a feeling of unrest, artfully and consciously striven for, which beclouds the clarity of the classic forlana.

Left: Ravel and conductor Paul Whiteman, in New York 1928.

Below: Ravel at a birthday party in his honour in New York City, March 8, 1928. From left: Oscar Fried, conductor; Eva Gauthier, singer; Ravel at the piano; Manoah Leide-Tedesco, composer-conductor; and composer George Gershwin.

Ravel, shortly before his last illness, 1935.

If one compares this rhythm and periodicity with that of the forlana in Johann Sebastian Bach's C major Suite for orchestra, the difference becomes very apparent. Bach writes the dance in 6/4 time with an upbeat. He also introduces the dotted rhythms, but they enter only in the second half of the first and the second measures, while they occur in both halves of the third measure, and only in the first half of the fourth. An even-flowing figure in eighths in the accompaniment smooths out these rhythmic irregularities, while the strokes of the thorough bass uniformly accentuate the third and the fourth beats of the measure.

In Bach the basic key of C major is darkened to the Mixolydian mode at the start by a B flat, and later to the Lydian mode by an F sharp; Ravel's *forlane* steps away constantly from the realm of the E minor diatonic scale, in spite of the stability of its association with a tonic, making use melodically, from among the notes of its scale, of only the tonic, the dominant, and the two neighboring whole tones of the tonic.

Because of its bizarre character, the *forlane* has often been the subject of conjecture about it's programmatic associations. Hélène Jourdan-Morhange sees in the piece only a solemn obeisance on bended knees, while an English essayist (Norman Demuth) claims it has been said that "it suggests the taste of pineapple." Vlado Perlemuter, who studied the *Tombeau* with Ravel, calls the *forlane* the piece that most faithfully affirms its allegiance to the past through the sound of its cadences, influenced by antiquity; he speaks of its ending, without the slightest retard, as a music-box effect.

The whole suite shows in each of its movements a skill of the most extreme refinement, and, at the same time, the full esthetic of renunciation. Here we have none of the rustling sonorities of the *Daphnis et Chloë* ballet, nothing of the transcendent virtuosity of the *Gaspard de la Nuit,* and absolutely nothing of the slightly coquettish charm of the piano waltzes, with their dramatic high points and swelling dynamic tides. The *Tombeau* is a jewel of classic form and of its expression turned inward on itself, a memorial of sublimated grief, and, simply, of sublimation itself. All self-torture, all renunciation of love, all tragedy over the loss of a mother and of fallen friends have here found concealment under a protective arch of artistry. Ravel's heart has been transformed into sheer music.

FOLK MUSIC AND MIMICRY

That the *Tombeau* dates from 1917 gives it a doubly enigmatic and poignant origin. The Great War had reached its apogee of frightfulness in that very France whose spirit Ravel had prized highly as such a civilizing influence. In Central Europe the omens of the collapse of all inherited traditions were increasing. In Russia the Revolution was soon to break out; Europe was approaching a crisis. The art world of Paris, through its creations, was giving warning of a catastrophe to which the daily life of the people of the city gave hardly any clue. Paris naturally felt some hardships from the war, but the population suffered comparatively few deprivations, and the theaters were crowded and the intellectuals never interrupted their debates.

Jean Cocteau himself, called up to serve with the troops, wrote a letter to Misia Edwards in which he speaks more of Erik Satie and of Igor Stravinsky than of the "aircraft that nibble the sky and eat out of your hand." He views the German prisoners of war as "domestics Count Kessler has driven off" and the big siege-gun emplacements as "landscapes camouflaged in the manner of Bakst or Picasso—cubism taking its revenge by bombarding Munich."

During the closing months of the Great War Debussy died in Paris under the thunder of the German bombardment. There had been for many years a state of admiring rivalry and acknowledged jealousy between him and Ravel. It was more the cliques surrounding the two men than their own inclination or aversion that nourished their differences and occasional discords. Debussy, whose more impressionable nature did not always distinguish what was his own from what he got from others, had early received stimulation from Ravel's music. Ravel, on the other hand,

more scrupulous in respecting the boundaries of artistic terri-
tory, himself joined in the general development of a style, as
did Debussy himself. His high regard for the older master
must have been tried sometimes by the latter's appropria-
tions. But Ravel remained true to Debussy. We know that
he asked that music of Debussy's be played at his funeral.

Debussy's death left no documentary traces behind
in Ravel's papers, but we can be certain that the news moved
him deeply and that it contributed to his growing feeling of
solitude. In 1922 he dedicated his *Duo Sonata* to the memory of the creator of *Pelléas and Mélisande*.

After the war, and because of the loss of his
mother, Ravel found himself in such a state of isolation that
it affected his artistic existence. The affectionate family
group in Levallois had lost its center. Although his devotion
to his younger brother Edouard was deep and sincere, it was
under the shadow of other relationships in which Maurice
could not share. For a while he lived together with his
brother in the home of the Bonnets, who were Edouard's extremely close friends. But this living together only seemed to
increase his wish to be completely away from everyone. He
dreamed of a home outside the city, and yet close enough to
Paris not to render his taking an active part in the artistic
and social life of the capital completely impractical.

For a part of the winter of 1919–1920 he was a
guest at the country place of his friends the Hérolds in the
Cévennes in south central France, the region of the icy
mistral. This aroused in him a desire for rural surroundings
and quiet. So he began to make inquiries among his friends
to learn if they might know of something, at least thirty
kilometers from Paris, to which he could retreat. Jokingly he
wrote to Georgette Marnold, the daughter of the critic Jean
Marnold, that sometimes he thought of looking for a lovely
monastery in Spain, but that this would be idiotic for an

unbeliever, and that, in any event, he could not compose "Viennese waltzes and other fox-trots" in such surroundings.

Every summer for many years he had partially satisfied his longing for Spain when he traveled to his tiny homeland to spend the warm months in Saint-Jean-de-Luz. The little cove at the mouth of the Nivelle beamed its witchery on him all his life. It was more than the rustic environs and the magnificent landscape combining the lofty Pyrenees and the wide Atlantic that drew him there. Although he was no infant prodigy but a creator early come to full ripeness, there is no doubt that as a mature musician he found assurance and incentive there, that the Basque elements he inherited from his mother reached out for nourishment at their source. Many of the visible and invisible characteristics that manifested themselves in his own mode of life and choice of surroundings, his habits, his individual private tastes, had their origin in things Basque. His love for bric-a-brac, for bizarre little ornamental objects, the way he put them together in his residences, had their roots on the Basque coast and in the little shops along the beaches of Saint-Jean-de-Luz and his birthplace Ciboure.

Ravel loved to lounge of an evening in front of one of the cafés around the Place Louis XIV and watch the Basque folk dances. A little orchestra would play gay dance tunes, and the musicians would slap a little Basque drum with their right hands while they deftly held the wooden nose flutes with three openings, called *txistu,* in their left.

These concerts almost always began with a fandango, the old dance, equally beloved in Spain and in the Basque country, that Curt Sachs thinks goes back to Phoenician origins. In Spain, where it emerged at the beginning of the eighteenth century, it is accompanied with guitars and castanets, and the couplets are sung. It stands in a brisk triple measure, and the players love to perform it with shifts in the rhythmic accents.

The Basques dance with an inimitable mixture of pride, grace, and modesty. When the music of the fandango strikes up, the girls slip out of their shoes in the middle of the square and perform the round dance steps gravely and happily with arms half bent, the hands held high toward heaven. The partner is always held with the eyes but never touched. Even the primitive farandole, which came to the Atlantic coast from giddier Provence, is given a more stately and measured character by the Basques. Possibly the folk tradition remembers that this dance once symbolized the escape of Theseus from the Labyrinth. Even more remarkable are the cries that are uttered by the dancers in Basque lands, rather weird singing tones that spiral up, sliding toward the heights without fixed notes. These are probably ancient signals of communication such as mountain people send each other from peak to peak.

Ravel eagerly absorbed this gay childlike music. He felt himself at home with the ancient Basque folk, and its enigmatic language, and its own native culture. As Isaac Albéniz had done before him, he adopted in his own compositions suggestions from this source. He had also, through Albéniz, become acquainted with the strangest of these Basque dances, which, like some Turkish, Greek, and Bulgarian folk tunes, run in an asymmetrical 5/8 meter in which the first eighth note is dotted. The dance is called *Zortziko*. Albéniz made a very charming piano setting of it, which Ravel often played. He took a lively interest in such rhythmic singularities.

He sought and found them often in Basque and North Spanish dance music. He knew well Charles Bordes' *Douze chansons amoureuses du pays basque français*. In this collection the *errefusa,* the "unsuccessful serenade," is an especially lovely example of the asymmetric bar of three plus two plus three eighth notes.

Had not his *Piano Trio* been written during a summer sojourn in Saint-Jean-de-Luz? It is not surprising that the first movement is governed by a meter that up to then European "art" music had not yet known but that is as customary in Basque and in Castilian folk music as it is in the Balkans among the Bulgars, the Romanians, and the Greeks. Possibly, too, the Arab infiltration into Spanish culture imported such peculiarities of tempo from lands beyond the coasts of the eastern Mediterranean.

Ravel was certainly not unimpressed by the 8/8 measure of the *errefusa* composed of units of three, two, and three. In the first movement of his *Trio,* however, this rhythm is also joined by a veiling of the key that seems to waver between Dorian A minor and Mixolydian A major. At the same time the bass operates as a quieting antipole. It begins on an organ point on E, which steps forward in contrary rhythm to the chords of the upper voice in four quiet quarters with a subdivision into eighths of the last quarter note.

Ravel was not a folklorist. The ethnological and scholarly sides of music left him utterly cold, although in the province of composition technique he advanced with scholarly exactness. Nor did he ever, like Bartók, Zoltán Kodály, or Leoš Janáček, travel far afield with notebook in hand in order to observe the peasants and get in writing old melodies in their unadulterated form. But he had a sixth sense, a clear, undistorted vision of the character of certain old folk songs and dances. And he sought these out with the equipment of modern knowledge of sound and rhythm, thus bringing folk music closer to its archetypal forms than the most painstaking scholarly reconstruction ever possibly could. Because of his introversion and his self-centeredness Ravel remained a child all his life. So the wide-ranging relationship he maintained with music of the people did not arise from a conscious turning back of the dial. It was, so to speak, an innate, congenital manner of thought. Ravel did not need to make an effort of will to enter into the folk inheritance, and his way of doing so was worlds away from any mere pedagogical or pedantic desire for exploration.

It is precisely through this artistically instinctive leaning toward folkloristic forms that the constant attraction of cultures geographically remote became clear to him. By this is not meant the exotic colors that he borrowed from the palettes of Rimski-Korsakov and Borodin when he drew his youthful sketches for the figure of *Shéhérazade,* but his settings of Greek and other folk melodies to which his friend Calvocoressi, one of the Apaches in the Paul Sordes group, first stimulated him. His work on these recreations of folk songs was spread over the period 1904–1914 and ended with the Hebrew chants *Kaddish* and *The Eternal Riddle,* but it had a sublimated continuation much later in the *Chansons Madécasses* and in the *Bolero.*

What charmed Ravel in folk melodies was their antique coloration through use of unaltered church modes. His settings always reach for the interval spans of these old modal melodies with great accuracy, while at the same time the characteristic Ravel chord with its three neighboring half tones frequently enters into and becomes an integral part of the harmony. In the *Quatre Chants Populaires,* which had been performed in the Moscow House of Song, Ravel also remained faithful to his basic principle that one should not "revise" folk songs or alter their melodic substance. The same album contains a Yiddish song *Meierke mein Suhn,* which preceded the *Mélodies Hébraïques* by four years.

Certainly his procedure in setting these folk songs is exactly the opposite of that applied to the Basque and

Spanish elements in the *Piano Trio*. In the songs there is an almost automatic entry into the musical sense of a prescribed melodic outline. In the *Trio* there is invention of melodic shapes that float in an aura that might be that of almost any folk base. In the former, therefore, the process may be compared to filling in colors on a drawing that has already been provided; in the latter, a bridge is thrown across from one inaccessible bank to another, almost a transsubstantiation.

But Ravel's genius for adaptation and substitution knows still another method, and that is the copying of a style. We know that his beginnings in composition were affected by two strong influences: first, the nationalistic Russian school, particularly Borodin; second, Emmanuel Chabrier. When he was a piano student at the Conservatory he, with his friend Ricardo Viñes, played for the master his *Valses Romantiques*. In 1913 he published an album bearing the title *A la manière de. . . . .* One of the two pieces in it is astonishingly faithful in its imitation of Chabrier's idiom, almost in mimicry of it. Apart from that, it is a paraphrase of a much-loved melody from Gounod's *Faust*. The other of these copies is *A la manière de Borodin,* a little waltz in the nationalistic Russian style yet still characteristic of Ravel.

The mimicry in which he indulged in these pieces reaches its highest intensification and its artistic justification in the *Valses Nobles et Sentimentales,* in which he was charmed by the example of Franz Schubert. A number of years later the same Viennese charm inspired him again to write a masterpiece, the choreographic poem *La Valse.*

Alongside the gift and inspiration that mark all these works there is a sublimation in them of a childlike impulse to play. It is a legitimate artistic device for one's own creations to make use of the same models that the old masters often employed. It is by copying old paintings that the student becomes a painter. Schönberg once asserted that he had only become original because he had consistently taken pains to copy things he considered good.

LA VALSE, 1920

It took a long time for Ravel to find his creative equilibrium again after the distractions of the war years. His homelessness drove him to making many actually aimless journeys. At the beginning of 1919 he took the cure in Mégève, a resort in Savoie. His letters at that time reported the curves on his temperature chart and the fantastic irregularities of his pulse. The torment of sleeplessness began, something that would never leave him for the rest of his life. On January 31, 1919, he wrote a card to Georgette Marnold with the laconic line: "I must believe that need for sleep is only a prejudice; I feel no worse."

September days saw him in St. Cloud. We know that in December he was a guest of Ferdinand Hérold, translator of Gerhart Hauptmann, in his country place in the Cévennes, west of Valence, where he was working on *La Valse*. It was late in April before he left this refuge, went to Eure-et-Loire, and then again to St. Cloud. Meantime the storm of hatred stirred up by his rejection of the Legion of Honor was receding. On December 12, 1920, *La Valse* had its concert premiere by the Lamoureux Orchestra in Paris.

Roland-Manuel asserts that Ravel's plan for glorifying the Vienna waltz musically was conceived very early. The ideas and plans for it originated before 1907 when he composed the *Rapsodie Espagnole,* and letters during the early war years complain of the need to refrain from a work that was intended to bear the title *Vienna*. During a period of extreme weariness and creative paralysis in 1919 Ravel received a fresh impetus from Diaghilev. The old plan was revived, with a performance the following year contemplated. Ravel, unable to compose in familiar surroundings, decided on the radical measure of spending the winter in a kind of seclusion. The Hérolds took him in for a stay of five months. It was a cold winter, and the Ardèche region in Languedoc, west of the Rhône, is majestic but forbidding.

About Christmas time Ravel sank into a deep, melancholy, and crippling depression. The turn of the year, with days beginning to get longer, brought him around this obstacle. On Twelfth Night he wrote to Madame Dreyfus: "I am waltzing frantically." And a week later to Marguerite Long, together with a delayed New Year's greeting, he wrote:

> I have begun work again as passionately as ever. I have resorted to a marvelous expedient. I am living as a hermit in the midst of the Cévennes.

The score, playing time twelve minutes, is a tour de force of mobilizing rhythmic and dynamic forms. It shows Ravel at the peak of his incomparable talent for orchestral and formal polish. Never has his orchestra displayed such variety and continuity of colors, of lights and shadows, of sensuous euphoria. And yet, the work eventually named *La Valse* is essentially tragic. Ravel's own commentary permits no doubt of it. He is said to have appraised it as "a fantastic and fatefully inescapable whirlpool," though this idea was merged into his original concept of a kind of apotheosis of the Viennese waltz. He added the stage direction that heads the score: "An Imperial Court, about 1855."

The year was certainly chosen deliberately. Austria was under the rule of Emperor Francis Joseph I, then twenty-five, whose long life ended in 1916 in the midst of the horrors of the World War. In 1855 a treaty between

Austria and Pius IX terminated the liberal reforms adopted during the reign of Joseph II. At the end of December, 1851, the Danube monarchy had entered one of the most reactionary periods in its history. A new era of absolutism set in. The Ministry of the Interior ruled the empire. In external policy tensions arose with Prussia and the German League. In addition, a quarrel with Napoleon III's Second Empire was fomented, a quarrel that ended in 1859 with an unhappy war, the defeats of Magenta and Solferino, and the loss of Lombardy at the peace of Villefranche.

It was a period of social glitter, of dancing on the volcano, whose tempo was set by Vienna as Austria-Hungary's center of absolute political and social power. Provocative women's fashions with deep decolleté, bright-colored frocks with crinolines, and huge hats trimmed with trailing feathers contrasted effectively with the gay officers' uniforms from Hungary, Croatia, Rumania, and Bohemia and with the colored frock coats and stylish long trousers of the rich bankers. Extravagance was as great in imperial Paris where the first World's Fair opened in 1855 and Jacques Offenbach of Cologne filled his Bouffes-Parisiens with frivolous music.

In Vienna the family of Johann Strauss was the musical ruler. Father Strauss entered the dance orchestra of Joseph Lanner in 1823 as a violist. Two years later began the series of triumphs of his dance melodies. Not only Vienna, all Europe went dance crazy. The old Privy Councillor Goethe in Weimar called the dance fury of the waltzers "Bacchic madness." It was not without an erotic basis, since in the waltz the man and the woman were permitted to put their arms around each other. At the Prussian court this undisciplined posture was prohibited. It came from rustic origins, from the Austrian ländler (country dance) and had a forerunner in the germans that Beethoven, too, liked to compose before he wrote actual waltzes. Franz Schubert and Lanner put their stamp on the Viennese type with one strongly accented beat followed by two weaker ones. Carl Maria von Weber, in his *Invitation to the Dance,* wrote the first apostrophe to the rhythm that then, in 1819, was still young and fresh. Berlioz made an orchestral setting of the Weber piece. Chopin, Schumann, and Brahms emulated their illustrious examples.

Ravel's piece is developed from a single rhythmic nucleus. It commences pianissimo with a broken seventh chord of F–A flat–C–D in the low register. It is one of the seven motives that are now evolved, taken apart, spun out, and transformed. Besides the principal key of D major, the keys of E flat major, F major and B flat major are announced as rivals. In one oboe melody appearing in the middle of the work one recognizes the diminished octave, which strains longingly downward, from the fourth of the *Valses Nobles et Sentimentales.* The concept of the piece is basically dynamic. A crescendo, at first hesitant, then interrupted just before the peak, enters again and this time more energetically and irresistibly. The summit is reached in a terrific whirlwind. Ravel's friends called these turbulent places in his work *La Grande Kermesse.* It really sounds as though a wild rebellious horde of noise-making figures were running around each other in a mighty, drunken market festival. Instead of elation, the riot has something frightening, deathly, in it. It breaks off suddenly as though lightning had struck its heart.

The score bears a sort of scenic directive: "Clouds whirl about. Occasionally they part to allow a glimpse of waltzing couples. As they gradually lift, one can discern a gigantic hall, filled by a crowd of dancers in motion. The stage gradually brightens. The glow of the chandeliers breaks out fortissimo."

At the stage premiere Bronislava Nijinska's choreography was limited to a tableau. It was inspired by a painting by the battle painter Eugène Louis Lami. It showed a festival ball in the Paris of the Second Empire. Nothing of the demonic quality of the music, nothing of the spirit of Émile Zola, disturbed the stage picture. The elegant couple was danced by Ida Rubinstein and Anatol Wilzak.

It was not before 1951 that George Balanchine in New York devised a choreographic interpretation for the "fatefully inescapable whirlpool" that the music expresses in its death-seeking ecstasy.

La Valse is dedicated to Misia Sert. But all her negotiating skill could not dispel the disappointment that Sergei Diaghilev felt over Ravel's new "choreographic poem." To be sure, it had been his plan to bring out *La Valse* on the stage in the 1920–1921 season, possibly with Stravinsky's *Pulcinella*. Ravel had set to work accordingly, though he was skeptical. He wrote to Misia: "Even my poor Daphnis had much to complain about over Diaghilev." But Diaghilev begged off. He could see no possible stage treatment for this music. In fact, the work remained restricted to the concert hall until 1928. No reconciliation between Ravel and Diaghilev ever took place, although until the death of Diaghilev in Venice on August 16, 1929, Misia Sert often tried to arrange one.

MONTFORT-L'AMAURY, 1920;
VIOLIN-CELLO DUO, 1922

If you take the train westward from Paris toward Versailles or Saint Cyr you come into a region of dreamlike gracefulness. It is the Ile de France, celebrated by poets, with its soft hills and deep woods, among which lies the hunting forest of Rambouillet hiding its manor houses of nobles and film stars. You travel some fifty kilometers to reach the little old town of Montfort-l'Amaury (Seine-et-Oise) . Here you go through narrow hilly streets, past a pretty little church in a very unpure Gothic style and with a Romanesque cloister. Further up is the steep elevation that marks the boundary of the village. There the street makes a bend and opens to the view of a house that might have come out of a grotesque box of toys.

It has a narrow outside staircase under a short umbrella-like steeple, all on a high artificial terrace. One-storied on the street side, two-storied on the garden side, with its wooden frame set over massive stone walls, it reminds one somewhat of certain old villas in the Basque country. On the garden side there is a view deep down into the valley, away over the roofs and towers of the town, over green fields and black pine forests, with a sky overhead in which the clouds mirror the pearl-gray gentleness of French daylight.

Here Ravel's desire to have his own permanent dwelling in the countryside was fulfilled. The house in Montfort-l'Amaury became available. It has six or seven rooms but with no inside communication between the upper and the lower stories. But the garden! And the situation! Exactly what he wished for. Near enough to Paris and yet remote enough to isolate him a little if he needed solitude for his work. The property was named, unpretentiously, "Le Belvédère."

Ravel took possession, became the owner of the house, and began to arrange and furnish it piece by piece. He lived there from May, 1921, on, engaging a Czech housemaid named Prohaska to tend him. His first letter from his rural home is addressed to the practical and helpful Georgette Marnold. It bears the date of May 12, 1921:

Dear friend: Last week I was in Paris for some days, most of all to see you, and I couldn't even telephone you once. I wanted to beg you to trouble yourself about the chest of drawers. My poor Czech has to hang her clothes on the trees in the garden or on a bush. The repairs are coming along. I can have my piano installed in a couple of months.

Alas, I shall not return to the war. Yesterday it was finally determined that I am 100% unsuitable. When I feel worse I cannot breathe too freely.

I continue to dirty my fingers. I remove the sparrow's nest only to find it rebuilt the next morning. But it is badly improvised. The eggs fall out and you find them as an omelet on the balcony.

Soon I shall have another occupation. *Daphnis* is to come out June 10, maybe even sooner.

Have you seen the Negroes? Sometimes they show a frightening virtuosity.

By the Negroes he meant a jazz band that was throwing Paris into ecstasy. Ravel showed a passionate interest in this form of exotic music, which was then beginning to electrify all Europe. The violinist Hélène Jourdan-Morhange, who frequently accompanied him on his walks in the woods around Montfort, also shared this love of jazz, whose first notable reflection, in the form of a blues, came several years later in the second movement of the *Sonata for Violin and Piano*. Ravel never made a systematic study of the blues style, but he did have the instinct to identify its characteristics in several examples he had heard. However, it is very probable that when he was working on the *Violin Sonata* —from 1923 to 1927—he knew the classic blues of W. C. Handy. The Negro band that delighted Paris so extremely in 1921 must have had the St. Louis style of blues in its repertory. Ravel's own blues style in his *Violin Sonata* is admittedly associated with the essence of this dance but is incomparably more polished. In it he applied to these typical harmonic and melodic forms, without questioning their merit, his chordal imagination. The whole *Sonata* is stylistically far removed from Ravel's earlier sound idiom. It con-

tains stretches of definite bitonality, the horizontal management of voices that Satie loved, and harmonies of gnashing
hardness, which Stravinsky had made all the vogue. It is a
process of dematerialization, announced earlier in the *Tombeau de Couperin* and now, much later, apparently encouraged by the "splendid isolation" of his proprietorship in
Montfort-l'Amaury. It is also possible that the influence of
Satie and Stravinsky signified the opening of a new creative
period in which the blues of the *Violin Sonata* marked a
high point.

The letters of the early period in Montfort also
give expression to a new attitude toward life, although it was
not free of cares. He wrote to his friend Roland-Manuel on
August 20, 1921:

Prohaska has suddenly walked out on me. She was
hardly gone five minutes when I got reports that she had been
seen in all the bars in Montmartre. Now I see the light regarding a certain nervousness that my table china had to endure and
about spells of dizziness that I had ascribed only to her Slavic
origin. All I need now is to find an embryo in the salt cellar.

My drains were stillborn, as the plumber puts it. There
is no remedy. This afternoon, a conference with the contractor.

One o'clock, and it's pouring. I must leave you. . . .
Armed with my storm lantern I shall reach my bedroom swim-
ming.

As already mentioned, there was no staircase between the two floors. The master of the house had to go
down through the balcony and by the garden stairs when he
went to sleep. Gradually the house acquired a profile. Ravel
sketched out his own wallpapers, had his chairs decorated by
branding in the style of the turn of the century, painted the
marble of the fireplace with odd designs, and began to collect crazy and trashy objects, including Gothic ashtrays,
pieces of fake Chinese porcelain, and a mechanical nightin-

gale that sang when it was wound up. The dimensions of the house were small, so the furniture had to be small as well—quite suitable to the master of the house. The list of contents remind one of an out-of-place child's nursery. It was a playhouse set up by a spirit of fantasy.

Ravel gave his microcosmic inclinations free rein even in the garden. He provided himself with dwarf plants, miniature trees, and small shrubs, such as are cultivated in Japan. One would imagine oneself in a dream of Jonathan Swift or in the fairy tale of Tom Thumb. Even the piano was covered with unusual things. Illumination was provided by two imposing metal lamps with the pressed milk-glass globes of the *belle époque*. Snuffboxes and all sorts of little containers of uncertain origin lay about. A tremendous feather, which might have come from an ostrich or a swan, was stuck in the inkwell. The corners were fitted with cabinets with several shelves filled with knickknacks of Meissen and French manufacture—some pretty, some ridiculous. Only the large wide-framed picture of his mother (*frontispiece*) gazed, serious and proud, on the "Curiosity Shop" her son had collected for himself.

Among all these infantile trifles prospered works of ever greater austerity and mastery. For months Ravel worked on a piece he frequently mentioned in his letters as the *Duo*. Once he reported to Roland-Manuel that he had begun the slow movement in blue and black so it could switch to poppy color in the middle. It was the *Sonata for Violin and Violoncello,* on which he had also worked during his summer sojourn in the Basque country and had finished while away on a trip.

The four-movement work was completed at the beginning of 1922. In February he wrote Georgette Marnold:

If you are well again, be sure to see *Dr. Caligari.* I was in despair because I could not get to see it in Marseilles Friday evening because the performance was forbidden. Nobody knows why. Two days later the ban was lifted anyway. Yesterday in Paris I was rewarded. They ran the film for me alone. I am a type just like Ludwig of Bavaria, but not quite that mad up until now. And now I have seen the art of the film for the first time.

Ravel was not the only contemporary who was enthusiastic over Robert Wiene's famous film. *The Cabinet of Dr. Caligari* in 1919 founded the movement of decorative expressionism, which, starting in Germany, proceeded to impress the whole world with its brand of film art. It constituted one wing of the invasion by German art that temporarily conquered even Hollywood, expecting to transform the art of the film by new stylistic methods. Today its rather childish demonism is considered a thing of the past. It is completely outdated. But Ravel had great admiration for the skill of this stylized cinematography, for its avoidance of right angles and of naturalistic presentation. By virtue of its spectral tone *Caligari* is also quite close to the subjects of *Gaspard de la Nuit* and must have appealed, with its novel and expressionistic form, to the changed Ravel of Montfort-l'Amaury. In his compositions of that time there are experiments in musical montage that sound as revolutionary and shocking as some of the ghostly sequences in the film.

The daring counterpoint of the *Duo Sonata,* its reckless coupling of two keys and its occasional forays into the new province of atonalism demonstrate how open Ravel was to the influences of the newest school. He understood how to reconcile the new harmony of Schönberg and Stravinsky with Satie's impulse toward simplicity in a musical statement, his so-called lean, bare or "stripped-down" style (*style dépouillé*). All this is most strikingly evident in the slow movement.

Now new images began to appear in Ravel's correspondence. Principally, he added some new companions to share his house. He, the dear friend of animals, adopted a Siamese cat that he came to love dearly and for which he soon provided female companions. There had long been many spiritual ties between him and the world of animals. Some of his friends even said that he looked like a fox. To Colette he seemed like a squirrel. Animals play an important role in his music, even above that of human voices. This trait of his character is one element in his complex yet childlike creative nature, just as is the special attraction folk songs had for him, and the manner in which he brought to realization his desire to lead a simple rustic life.

But there were also some less cheering experiences in his daily life. In July, 1922, he wrote to the poet and musicologist Jean-Aubry: "I have been in Montfort two days now, trying to get some sleep, which still eludes me. I expect I shall succeed if I lie down often enough." The curse of sleeplessness, which the war had brought him, increased from year to year. He complained of insomnia everywhere on the many journeys he made to Amsterdam, Venice, and London. He spent many whole nights awake, in conversation, if possible, with friends whom he would accompany home by roundabout routes. Out of pure fear of long, lonely nights, he would often go to Paris to visit the theater, hear a concert, or see friends. He even rented a permanent room in the Hotel d'Athènes, not far from the residence of his friends the Godebskis.

PICTURES AT AN EXHIBITION, 1922; RONSARD À SON ÂME, 1924

Several other matters besides composing and the renovation of his house occupied Ravel at this time. He even took on a pupil or two, in spite of his previous convictions and habits and his lack of inclination toward teaching as a calling. For him it was always a question of personal contact that made him decide whether to give anyone lessons. In the case of Maurice Delage, his friend since youth, the reason was that he had been acting as a friendly adviser. With Roland-Manuel and with Manuel Rosenthal in 1923 there was a true pupil-teacher relationship, out of which a real friendship developed.

In 1909 the mail brought him an inquiry from abroad. The Englishman Ralph Vaughan Williams, though older by two years, became a pupil of Ravel for a short period, and afterward clearly showed the influence of the Frenchman in his compositions. Some years later George Gershwin, then already highly successful, expressed a wish to work with him, but Ravel declined, saying that he thought that it would be better to write honest Gershwin than imitation Ravel.

Another side occupation, pursued with much stronger inner conviction, was that of orchestration. This is the closest possible link with the musical material of another, a kind of esthetic association that otherwise only the art of the actor or the singer enjoys, that is, complete identification together with unlimited freedom of interpretation. Ravel had already tried out his coloristic mastery on Erik Satie's prelude to *Fils des Étoiles,* a drama by Sar Péladan. Soon after that, at Clarens, together with Stravinsky, he arranged some excerpts from Moussorgsky's *Khovanschchina* for orchestra.

That effort was followed by orchestrations of material by Debussy, Chopin, Schumann, and Chabrier. Then he accepted a commission from the conductor Sergei Koussevitzky to do an orchestration of Moussorgsky's greatest piano work, *Pictures at an Exhibition.* He wrote this for woodwinds in threes plus alto saxophone, brasses in threes plus tuba and a fourth horn, two harps, a celeste, glockenspiel, xylophone, bells, tam-tam, rattle, whip, and, of course, a large string orchestra. It is often said that Ravel's orchestration made a new work out of Moussorgsky's piano piece. Ravel himself took the view that there is no badly orchestrated, only badly written, music. For this reason he refrained, when making his orchestral version, from correcting certain technical weaknesses in Moussorgsky's writing. On the contrary, he strengthened them in his treatment. At any rate, the orchestral form more than approaches the expression of Moussorgsky's complicated and extremely thick chordal structure. On the whole, the score is an ideal example of artistic empathy, giving the impression that Ravel had completely identified himself with Moussorgsky's own creative thinking. This is especially true in the *Samuel Goldenberg and Schmuyle* and the *Great Gate of Kiev* sections.

Ravel's intense susceptibility to Russian music made him an early champion and friend of Stravinsky. During the period 1910–1932 an intimate understanding and perhaps even a mutual interchange of ideas existed between the two musicians. This extended beyond purely coloristic aspects into their harmonic and rhythmic speech. Without the models certain passages of Ravel provided, Stravinsky's ballet scores before *Le Sacre du Printemps* are hardly conceivable.

Stravinsky paid tribute to Ravel's clear-sightedness in his Harvard lectures on "Musical Poetics" in 1939. There he took issue with the charge, formerly widespread, that his music was revolutionary:

When *Le Sacre* came out, all sorts of opinions of it were bruited about. In the tumult of contradictory interpretations, my friend Ravel, almost alone, raised his voice to clarify the discussion. He recognized, and so spoke out, that the novelty of the *Sacre* lay not in its style, or its instrumentation, or in the technical arrangement of the score, but in its musical essence.

On the other hand, Ravel, in his *Duo Sonata for Violin and Violoncello,* adopted some of the style characteristics and technique of the younger Russian. There had also been a similar interchange for a short time between Stravinsky and Debussy.

In 1923 Ravel heard the last of Stravinsky's works that was to make a strong impression on him, *Les Noces.* On June 26 he wrote a memorandum to Roland-Manuel:

Dear Friend: Last Thursday I heard *Les Noces*, in spite of being stupefied by Dr. Dujardin, who injected cocaine into my foot. You are right. It is a brilliant work. I even think it is Stravinsky's greatest to date. The production is the masterpiece of the Russian season. I owe you thanks. Without your insistence I might have missed this great joy. Apart from that, I brought away from it a worsening of the condition of my rear paw. I must rest at least until the end of the week. I hope to have the pleasure of seeing you in my room at the Hôtel d'Athènes, where I shall be spending my convalescence.

During those years Ravel maintained contact with many of the French musicians of the younger generation, especially with Darius Milhaud, Francis Poulenc, and Arthur Honegger, the last of whom had practically become a Frenchman after his many years' residence. As a very young man, Milhaud had attended the rehearsals of *L'Heure Espagnole* and had ever since shown a marked critical interest in Ravel's music. On the other hand, Ravel had been strongly enthusiastic about Milhaud's *First Violin Sonata,* which consequently was accepted for performance by the Société Musicale Indépendante. About Poulenc, Ravel had made a very penetrating judgment, which was repeated by Claude Rostand: "The good thing about him is that he creates his own folklore." Above all Poulenc admired Ravel's orchestral skill, especially when he orchestrated his own works, such as *Ma Mère l'Oye, Le Tombeau de Couperin,* and *Alborada del Gracioso.* Honegger, among those invited to the villa La Belvédère, was especially close to him.

That famous little bar in rue Duphot, Le Bœuf sur le Toit, had been made a meeting place for artists and intellectuals by Cocteau and his friends. There were heard the pianists Jean Wiener and Clement Doucet, who, with their interpretations of Mozart, were at home in many European concert halls. But at Le Bœuf they played, sometimes together, sometimes separately, a repertory that extended from Bach to jazz and that Wiener enriched with his own modern and very witty jazz compositions. Ravel was one of the regular visitors to this pub, the only place in the Paris of the twenties that afforded this unique and characteristic blend of French avant-gardism and American night life.

At this time Ravel shared with Stravinsky an inclination toward radical experiments in music. These were not so much toward harmonic boldness or the liquidation of tonality, which had already gone beyond their early high points in France, but were much more toward leading music back to its simplest stylistic formulae. This was a classicistic trait, undoubtedly prepared for by Satie and eagerly followed by the young musicians among his following after World War I.

At the beginning of 1924 Ravel set to music one of the loveliest poems of the French Renaissance, the song of Pierre de Ronsard "to his soul." The poet addresses it: "Much loved occupant of my body, thou weak, pale, slender, lonely one, now thou goest down into the realm of the departed." And he closes with the plea that his sleep not be disturbed. For this unusual subject Ravel found an equally unique form. The piano accompaniment sets fifths after each other, like an organum from the early years of polyphony. The melody, later taken up by the alto voice, is mirrored as on the surface of a pond. The song runs along almost without any dynamics, with only the slightest swellings between piano and triple piano. At its end Ravel builds a tower of fifths until a chord of eight notes stands there, the lowest note of which, A, rubs softly against its top note, A sharp. It is a jewel of the "stripped-down" style, well worthy of his having invited some friends in to hear its baptism.

The singer Marcelle Gerar was to sing it. Ravel dedicated the precious work to her. He wrote her on February 8, 1924:

I am sure you understood that I sent you my telegram after mailing my letter, even before I got your letter. I had to wire in all directions to make the invitation retroactive. Such are the little discomforts of country life. There are worse.

I haven't told you anything about the baptismal ceremony. I hope you haven't inferred from this that it might be distasteful to me. Quite the contrary, and, if it is all right with you, I will invite my friends the Delages as well. That way, with Roland-Manuel present, the Montfort School will nearly all be there. Only Vaughan Williams will be absent. It is too late to get him to come from London.

You haven't told me if we should dress. I would not mind. I keep an evening jacket here and another in Paris. But if I don't hear from you to the contrary, I shall write the Delages to come in street clothes.

The private concert took place at Marcelle Gerar's. The otherworldly harmonies of the song *Ronsard à son Âme* were heard for the first time by this narrow circle of friends. Today they are among the forgotten treasures of Ravel's music. For the rest of the year 1924, which brought a journey to London for the composer, now known throughout

Europe, he devoted himself to work on an opera, *L'Enfant et les Sortilèges,* which is discussed in the next chapter.

CHANSONS MADÉCASSES, 1925

In 1925 Ravel wrote a small but important work in which again he invoked the spirit of exotic music, but this time more personally than was the case in the *Shéhérazade* compositions of his youth. Yet, in even more sublimated form the earlier impressions of non-European music, which he had received as a child, sound forth again and again in this work, the *Chansons Madécasses*.

Ravel wrote about the works he created at Montfort-l'Amaury during the twenties with greater warmth than he displayed for most of the others:

The *Sonata for Violin and Violoncello* was written during the time I was getting settled at Montfort-l'Amaury. I believe that this sonata marks a turning point in my career. Bareness is here driven to the extreme. Restraint from harmonic charm. More and more an emphatic reversion to the spirit of melody.

The *Chansons Madécasses* seem to me to introduce a new, a dramatic, indeed even an erotic element through the subject of Parny's verses. It is a sort of quartet in which the singing voice plays the role of the principal instrument. Simplicity reigns, the independence of the voices, that will be found even more stressed in the *Violin Sonata*.

In the writing of the *Sonata for Violin and Piano,* two fundamentally incompatible instruments, I assumed the task, far from bringing their differences into equilibrium, of emphasizing their irreconcilability through their independence.

Evariste Parny, whom Ravel mentions here, was a poet of the eighteenth century who lived in the tropics and, with his love lyrics, introduced a new romantic note into

French literature. Ravel set three of his poems to music on a commission from the American, Elizabeth Sprague Coolidge. She was one of the most generous supporters of contemporary music, having commissioned, among others, Bartók, Casella, Hindemith, Prokofiev, Schönberg, and Stravinsky. The instrumentation for the Ravel songs was prescribed. The voice was to be treated as an instrument to which are added flute, cello, and piano.

In the sharp differentiation of these four tone colors that strive to go their own ways Ravel here reached the peak of melodic inventiveness and coloristic mastery. The cycle of songs is one of the most beautiful the twentieth century has produced in the realm of erotic lyricism. In the composition Ravel has evolved such a richness of form from a minimum of intervallic and rhythmic germs that the three pieces, the tender love call, the war cry, and the evensong, seem to have sprung from nothing. As in the *Duo Sonata* there are long passages governed by bitonality.

Ravel's work almost always avoids love and death, the two most frequently encountered emotional motives for the creation of great art. He, the great unbeliever, preserved his skepticism against these basic emotions, even when he had shed the dandyism of his youth and experienced the stresses of his war years. There are, in fact, no composers of high rank who have so completely excluded such religio-metaphysical subjects. Even the skeptic Debussy was able to set to music the *Martyrdom of Saint Sebastian*. One can search in vain in Ravel's vocal music for any religious subject. There are mysterious links between religious feeling and the tragic experience of death and the exaltation of love; Debussy's *Pelléas and Mélisande* is an opera in which the sublimated experiences of love and death have metaphysical undertones. It is true that in Ravel there are erotic strains in his most successful work for the lyric stage, his *L'Heure Es-*

pagnole, but the sexual element remains playfully frivolous. It is limited to a kind of sportive feeling. It stands entirely outside the deeper meaning of human existence and never for a moment touches the spheres of tragedy and death. It is only in the pseudo-antique shepherd ballet *Daphnis and Chloë* that Ravel approached music of unbridled passions.

In the *Chansons Madécasses* he stepped, as it were, over the limits of his own nature. Emotion appears simultaneously with the stripping from the music of all ornamental accessories. As so often with Ravel, these three songs embody music of symbol and inner conception that seems to originate in a sympathy for a landscape and a race that are foreign and strange. The pattern is the representation of something wholly imagined. By way of an almost supernatural empathy, Ravel understood and participated in the spirit of these passionate songs, which, incidentally, Evariste Parny professed only to have translated into French. This skill of adhering to a pattern of imagined reality is typical of Ravel. Creatively he was always in the grip of an intuition quite unique, which made the inner essence, the core of a subject, clear to him and inspired his creativity. For this reason, as Debussy once claimed, Ravel wrote Spanish music that was more typical of Spain than the music of native Spaniards, and this long before he had even become acquainted with the country.

This facility has caused his critics to commit numerous errors. The choreographic symphony *La Valse* had its concert premiere in December, 1920. At that time many of the listeners professed to hear in it a reflection of an actual visit to Vienna. In fact, Ravel had been invited to the Austrian capital in 1920, where he was surprised and delighted to encounter a friendly attitude toward his music. He met Arnold Schönberg, Alban Berg, and Alma Maria Mahler and he described with pleasure an exceptionally flattering experience. He bought a leather portfolio and asked that it be sent him to his hotel. After he had spelled his name for the saleswoman, she asked if he were the composer of *Jeux d'Eau*. When he admitted it, she refused to take his money and presented the portfolio to him out of gratitude for the joy she experienced in playing this music. But *La Valse* had been completed before the start of this trip. The score could not have turned out more Viennese if Ravel had known the waltz capital before.

But, as with everything in Ravel's life, this intuitive faculty of recognizing unfamiliar things, had its exact opposite. We know his imitative skill from the pieces *À la manière de. . . .* In other cases we know actually from his own word that he made it a practice to copy and study formal structure.

The life in Montfort-l'Amaury, even though it suited his wish for isolation, was not healthy for Ravel's constitution, especially the cold and damp autumn and winter. Basically, he was a sick man after the war. He was always consulting doctors about his sleeplessness. Although physical exertion was difficult for him, travel refreshed him, even a journey as taxing as that to America in 1927. As a soldier, he had to combat many physical ailments, until at last he was released from military service as unfit. He was a violent smoker, lighting one strong black Caporal from the butt of another. In addition, he loved heavy wine and highly seasoned food.

But, in spite of all his bodily indispositions and the conflict between his gentle nature and his rather raw rural surroundings, the years in Montfort-l'Amaury were rich in creative accomplishment. One gets the impression that his lonesome life in the little house with its steeple and decoration released something within him, as though it made him free and caused the stream of inspiration to flow with less restraint.

L'ENFANT ET LES SORTILÈGES, 1925;
TZIGANE, 1924

Ravel had an openly expressed liking for the stage. His music, in many of its most soaring flights, is of the theater. Even what he wrote about Wagner, about Mussorgsky's *Boris Godunov*, about Vincent d'Indy's *Fervaal*, evidences the attraction that stagecraft and dramatic possibilities had for him. Plans for operas and ballets constantly occupied his thoughts, and often he carried these quite far toward completion. We know about his sketches for Gerhart Hauptmann's *Sunken Bell*, about the plan for an opera based on Maurice Maeterlinck's *Interior*, and about his youthful dream of an opera to be called *Shéhérazade*, of which only the overture was realized. The successes of his first two stage works, the comedy of love *L'Heure Espagnole*, and the ballet *Daphnis and Chloë*, were not entirely spontaneous. Nevertheless, both works have stood the test of survival.

In 1917 Jacques Rouché, the director of the Paris Opéra, offered Ravel, then just discharged from military service, a libretto to set to music. It bore the working title *Ballet for my Daughter*. The author was Colette, then already at the height of her fame as a novelist, whom Ravel had met long before at the salon of Mme de Saint-Marceaux.

After Ravel's death, Colette wrote of her friendship for the composer and her collaboration with him:

There came a day when Monsieur Rouché invited me to write a libretto for a magic ballet. I cannot explain how it was that, although I usually write slowly and with difficulty, I delivered the text of *L'Enfant et les Sortilèges* to him in less than a week. He liked my little script and suggested some composers to me, to whose names I listened as politely as I could.

But, after a short silence, Rouché asked: "But suppose I suggested Ravel?"

I immediately and loudly stopped being so polite and no longer restrained the expression of my approval.

Then Rouché added: "Let us not conceal from ourselves that it might take quite a long time for him to say yes, even if we hope and assume that he would."

He did say yes. He took my libretto home with him, and then we heard nothing more either from Ravel or about *L'Enfant et les Sortilèges*. Where was he working? Was he working? I did not clearly understand what the creation of a work demanded of him, how a slow-burning frenzy took possession of him, isolated him, and robbed him of all awareness of hours and days. The war spread an impenetrable silence over his name, and I gradually reconciled myself to thinking no longer about *L'Enfant et les Sortilèges*.

Five years went by. The composer and his completed composition emerged out of the shadows. But Ravel did not treat me as a specially privileged person. He gave no indication of willingness to play the score for me, or even extracts from it. He seemed to be concerned only about the "Miau" Duet between the two cats and asked me with a serious air whether I saw any advantage in substituting "Mouain" for "Mouao" or vice versa.

In the end Ravel used entirely different miau words for his feline musical duet. The passage, a duet for mezzo-soprano and baritone, is a masterpiece of vocal witticism and onomatopoeia. How easily a lesser intelligence could have overstepped the bounds of good taste here! The enchantment that this highly original, actually entirely unprecedented, text exercised on Ravel all the time he was at work on it is reflected in his letters.

Ravel was tied to a deadline. Raoul Gunsbourg had agreed to give the premiere performance in his opera house in Monte Carlo and had set a final delivery date of the score.

Gunsbourg, born in Bucharest in 1859, was an interesting personality who had some traits in common with Sergei Diaghilev. From the turn of the century on, he had made several appearances as a writer and an amateur composer, writing operas on Russian themes, such as *Old Eagle* after the tale of Maxim Gorky, *Ivan the Terrible* after Alexei Tolstoy, a music drama *Satan,* which he described as a *drama philosophico,* and a farce after the *Lysistrata* of Aristophanes, as well as an adaptation of the biblical *Song of Songs* of King Solomon. His career as a theater director was begun at the St. Petersburg Opera and then continued in France. In 1892 Prince Albert of Monaco engaged him as director of the opera house in Monte Carlo. During his incumbency there, which extended through both world wars and did not end until 1950, he brought distinction to the stage of the little principality's theater, where he had Enrico Caruso, Feodor Chaliapin, Beniamino Gigli, and the other star singers of the epoch make regular appearances. The Monte Carlo Opera also became a leader in first performances of opera. Among these were César Franck's *Gisèle* 1896; Camille Saint-Saëns' *Hélène* 1904, *L'Ancêtre* 1906, and *Déjanire* 1911; Jules Massenet's *Le Jongleur de Notre Dame* 1902, *Chérubin* 1905, *Thérèse* 1907, *Don Quichotte* 1910, *Roma* 1912, and *Cléopatre* 1914; Arthur Honegger's *L'Aiglon* (partly composed by Jacques Ibert) 1937.

Ravel's score was to be completed by December 31. A few laconic cards and letters to friends describe his situation. One, to Georgette Marnold, on August 29, says:

The news is very simple. While I am not putting on any weight, still I am not getting thinner. I am working a lot but producing little. And I am not a bit sorry that I denied myself any vacation when I hear from all quarters that it is raining just as much as it is in Montfort.

Three months later he wrote to Marcelle Gerar:

Please abandon all hope, my dear friend, because soon I must go to Paris, but on the four o'clock train, to work with Pierné on *Tzigane*. You would never believe how important nine hours are to me at this moment. I cannot even get to the Châtelet next Sunday. I never move, or only rapidly, as you see. I mix with no one but my frogs, my Negroes, my shepherdesses, and other insects.

Ravel added a few words about the style and technique of his work to his commentary on the *Duo Sonata* for violin and violoncello, in whose esthetic of restraint and rediscovery of melody he recognized a turning point of his career:

On another level, *L'Enfant et les Sortilèges,* a lyric fantasy in two scenes, obeys the same precepts. The striving for melody, which governs it, finds itself supported by the treatment. It pleased me to elaborate it in the spirit of American operetta. Madame Colette's libretto justified this freedom by its magical content. Here it is song that dominates. Without disdaining instrumental virtuosity, the orchestra nevertheless remains in the background.

The reference to American operetta is striking. It was before the coming of the "musical," Jerome Kern's *Showboat,* or George Gershwin's *Porgy and Bess.* At that time only a kind of revue, to be seen also in the music halls and variety houses of Paris, was meant by the term. Ravel became acquainted with America itself only three years later. But what he did know and eagerly admired were the jazz bands that had bobbed up in Paris even before the First World War and had drawn all the young Paris intellectuals to them after 1918. Debussy's work, even before Ravel's, testifies to fascination with this Negro music.

In the magic opera the jazz style became an integral

component. But Ravel spoke even of this work, which sprang, more than almost any other, from a deeper source of his being, with the same striking detachment that he always exhibited toward his completed works. The librettist Colette reacted far otherwise. She undoubtedly sensed in this music the undertones of tension, grief, and sorrow that were hidden behind the perfection, the dryness of melody, the irony in the chord sequences, and the fluency of the rhythmic combinations. Her report of the renewed encounters with Ravel and of the impression made on her by this composition is not only the work of a writer, it is marked by a strong and deep feeling:

> The years had taken the conceit out of this little undersized man, as they had his pleated shirts and his beard. White and black streaks intermingled and gave his hair a feathery look. In speaking, he put one delicate mousy hand over the other and swept everything with his little squirrel eyes.
>
> The score of *L'Enfant et les Sortilèges* is famous now. How can I describe how moved I was at the first jingle of the tambourines that accompanies the entrance of the shepherd boys? The moonbeams in the garden, the flight of the dragonflies and the bats. . . . "They are amusing, aren't they?" asked Ravel. Meanwhile, my throat choked up with tears. The creatures bent over the child, whispering forgivingly in phrases hardly formed into audible words.

In *L'Enfant et les Sortilèges* the misbehaving little boy, driven by an ungovernable impulse for destruction, rebels against his environment. In her libretto Colette indicates that the immense size of the pieces of furniture emphasizes the smallness of the little evildoer, that his four-footed victims menace him in his dream, but that, finally, his sympathy for the little wounded squirrel brings him redemption.

All his life Ravel moved in a world of children and

animals. He suffered endlessly from the discrepancy between his own size and that of the rest of mankind, but it provided him with the creative stimulus to overcome this gap. The worship of his mother was the center of his life until his forty-second year. The love he cherished for all things Basque, for the Spanish atmosphere, even more for its folk songs and folk dances, was an artist's sublimation of his devotion to his mother. He was so fervently attached to that tender and lovely woman that no sentiment for any other woman could ever fill his heart. He projected the kind of tenderness that only his mother elicited even into his friendships with other women. The only affectionate dedication he ever inscribed to any woman was one in the Basque tongue on a photo he presented to Marie Gaudin, the friend of his youth in Saint-Jean-de-Luz. It was certainly no mere coincidence that she, too, was a Basque and bore the same name, Marie, as did his mother.

And so we have this mother image in Colette's play of dream and magic. It is only hinted at briefly, as would be figures in a dream. It reprimands the lazy boy with kindly severity and admonishes him to remember the vexation he is causing his mother. Immediately the turmoil inside him boils up. At the height of his destructive fury the objects around him come to life. A threatening spirit world populated by the animals, the furniture, the ornaments, and the creatures of fantasy rises up against him, warns him back to his proper place, punishes him with fear, until the low cry for help, "Mama," crosses his lips. They all pick up the word, sing it in chorus, and at last forgive him and restore him to life.

The overture is marked by the thin chamber-music style of the entire work: two oboes run parallel as in medieval organum. A principal melody in harmonics on the double basses, in Dorian mode, moving quietly in quarters and eighths, is added to their fifths and fourths. It is a modest triumph of the "stripped-down" style that Ravel had developed in Montfort-l'Amaury.

The curtain rises. The child is being perverse. The presence of the mother is suggested. With her entrance the musical background changes: chords of falling fourths beginning on upbeats, mixture of keys, hammering on the piano. With gentle warnings she leaves the stubborn small boy. Now the acoustic picture sharpens. Presto, bitonality, triple forte. He smashes dishes, wounds the squirrel, pulls the cat's tail. Smoke and ashes rise out of the fireplace. He slashes the wallpaper with the poker. The boy is in a veritable ecstasy of destruction, pulls off the pendulum of the clock, tears up his school books and notebooks. When, exhausted by his own frenzy, he tries to sit down in the armchair, its arms spread out and it hobbles away like a huge toad and vanishes. To the child's utter stupefaction sorcery has begun to work.

Now their enchantment brings the objects release. Little and big articles of furniture get together in an Olympian fury. They take a menacing stand toward the creature who has disturbed their peace. The nightmare begins with a sarabande between an armchair and a sofa, which Ravel colors with the sounds of a cembalo. To accomplish this he provides the orchestra with a lutelike piano, on which, according to need, the strings can sound hammered or plucked.

With terror, the youth realizes, from the sport in which the furniture is engaged, that from now on no couch, no cushion, no chair will be there for him to rest on. After the furniture duet there follows the lament of the grandfather clock, which has lost its pendulum. To this is added a strange duet between the black Wedgwood teapot and the china teacup, a dance, half spoken, half sung, in a mixture of slangy English and pidgin Chinese. Musically, it is a fox-trot growing from the seeds of early jazz. The middle section of this piece, tense with dissonances and abrasive seconds in the celeste, is, however, purely pentatonic in a pseudo-Chinese manner.

After this fox-trot, a coloratura aria by a character representing Fire flashes like neoclassic lightning, a raging element that a gray, speechless figure representing Ashes endeavors to still. Now it begins to turn dark. The boy shivers out of chill and fear.

The round dance that follows fails to quiet his apprehension. Shepherds and shepherdesses step out of the decorative patterns on the wallpaper. They dance a melancholy ballet with bagpipes and tambourines, accompanied by an organ point in double fifths fashioned out of the tonic, dominant, and subdominant. Never has Ravel better reproduced the naïve and somewhat sentimental mood of old French folk song than in this little chorus of pastoral pensiveness. The child lies down on the shreds of his books and begins to weep.

Now comes the moment for the lyric high point of this magic tale. The boy weeps, and out of the torn pages of his book rises his first love, the fairy-tale princess. Her song in E flat major unites with the accompanying tones of the flute in crystal-clear two-part writing. Later it is enlivened by arpeggios in the clarinets. The boy, in despair, answers her that she must return into the void to which his destructive fury has condemned her. His beloved leaves him. He searches in vain among the torn pages of his storybook to find the ending of his lovely fairy tale. His sorrowful little song leads back to the opening key of E flat major. He kicks his hated school books away from him and so invokes the most spirited of all the scenes that Colette and Ravel devised. Arithmetic itself steps out in the person of a little old man, threatens the unwilling scholar with problems to be done, singing in a high tenor falsetto, and is answered, as if in an antiphonal chant, by the Numbers themselves, who sing in a tiny unison chorus. It is a spookily comic rondo, which winds up in a mighty increase of tempo and dynamics. This whole first scene closes with Ravel's famous duet of the cats.

Now the scene changes. We are in the garden. We hear the bizarre voices of the frogs. Their croaks originally stood in the score Ravel had begun for Gerhart Hauptmann's *Sunken Bell*. We hear too the singing tree, the slow American–type waltz that the dragonflies dance, but into which the bats, the frogs, and other animals intrude. These are sounds of nature, such as only a sound wizard of the highest skill could conjure up with such economy of means. With the rhythm of the waltz the orchestra grows in warmth. After having remained almost silent in the first scene, the strings raise their voices. The dance the animals perform in the garden grows ever more tender and oblivious of the world. Suddenly they catch sight of the boy and fling themselves upon him to take their revenge. However, it is at this point that he is discovered binding up with his handkerchief the wounds of the squirrel. And so the spell is broken.

What was the last word one heard the boy utter? It was a cry for help, a call from loneliness: "Mama!" The animals hear it, whisper it in chorus, sing even louder, until the falling fourths of the call to his mother take possession of the orchestra, and the lights in the little house go up. The animals, now forgiving, carry the rueful little sinner back to his mother. Now they sing the song of man's good will, a free fugal chorus that begins *a cappella*, then draws in the whole orchestra, which once more picks up the archaic organum fifths of the opening measures. The circle is closed. The falling fourth of the word "Mama" ends it.

In this work Ravel truly found his way back to all mothers, and therefore *L'Enfant et les Sortilèges* is without doubt his *opus summum*. It embraces all the characteristics of his personality, psychological as well as musical. The fairy-tale theater released him in the same way the lad in Colette's fairy-tale poem was released. Roland-Manuel recognized this child as Ravel; he has drawn attention to the animosity that ruled Ravel's spirit in the years after World War I. Later, Roland-Manuel also wrote down Ravel's esthetic creed, as the latter had formulated it in many conversations with him. The text was subsequently approved by Ravel:

I have never felt the need to formulate the principles of my esthetic creed, either for myself or for others. If I were obliged to do so, I would crave permission to adopt the simple explanations that Mozart has given. He was content to say that music can do, dare, and describe anything, provided only that it gives joy, and, once and for all, remains music.

At times people have been pleased to ascribe to me contradictory intentions regarding falsehood in art and the dangers of frankness. The fact is that I refuse, absolutely and unequivocally, to confuse the conscience of the artist, which is one thing, with honesty in art, which is another. The latter is of no value unless the former helps it to become manifest. Good conscience requires that we develop into good craftsmen. Therefore, my aim is technical perfection. I can strive for it unceasingly because I know I can never attain it. The important thing is to come ever closer to it. No doubt art can produce other effects. But, in my view, the artist should have no other goal.

The magic opera had its first performance on March 29, 1925, in Monte Carlo at Gunsbourg's theater. On the podium was a young conductor whom Gunsbourg had brought to Monte Carlo and who later made the leap from there to Milan's La Scala: Vittorio de Sabata. Its success was immediate and without reserve. Only in Paris, where the Opéra Comique produced the work almost a year later, were there protests against the cat scene and against the jazz sounds, which the audience was accustomed to hear from

Milhaud and from Honegger but did not expect of Ravel. Roland-Manuel reports an occurrence indicative of the indifference Ravel displayed toward the reception given his works. At one of the last performances of *L'Enfant et les Sortilèges* in Paris Ravel is said to have offered the key of his box to an indignant participant in the whistling that greeted the music, so that he could make his whistling more audible.

Tzigane and the song *Ronsard à son Âme* were composed during the work on the magic opera. *Tzigane* is a showpiece for violin and orchestra that makes the highest demands on the technique of the performer. In fact, all the difficulties of virtuoso violin music of the nineteenth century were exceeded by it. The violinist, Jelly d'Aranyi, for whom it was composed, received the score only a few days before its first performance.

TOUR IN AMERICA, 1927–1928

With world renown came journeys, invitations to foreign countries, and engagements to conduct some of his works, or at least to be present at their premieres. He had gone to Vienna at the beginning of 1920. In 1923, Amsterdam, Venice, and London called him, then London again in 1924. Then came some quieter years in Montfort-l'Amaury, interrupted only by a couple of excursions to Stockholm and Edinburgh. In 1927 the Salle Pleyel in Paris was opened with a celebration. They engaged Ravel and Stravinsky for the festival concert. Ravel conducted *La Valse;* Stravinsky his *Firebird* suite.

Meanwhile a correspondence began that had for its aim the persuasion of Ravel to make a tour of North America. In 1920 the pianist Elie Robert Schmitz, who, in spite of his Rhenish name, was a born Parisian, had founded a Franco-

American music society, the purpose of which was to organize the exchange of artists between France and the United States. The Society was modestly named *Pro Musica*. Apparently Ravel at first, after much hesitation, thought of accepting the invitation. He imposed the most burdensome conditions and delayed signing the contract until the very last moment. Among other difficulties, he was afraid he would not be able to obtain in America the Caporal cigarettes that he smoked exclusively. It required diplomatic representations to assure him he could enjoy these for the length of his stay in America.

Ravel had another physical checkup. His sleeplessness, the history of which went as far back as the last year of the First World War, still plagued him. Unexplained bouts of fever, coughing, and attacks of nerves are constantly mentioned in his correspondence. In addition, he had specific ailments in 1927, so that he looked up Professor Pasteur Vallery-Radot, the specialist who was treating his prostate. In early autumn he went to swim for a few weeks in Saint-Jean-de-Luz and apparently found his fatigue increasing to an extent he had not foreseen. On October 15 he wrote the conductor Ernest Ansermet that his departure for the United States was set for the end of November. He was to be en route for five months, rushed from one city to another, crossing the huge continent several times, a sacrifice to his fame, from Los Angeles to Montreal, from New Orleans to Vancouver.

The trip is amply documented in letters. The concerts in which he appeared interested him far less than the experiences he had. Among the addressees we find over and over again the names of his brother Edouard, his friend Hélène Jourdan-Morhange, Roland-Manuel, Garban, and the ladies Dreyfus and Casella.

At the pier in New York an acquaintance awaited him, the painter Bolette Natanson. The first words he called out to her, from the deck of the ship, were: "Wait till you see the crazy neckties I brought with me."

The first news he sent his brother about his debut was from the Pullman car from New York to Chicago. The card, dated January 16, 1928 says, laconically:

I arrive tomorrow morning at 9:45, just 20 hours. The New York concert went well. Articles of praise, some a whole page. It is only the New York French newspaper that doesn't mention me.

And in a postscript: "It is spring in New York as it is in Boston. Snow in between." On January 20 there is a more detailed report, again to his brother:

Have just telephoned the hotel desk that I am not here. Now I'll have a few moments of peace. Day before yesterday, chamber music recital. It went well today. As I took my bow, the brasses blew me a salute. In Chicago I found the spring, but yesterday within an hour icy cold and devilish wind that cuts the face, and water and ice smell like *eau de javelle* (chlorine). The city is extraordinary, much more than New York.

Tomorrow evening a second symphony concert. Right after, departure for Cleveland, where I arrive the next morning.

Cleveland the 26th. Had no time to finish. Second concert went well. 3500 persons stood up. Another salute. Departure.

We know that Ravel was an enthusiastic moviegoer. He was delighted with impressionistic films, especially *The Cabinet of Dr. Caligari*. It is no wonder that he looked forward to the next stop but one on his journey and that he was attracted more to Los Angeles than to the far more beautiful city of San Francisco, where he was scheduled to appear after Cleveland.

He wrote on February 7, 1928:

My little Edouard: This time it is summer, 35 degrees (centigrade), glorious sunshine. A great city, all full of flowers. They are flowers that grow only in greenhouses for us. Tall palm trees. . . .

Stroll in Hollywood, the cinema city. Various stars. Douglas Fairbanks, who fortunately speaks French. Very pleasant trip from San Francisco to Los Angeles, on the rear platform almost the whole way. Forests of eucalyptus. Tall trees that one could mistake for oaks, but they are holly. Different kinds of mountains, some rocky, some bright green. It is annoying to think we must go through bad weather again.

A package of letters waiting here for me, news from all the world but none from you. Concert tomorrow evening. In the afternoon I'll take a look at the studio of the film lions.

I was to have breakfast with Charlie Chaplin, but I think it would be less amusing for him than for me. He doesn't speak a word of French.

On the trip in a Pullman of the Southern Pacific Lines on February 10 he informed Hélène Jourdan-Morhange:

One more night on the train (that makes two; there were three from Chicago to San Francisco) and I arrive in Portland, in Vancouver, in Minneapolis, and then a third time in New York, where I am afraid I'll find it freezing.

I see magnificent cities, bewitching landscapes, but the triumphs are exhausting. In Los Angeles I walked out on the guests impolitely. I was starving of hunger.

Meals in foreign countries were a trial and a problem to the Frenchman's palate. An undated letter to Edouard from somewhere between Chicago and San Francisco complained of this:

Ate recently in Chicago at Mrs. Rockefeller-McCormick's, a millionairess. Hurried back to the hotel to order up a beefsteak. Have dined here with Mrs. Kim, who has the loveliest

219

Lautrecs, Gauguins, Degas, etc., good wines, and a famous cognac. Am going to dress now. Shall write you a short note from the train to San Francisco. Hope I'll find news from you.

The next dated message, again to his brother, is of February 21, from the Denver–Minneapolis train:

Last evening Denver. A good night. Nine hours sleep. Arrive soon in Omaha to change trains. Departure this evening about ten, after hearing the famous Omaha jazz. Denver, where I spent three days, is 1,600 meters high (gold and silver mines). The air is very pure. Always sun. Looks as though it might cloud over. I am afraid I'll find it freezing cold next week in New York.

Over and over again this fear of a return to a cold climate. One remembers his letters as a soldier, his frostbitten feet, his attacks of fever and coughing. The climatic contrasts between Southern California and Canada, between seaport cities and those in the high Rockies, the blizzards of New York and the burning suns of Texas and Colorado, must have exhausted this delicate physique.

No cheerful note was sounded in a card to Roland-Manuel on February 24, this time from a Union Pacific train:

Dear Friend: Tomorrow I am turning homeward, to New York, though my actual homecoming will not be before the month of May. After perspiring in a bathing suit in Los Angeles, but since then meeting spring everywhere, even in Canada, here I am again in icy frost with snowstorms again. Ran rapidly through Chicago this morning so as not to freeze my hands again. Thanks to the trains I slept almost unbrokenly through two days and two nights.

Ravel was apparently having a communicative day. Letters to Hélène Jourdan-Morhange and Lucien Garban from the same train carried the same date. To the former:

Found your letter in Minneapolis day before yesterday
with great joy. There was one from my brother too, the first.
. . . Tomorrow morning in New York. I'll distribute your
tokens of friendship, souvenirs and kisses, right from the station.
I'll arrive in France only in early May, unless I have to leave my
hide here. I can rest only in the trains. The previous night and
day I slept both before and after breakfast.

And to Lucien Garban he repeated his complaints
about snow, frost, and icy winds, and his assurance that he
will return in May "if there are any pieces of me left over."

The letterheads of the great railway lines continued
to appear on the paper on which Ravel wrote news to his distant friends in Europe. In April it was the Crescent Limited
that brought him from New York to New Orleans. He wrote
his godmother Dreyfus on April 4:

Your letter reached me in New York where I spent
three days more. Monday, New Orleans, where I arrive tomorrow, solely to cast a sentimental glance at this old French colony
and taste the *pompano en papillotes* that is marinated in French
wines. Oh, if you only knew what this Prohibition is like!

Shall leave there in the evening for Houston for two
concerts and auto ride along the Gulf of Mexico. So three nights
on the train. From there to Grand Canyon: two days rest, no
concerts (from Houston to Grand Canyon two nights).

Then I leave Arizona and go direct to Buffalo and
New York (four nights this time). New York to Montreal and
back, then embarkation on the *Paris* that leaves at midnight (I
arrive April 21 at 10:30).

And then he added a white lie, obviously to reassure
the kindly old lady. He wrote:

And I shan't be all used up, as someone has told you. I
have never felt better than during this mad tour. At last I have
discovered why: because I have never led such a rational life.

221

The last bulletin, dated April 14, 1928, was to Roland-Manuel. It was another letter from the train to Buffalo:

I am ending this little excursion that will have taken me ten days! Two plus four nights in the train Houston–Grand Canyon–Buffalo (about like Paris–Constantinople–Stockholm). The seventeenth century would have loved these mountains. They look more like gigantic and harmonious structures where the plesiosaurians and the pterodactyls have left traces of their footprints behind them!

Ravel traveled with heavy luggage, whose transport to hotels gave him a problem. In Chicago, where he had to conduct the symphony orchestra, he noticed, just before the beginning of the program, that he was missing his patent-leather shoes. The audience had to wait a half hour until his outfit was complete. Germaine Schmitz, the pianist's wife, helped him to unpack his twenty pair of pajamas and fifty shirts, the pastel colors of which delighted American musicians at rehearsals.

New York made a tremendous impression on Ravel, probably because among the skyscrapers he was more than ever conscious of his own diminutive bodily size. It is characteristic of him that he made his promenades through the streets—hours long—principally at night.

At first he refused to make an appearance as a pianist. He said he was not a professional pianist and did not wish to perform a circus act. Finally, however, he agreed to play the *Sonatine* and to accompany songs. In New York he performed the *Violin Sonata* with Joseph Szigeti, then at the height of his fame. With *La Valse* he had remarkable success as a conductor in Boston. But the biggest ovation he received was at a Koussevitzky concert that he attended as a listener. The audience recognized him and applauded him for ten minutes but could not persuade him to go to the podium to take a bow.

Among the younger American musicians on whom Ravel's music exerted creative influence were Aaron Copland and David Diamond (who wrote an *Elegy in Memory of Maurice Ravel* in 1938). George Gershwin was another who sought him out. He was presented to Ravel in New York at the home of singer Eva Gauthier. There he learned that Ravel thought very highly of his *Rhapsody in Blue*.

Two other reports describe meetings in America with Ravel. Madeleine Goss, who later wrote his biography, noted:

Ravel was accurate in every detail. Small in frame and stature, he always dressed his slender body in the latest and most fashionable mode. No effort was too much for him to make to produce the effect he wanted, whether in working out an awkward detail in a composition, or accomplishing a harmony between his cravat, his socks, his handkerchief and the pattern of a suit of clothes he was wearing.

. . . No violent emotions or overpowering passions clouded the clear mirror that reflected his art. He was the bed of a stream through which music flowed. . . . His attitude toward his own music was impersonal as though it were the work of someone else. He could seldom be persuaded to listen to his own music. At a concert he would disappear into the lobby for a liberating cigarette (*cigarette libératrice*). He was indifferent to success. The idea he was making a career never occurred to him. He made music because he had to, just as an apple tree grows apples (*comme un pommier fait ses pommes*).

Everything he did, even when he was telling an anecdote, was influenced by his insistence on perfection. He had an uncommon gift of mimicry and could reproduce bird calls and animal voices with singular realism. If anyone paid him a compliment, he would cover up his pleasure and his embarrassment by turning aside with a comical bird or animal call.

An interview by the musicologist David Ewen appeared in the music journal *Etude*. It said, in part:

I am not a modern composer in the strictest sense of the word, because my music is an evolution, not a revolution. While I have always been receptive to new ideas in music, I have never tried to throw the laws of harmony and composition into the discard. On the contrary, I have always drawn inspiration generously from the masters. I have never stopped studying Mozart. To the greatest extent possible my music is built up on the traditions of the past and grows out of them. . . .

I have never been the slave of any style of composition. I have never followed any particular direction in music. I have always believed a composer should bring to his writing what he feels and how he feels it—without giving thought to what the current fashion might be.

Great music . . . must ever come from the heart. Music that is made only with technique and intellect is not worth the paper it is written on. This has always been my argument against the so-called modern music of the younger rebellious composers. It is the product of their heads, not their hearts. First they devise complicated theories, then they write music to satisfy these theories.

They construct logical reasons why the music of our time must be choppy and dry, mathematical and intellectual, as an expression of our machine age. . . . How can one compose music by logical syllogisms or mathematical formulae? If one does, it loses its most distinctive quality as the expression of human feelings. Music should always be first emotional, and only then intellectual.

I agree that the radical style of the young and very interesting composers exerts fascination, and also that it displays power and a considerable measure of originality. But it has no heart and no feeling. We react to it intellectually, not emotionally. This is why, from my point of view, these experiments are a failure artistically, even though there is much to be said for them. . . .

I do not understand the arguments of composers who tell me the music of our time must be ugly because it expresses an age that is ugly. Why does an ugly age need expression? And what is left of music if it is robbed of its beauty?

Theories are all very nice, but a composer should not write his music by theories. He should create musical beauty straight from the heart and feel intensely what he composes.

This is challenging doctrine, an extremely French theory. Ravel could not define in words what beauty is. That his music itself contains foundations for a new definition of the concept of beauty has been demonstrated by its lifetime of acceptance, as well as by its occasional failures and their psychological causes. What Ravel admired, outside the realm of music, contradicted so frequently prevailing standards of beauty that one might quote him equally for a cult of ugliness, extravagance, and buffoonery. Perhaps it was the impression made on him by the strange and wild continent of America that confirmed his longing for his homeland, his *douce France* and its clear laws of artistic form, and made him reveal what was in his heart.

On the pier in Le Havre the morning of April 27 stood seven of his friends to whom no one could deny the joy of greeting Ravel on his return. They had put together a huge bouquet of flowers skillfully wrapped in paper lace. As Ravel came off the gangplank of the *Paris,* one of the ladies facetiously knelt down and handed it to him. Beside the loyal friends of his youth, Maurice and Nelly Delage, stood Hélène Jourdan-Morhange, next to her the notary Coste. His brother Edouard, making eight in all, had brought along the faithful Bonnets from their villa in Saint Cloud, and, of the newest friends, the mezzo-soprano Marcelle Gerar. Ravel concealed his emotion, saying: "I would have liked it better if you had all stayed at home. . . ."

THE LEYRITZ PARTY, 1928

Marcelle Gerar had been one of Ravel's close friends for quite a while. Soon after the tour of America

Ravel met at her house the sculptor and interior decorator Léon Leyritz. Leyritz spontaneously expressed a wish to do a portrait bust of him. Ravel replied: "I am ready, but on one condition, that I do not have to sit for you." So Leyritz was invited to attend the rehearsals of the *Violin Sonata* on which Ravel was working with the performer. The sketches that resulted were sufficient for the plaster cast. It was soon finished. Then Leyritz asked if his subject would look at it to be sure the proportions were right. Ravel told him to come "tomorrow between 10 P.M. and 3 A.M." When he saw the bust he decided: "It is my best portrait."

Marcelle Gerar decided she should prepare a festive reception for a work of art that had begun under her roof. She had first met Ravel when she was organizing little concerts of French music during the twenties in a pub in Montparnesse, the Caméléon. Ravel attended one of these evenings, and the introductions were made by Roland-Manuel. Then Ravel invited her to Montfort-l'Amaury and had her sing *Shéhérazade* for him. To her great disappointment he remained silent. But soon after that the mail brought her the song *Ronsard à son Âme,* with its dedication to her. In April, 1924, she sang the premiere in London, with Ravel playing the accompaniment. *Tzigane,* played by Jelly d'Aranyi, was on the same program.

Marcelle Gerar has given a description of the little party that took place one lighthearted Sunday, June 10, 1928, in Ravel's house, La Belvédère, and became known as *L'Impromptu de Montfort-l'Amaury.* It was organized as a surprise garden party, but not without giving the master of the house due warning. Ravel declared himself ready to provide "cocktails, wine, and peas from the garden," and only worried that he might not have enough dishes. Then came the horde of guests to admire Leyritz' portrait. You see them in the photographs, at table on the big terrace in front of Ravel's bedroom, the table covered with a checked and flowered tablecloth, wine bottles, glasses, carafes, and country bread-baskets. There stand the Godebskis, Delage, Roland-Manuel, Jacques Ibert, Gil Marchex, P.O. Ferroud, Arthur Honegger, the Spanish pianist-composer Joaquin Nin, the conductor Vladimir Golschmann, the singers Jane Bathori and Marcelle Gerar, the violinist Hélène Jourdan-Morhange, the composer Alexandre Tansman, the poet and writer Léon-Paul Fargue, René Kerdyk, and naturally the sculptor whose work this party was to celebrate.

He brought out the stone bust and Kerdyk recited a long poem telling about fawns in the garden, Mother Goose, Daphnis and Chloë, the deceased princess, and the play of waters. In it he also included the American cities, as well as "Spanish Time." The animals in *Histoires Naturelles* performed a grotesque serenade. It ended with the words: *Un dieu vivant sourit à son masque de pierre . . . et le déjeuner est servi.* ("A living god smiles at his image in stone . . . and lunch is served.")

Meanwhile the sky clouded over and everyone wondered how all these guests could be served in the tiny rooms of La Belvédère. But the weather took pity on them and lunch was finally reached, prepared by Ravel's housekeeper Madame Revelot and majestically served by Honegger and Roland-Manuel. Ravel put on Mme. Gil Marchex's cloak and Hélène Jourdan-Morhange's hat and did a dance. Finally some of the guests who had to be in Paris early left, but the most faithful traveled with Ravel to nearby Rambouillet where they had an apéritif and then went on to dine together in Versailles. Ravel took the steadiest ones from there to a cabaret, where, about four in the morning, Léon-Paul Fargue got them all involved in a subtle discussion of art.

The Leyritz bust stands now in the foyer of the Paris Opéra. The white stone portrait, a little larger than life, seems to have been hewn with a knife. It shows the fashionable and slightly stylized expressionism that can easily lead from nature into geometry. The flat surfaces of the face are interrupted by curves and incisions. Lights and shadows alternate effectively. One gets the impression of a softened Archipenko and is reminded of the Storm exhibitions of the twenties in Berlin, where William Wauer's stylized bodies were shown.

Several years later Leyritz had a strong influence on Ravel's external mode of life. He decorated a city residence for him that showed the expressionistic traits then in fashion. In the tragic last years of Ravel's life he was Ravel's most intimate friend and his traveling companion.

The guests at the "Impromptu of Montfort-l'Amaury" could admire the bizarre furnishings of the house and "the most unlikely knickknacks," which Hélène Jourdan-Morhange has described in her book on Ravel. The doll under a glass bell came from Suzanne Roland-Manuel; after the waltz ballet it was baptized Adelaide. A pretty little porcelain sofa was from Germaine Tailleferre. Ravel's special delights were a little sailboat that could be made to bob on paper waves, a cheap piece of trash that he found at the Japanese exhibit, and a cathedral-shaped inkwell. At one point he brought in on a painted pedestal a curious globe that seemed to be made of smoked glass. When they admired this work of art, he laughed at them and explained: "Well, it's only a burned-out electric bulb."

After the "Impromptu" strange rumors were circulated in Montfort-l'Amaury. Jacques de Zogheb, a neighbor, heard them. Ravel questioned him as to what he had been told. Zogheb reported that in the town it was believed that fifty guests had undressed themselves and celebrated an unusual bacchanal. "That's just what my housekeeper heard at the market," said Ravel. "Isn't that a shame!" Zogheb felt the shame to be that he had always been invited only to very boring gatherings at Ravel's and not to such an interesting one. Otherwise, Zogheb was one of the warmest admirers of Ravel as a man. He never heard of his telling a lie, nor of his ever being interested in receiving honors. Zogheb also reported a remark the composer made: "People talk about my being hardhearted. That's not true, and you know it. But I am a Basque. The Basques feel deeply, but they don't say much, and then only to a few." Being asked whether Wagner or a French master would leave the deepest traces on the history of music, he replied: "Wagner." About Claude Debussy's *Prelude to the Afternoon of a Faun:* "On hearing this work I really understood what music is." And finally the admission confirmed by many observers during his lifetime: "Basically, the only love affair I have ever had was with music."

X 1928–1937

BOLERO, 1928

One of the dancers of Russian background whom Diaghilev brought to Paris in 1909 was Ida Rubinstein, a pupil of Michel Fokine. This extraordinary woman was the inspiration for a number of works that Claude Debussy, Gabriele D'Annunzio, Arthur Honegger, Paul Valéry, Paul Claudel, Igor Stravinsky, and André Gide created for her. In 1927 she came to Ravel with a request to orchestrate a few dances from Isaac Albéniz' *Iberia* for her. To his surprise, Ravel learned through the composer Joaquin Nin that Fernandez Arbos had already begun work on an orchestration of the music. For this reason the plan had to be abandoned, but Rubinstein had already arranged that another work be substituted for *Iberia*. It was out of this situation that *Bolero* was born. It had its premiere at the Opéra on November 22, 1928. The single female dancer, accompanied by twenty male dancers, was Ida Rubinstein, to whom the work is dedicated. The choreographer was Bronislava Nijinska and the conductor, Walter Straram. In addition to the Ravel premiere there was a ballet, *La bien aimée,* for which Darius Milhaud had orchestrated some pieces by Liszt, and another to music by Bach in an orchestral version by Honegger.

The *Bolero* became Ravel's most performed and his one widely popular work. The criticism of it most worthy of note is by its composer, who said to Honegger: "I have written only one masterpiece. That is the *Bolero.* Unfortunately, it contains no music." No music! Perhaps not, if by music is meant the increasingly complicated forms, spun out from one shape to another, that have developed out of European polyphony, the growing independence of basic key, the avoidance of repetition, and the incessant use of surprise through the introduction of new themes.

Ravel's *Bolero* departs from a thousand years of tradition in the development of music thinking in the West in that it avoids not only polyphony, but also the very use of variation in the current thematic-motivic sense. The whole piece is nothing but the insistent repetition of the same theme, which is composed of two sections rooted in C major. This basic key is left solely in the coda and only for a brief time span. In addition, the work is built on a two-measure rhythm, which is a deviation from the traditional bolero rhythm.

As a dance form the bolero is a product of the seventeenth century, a piece in moderately rapid three-four meter that preferably involved dotted quarters plus eighths, and later also, in the manner of a polonaise, eighths plus sixteenths. One line of its ancestry leads back to the minuet, another to the *seguidilla.* The nineteenth century discovered its use as art music. In France Auber and Berlioz, in Germany Weber, and in Poland Chopin have made use of the rhythm and form of this dance, which, as a folk dance, is prevalent in Andalusia and Castile.

Ravel adds to the basic rhythm (which consists of an eighth plus a sixteenth triplet, an eighth plus a sixteenth triplet, and finally an eighth plus an eighth, and variants thereof) an instrumental peculiarity of the rhythm as it is danced in Spain. The triplet in sixteenths is meant for the castanets and in the bolero is introduced by the dancers who play them. In the first four measures Ravel has this rhythm appear, so to speak, thematically on the drums, supported solely by a pizzicato in the violas and violoncelli on the strong beats of the measure. Then for sixteen measures the first flute takes over the quietly rocking theme, which first returns faithfully to the tonic, C, then presses to the region of the dominant, G, and then by rapid steps returns to the tonic. The second half of the theme widens the range of the melody and at the same time gives it a peculiar quality reminiscent of church modes, and that is the fluctuation between the centers of tension of the basic key. The gentle color of the solo flute, after two transitional measures, is darkened by the solo clarinet, which then repeats for sixteen unaltered measures what has already been heard.

At the same time the second flute, on the note G, shares the rhythm of the drum. After two further transitional measures an elaboration of the melody, with somewhat altered rhythmic character, takes place in the bassoon. It starts from the note B flat, expanding the C major triad into a seventh chord. Then in the fourth measure, through the tone D flat, it is expanded to a chord of the minor ninth. No modulation of any kind has, however, taken place. The impression given is similar to that of exploring the harmonics over a firmly held root. In the last half of the melody in the bassoon there also appears an A flat as a chromatic neighboring tone shortly before returning to the tonic. But in this way the stress is removed to the region of the subdominant, and in remarkable obduracy the bassoon melody presses down from here to E flat and D flat, which is, however, now with lightning speed converted to a leading tone reaching downward toward C.

The effect of this passage in sixteenths, F–E flat–D flat–C is once again archaic, reminiscent of the church modes, modal and exotic all at the same time. During this entire bassoon solo, indeed beginning two measures before, almost unnoticed, the harp, with two major seconds, has entered into the prism of colors. This very motif of the major second is continued by the harp on various steps of the scale and widened, as an interval, to a major third and a fourth. Now the color again changes. What the bassoon has sung in the tenor range now appears in the constricted treble range of the E flat clarinet, while the harp motif expands to the three-note cluster C–D–E, or B flat–C–D.

Not until after No. 4 in the score does the principal theme return in its original form, this time as a solo for the oboe d'amore, while the drum rhythm is carried along no longer by the second flute but by both bassoons. The palette of strings draws in the violins and double basses. When the melody is repeated, the flute and the first trumpet, muted, take it over from the oboe d'amore, while the horns replace the bassoons in producing the rhythm. Now the strings still play pizzicato, not only the ground note and the tonic triad, but an accumulation, tending to the pandiatonic, of notes from the C major scale, that is, sounding the entire C major scale at once. By reason of the wide disposition of the chord layout the sound remains light, flexible, and only attractively dissonant.

The section after No. 6 in the score adds the tenor saxophone as a new color, which takes over the development of the melody from the solo bassoon of the beginning. It is answered in the second half of the melody by the sopranino saxophone. Ravel's idea of providing all the instruments of the orchestra in turn with melodic and rhythmic assignments shows itself in ever new aspects. Thus, flutes, clarinets, oboes, and horns are inserted and given purely rhythmic accents. Later, bassoons, finally trombones and tuba, too, step in. This is also an original property of this score, that the rhythm gains autonomy in a manner that had been forgotten for centuries in European music.

In the section after No. 8 in the score the first shock occurs. The celeste performs the theme in octaves doubled with the first horn. At the same time it is heard in two piccolos, one at the fifth, the other a major sixth higher. We thus hear it in three keys: C major, G major, and E major. The effect is derived from organ mixtures. It is the simplest and, therefore, the most convincing application of discoveries that Stravinsky and French composers like Darius Milhaud had made in polytonality. The passage sounds, at one and the same time, like the babel of a marketplace and like festive waves of music. Everything takes place in a high treble range, while the lower positions are reserved for the rhythmic persistence. Only when this passage is reached does the listener become conscious of a development that until then, with great discretion, has been kept below the surface. From the opening pianissimo Ravel prescribed a single slowly rising crescendo during the gentle laying on of hues that takes place on the level both of pure dynamics and of the accumulation of colors.

With the section after No. 9 a mezzo-forte is reached. In the period after No. 10 in the score the heavy voice of the solo trombone is added to the alternating monologue of the woodwinds and horn that rules the following section. In the section after No. 12 the violins take over the melodic leadership for the first time and share it in octaves with the high woodwinds. Now the dynamic peak approaches, and in sections 13 to 16 it increases steadily. Now no longer gently plucked, the strings are ruled by the full bow, and they achieve a maximum of tonal volume by quadruple stops. The harp, the percussion, and the heavy brass add their massed volume to the orgy of sound now beginning, which, as a final shock, reaches a completely unforeseen E major in the eighteenth section. The key is held for eight measures, then is abandoned with equal abruptness for a return to C major. On this last summit the trombones, with their primitive quality, howl in glissando for the last five measures until the C major chord rumbles over everything in the final explosion.

The ideal of perfection has ripened to truly maniacal individuality in the *Bolero*. The work is a triumph of orchestration, of color and dynamics for their own sake, of instrumental clothing. A single phrase, a single concept, stretched out over twice sixteen measures, is converted into a form that evokes both arcane historical and remote geographical origins. It is only the coloration that makes this music interesting, the growing and swelling laying on of effects, the tension that is amassed in the orchestral timbre and in the dynamics, the nuances of parallel running keys, which Béla Bartók, equally gifted, later used in the *Giuoco delle Coppie* of his *Concerto for Orchestra*.

As always after a composition left his writing desk, Ravel was indifferent to this score. When he was told that at the premiere a lady had called out: "He is mad!" he answered, smiling, that she understood the piece.

PIANO CONCERTI, 1931

The autumn of 1928 brought Ravel one of the few honors of which he was proud. On the recommendation of Professor Hugh Percy Allen he was made, on October 23, an Honorary Doctor of Music of Oxford. It is a distinction conferred only on composers. Ravel was accompanied to the celebration by his brother, there to be delighted with the rose silk academic gown for which he had to be fitted. Smiling a little bashfully at himself, he let himself be photographed as a D. Mus. (Oxon.) in full regalia. The citation lauds him as *patriae suae dulcissimae decus atque delicias* and *vir tenero vegetoque ingenio pollens* and emphasizes that *Daphnis and Chloë* is a work *qui doctis omnibus persuadet Pana non esse mortuum*. ("The glory and delight of his beloved country, a man mighty with talent both lively and tender, who persuades the learned that Pan is not dead.")

By 1928 the fame of the *Bolero* had made Ravel a popular figure. Even in his Basque homeland they began to be proud of him. The seafront at Ciboure, where the house of his birth stands, was renamed Quai Ravel. From Saint-Jean-de-Luz, where he went again to spend some vacation weeks, he went to a Ravel festival established in nearby Biarritz, the bath resort of kings and queens.

Toward the end of the year Ravel's creative power strikingly manifested itself again. He set his hand simultaneously to scores of two concerti for piano and orchestra that had begun their lives, so to speak, in one breath. A short trip preceded this double labor. Ravel, for the first time, visited Spain, the land he had recreated in so many of his works, journeying as far as Saragossa. One is aware of the crisis mounting in him. After the *Bolero* his productivity had suddenly come to a full halt, but it is as though the contact with Iberia suddenly lifted a restraint. On one side of him was the pad on which he was writing the *G Major Concerto* for two hands, on the other that on which he was carrying out a commission for Paul Wittgenstein, the one-armed Viennese pianist and brother of the philosopher Ludwig Wittgenstein. The results are surprising because of their complete stylistic difference. Not only the technique of the piano writing, but also the content and expression, are radically different.

Certainly the pieces have traits in common. The influence of jazz is immeasurably stronger in the work for one hand, but it is also noticeable in *G major Concerto*. Both reflect the fast-moving, varied, and turbulent life in North America, which made such a deep impression on Ravel's sensitive spirit, and both are sublimations of influences to which he was subjected, either unconsciously or with complete awareness.

We know from Ravel's own admissions that in some

cases he borrowed from and used as models the work of another writer. In the *G major Concerto* the slow movement is modeled after the Larghetto of Mozart's *Clarinet Quintet,* K. 581. On other occasions Ravel had relied on Saint-Saëns, or simply on folk examples. All this can well be understood in the light of his esthetic of substitution, which was the case in both his private life and his verbal and written expressions. Sometimes he wrote music that seemed to be the sublimation of the essence of a region or a race. In such cases the model was an imagined representation of the original. In the case of Basque folklore it was the nourishing element of his youth, the image of his mother. Jazz was a later influence of a similarly domesticated exoticism. Mozart's spirit animated him as a concept of a life-giving form. These three dissimilar ingredients were brought together by Ravel in the two concerti.

The G major work was finished a little sooner than that for the left hand, where his instrumental creativity is positive and dramatic. The work on the compositions took longer than was customary with Ravel. Only in the autumn of 1931 were the last notes of both scores written. Ravel said of them that basically the music of a concerto should be gay and brilliant and could dispense with drama and depth. At first he meant to call the *G major Concerto* a *Divertissement.* The piano solo in it is treated in a virtuoso style equal to that of the orchestral treatment, which is markedly brilliant, especially in the wind parts and especially in the trumpet part. With this leaning toward virtuosity the *Concerto* is close to the somewhat earlier *Violin Sonata.* It is in three movements, and among the most virtuoso passages is the cadenza with its trills and arpeggios.

The *D major Concerto* is much more serious in character. Ravel wrote it in one movement. He himself admits that the special technical requirements led him to make use of a more traditional style. He points out that the broad passages in jazz idiom are also developed from the themes of the beginning. In doing so he makes use of an apparent improvisation that leads into the jazz section. The desire to make a one-handed piano part sound as full as if it were written for two hands is consistent with Ravel's esthetic of substitution, which here is developed to the acme of its perfection.

The premiere of the *D major Concerto* by Paul Wittgenstein took place on November 27, 1931, in Vienna. Marguerite Long played the *G major Concerto* for the first time on January 14, 1932, in Paris. The program, which Ravel conducted, was composed entirely of his compositions. After the premiere he and Marguerite Long set out on a tour that led them through the principal music centers of Europe.

LAST YEARS, 1930–1937

Apart from a few concert tours in France and Belgium, Ravel in 1930–1931 led a quiet life of slow and careful labor. In the spring of 1930 he heard a performance in Paris of his *Bolero* by the New York Philharmonic conducted by Arturo Toscanini. He upset the famous conductor by the matter-of-fact criticism that he was not in agreement with Toscanini's tempi. Ravel considered them twice too fast.

On May 8 he begged Ida Godebska to excuse him from staying on for a reception:

I have begun to cut down my sleep. If I was seen at the Opéra it was because I knew that Toscanini takes a ridiculous tempo in my *Bolero* and I wanted to tell him so, though this amazed everybody, most of all the great virtuoso himself. . . .

Wittgenstein needs his concerto by the end of next month, and it is still far from finished.

In July there was another Ravel Festival in the Basque province. In his presence a tablet was affixed to the house of his birth.

At the beginning of 1932, about the time of the premiere of his *G major Piano Concerto,* a film company approached Ravel. They were planning a film of *Don Quixote* with Feodor Chaliapin in the title role. The producers, who later turned out to be a lot of frauds, had assured themselves of big names: the fashionable author Paul Morand was working on the script, and Ravel agreed to do the music. When the whole venture collapsed, there still remained three songs for baritone that Morand and Ravel had given to Don Quixote as homage to Dulcinea. These were a romantic song in the meter of the Spanish *quajira,* alternating between three-fourths and six-eighths, an epic song in the Basque five-fourths meter of the *zortziko,* and a drinking song in the rhythm of the Aragonese *jota.* They, the last compositions Ravel ever finished—are light and unpretentious, filled with the spirit of the Spanish and Basque land and culture, which had been the breath of life to him.

In October, 1932, Ravel was riding in a taxi in Paris when it collided with another vehicle. Ravel received a head wound, lost a couple of teeth, and for a while showed symptoms of a slight concussion. Slight? That is what the doctors believed. He tried every possible kind of therapy, took electric treatments, was pierced with gold needles in the Chinese fashion, and was even hypnotized. But after the day of the mishap there were no more completed compositions. Ravel continued to work on sketches for all kinds of works. One was the draft of a ballet opera on a tragical tale from the *Thousand and One Nights,* as suggested by Ida Rubinstein, the title to be *Morgiane.* But Ravel's concentration span had diminished so badly that no coherent music came into being. He could still play music and record it, as he did the *Chan-*

sons Madécasses, of whose success he informed Madeleine Grey with delight.

The year 1933 brought cares into his intimate circle of friends. In Germany racial persecution had been adopted as official policy. Ravel was not a political being and paid little attention to the events of the day, but, from an innate sense of justice, he stood on the side of people who were oppressed by the power of might. He could feel no sympathy for any regime that persecuted his closest Jewish friends.

The summer of 1933 saw him again in Saint-Jean-de-Luz. He enjoyed the familiar homelike surroundings. He strolled through the old streets and saw the house in which he had spent innumerable vacation weeks. There still stood the lovely corner house in the Place Louis XIV where, in 1901, the *Jeux d'Eau* was born. Not far from it, in the rue Gambetta, the Gaudin family had its house, where he had frequently been a guest until their two sons, to whom he had dedicated the rigaudon from the *Tombeau de Couperin,* had fallen in 1914. Marie Gaudin, the friend of his youth, still lived there. To her he had inscribed a copy of the *Tombeau* and had given a proof of the *Violin Sonata,* with his corrections on it, and an amateur snapshot that bore the inscription in Basque: "For Marie, my deepest friendship."

That summer he went to the beach with her. He wanted to show her how to skim pebbles on the surface of the water. But his arm could not make the movement he planned. Instead of throwing the stone toward the sea, he hit his friend's mouth with it. He tried to swim, but he could no longer control his limbs. An arm moved instead of a leg. He realized with horror that he could no longer control his body.

Then for a while it seemed that the condition improved. The illness was capricious, led him and his friends astray, permitted him hours of apparent recovery, after which the relapse was so much more torturing.

Ravel returned to Paris and Montfort-l'Amaury for the season. The winter brought fresh difficulties. In January, 1934, his doctor, Professor Dr. Vallery-Radot, wrote a most concerned letter to Hélène Jourdan-Morhange, recommending that every means should be sought, even through his brother Edouard, to persuade Ravel to take a week's complete rest. This was the same doctor who had given Ravel the checkup before the tour of America. Now, in the light of the later developments, his findings then had included some menacing discoveries: rickets and inadequacy of the kidneys, combined with a clinical record of sleeplessness. Vallery-Radot now pronounced his first diagnosis: "He feels nervous, overworked. First sign of ataxia, which means confusion in movements, making one gesture instead of another."

On January 30, 1934, Ravel complained of extreme weariness. The doctor recommended a complete mental rest and a stay at a health resort at an elevation of a thousand meters. In March the composer went into the Clinic Monrepos on Mont Pélerin near Vevey on Lake Geneva. Here he received the news of the death of the mother of Maurice Delage, his oldest friend. To write him he needed all his will power and persistence. The message of condolence was one of his last letters:

How I sympathize with you, my poor old chap, I who think more and more about my relatives. At least you have not suffered as much as your poor old Mama. Come soon. The house is a little clinic. It is absolutely what you both need. I hope it will be soon. I embrace you both.

The Delages obeyed the invitation. But they were deeply disturbed to see how Ravel looked in Vevey, especially when he told them it took him eight days with the help of the Larousse lexicon to finish the letter he wrote.

It was not only his limbs that refused to obey him. He had to learn to write again, and, beyond the handwriting, it was the shape of the letters themselves that escaped him. The attending physician, Dr. Michaud, diagnosed:

Sleeplessness, clouding of memory, weariness, lack of concentration, condition of anxiety, errors in handwriting. Has forgotten how to write certain letters of the alphabet. Is obstinate. Anxiety plays a large part in his uneasiness. Constant feeling of fear. I tried to persuade him not to be concerned about his reactions.

At the same time Ravel was sociable, sometimes even cheerful. Some days he spoke as though he were well. When the Delages settled in at the Pension Stucki, he came to visit them every day and announced himself with the old Apache signal from Borodin's *B minor Symphony*. There were only certain concepts that eluded him. He had to describe them to make himself understood. So he spoke of certain friends whose names he could not recall, using descriptive phrases: "His name is . . . he is the composer . . . his wife drives the car. . . ." Then the others understood he meant Darius Milhaud, whose wife Madeleine had to be chauffeur to her almost crippled husband.

The cure at Lake Geneva was not successful. His friends drove Ravel back to Paris and to the little residence that Léon Leyritz had furnished for him in 1928. It was in the familiar Levallois district, not far from the west bank of the Seine, but beyond the Porte de Champerret, in an industrial area where Citroën and other automobile factories are situated. One reaches it by Métro to the Louise-Michel stop, then goes left to rue Danton. This is joined by a complex of little streets, one of which crosses the rue Camille Desmoulins. At the corner of rue Louis Rouquier there is a house prettier than the others, next to and opposite garages. It is two stories high, with a nearly flat roof, and built of white brick rather in the Dutch style.

Today it bears a tablet on its front: "The composer Ravel lived here 1905–1937." The inscription is wrong. The house was only built in 1909, but the Ravels lived directly opposite in No. 11, the corner house.

In the second story of the 1909 house is Ravel's apartment. Two rooms and a bath, quite modern but oddly decorated in its strict adherence to the fashion of 1928. Everything is wood paneled. Next to the big couch there is a corrugated aluminum partition and at its foot a bar that can be hidden in a wall cupboard. In front of it are two high bar stools. There is a large circle sunk in the bedroom ceiling above a metal disc that reflects the light of the electric bulbs it conceals. In addition: a round glass table, two modernistic chairs, wall cupboards and bookshelves holding books, among them Ibsen's *A Doll's House* and a *History of the Customs of Paris*. In a glass case full of knickknacks one can see a toy village, many animals, a seal that balances a ball on its nose. After Ravel's death a copy of the Leyritz bust and a small expressionistic sculpture were placed on a bookshelf. There was also a bronze of the death mask on the chest of drawers and a cast of his small, attractive, ladylike hand with its energetic bony fingers.

The master bedroom is in the corner overlooking the intersection of the two streets, and next to it is the tiny studio. It has a window with bull's-eye windowpanes that magnify everything fourfold. Through them one can get a distorted view of the ugly street and of the side of the house next door, so that instead of seeing one auto at a time passing by, one sees a stream of traffic. There are two narrow aluminum armchairs in the studio. On the walls, paneled in a silver-gray wood, are some Japanese drawings in India ink.

Under the window there is a dropleaf table that served as a writing table. Somewhere there is a little peacock and a glass bell with a spiral shell under it. The bathroom is the way Ravel left it: an empty bottle that contained Eau de Cologne d'Orsay, a pretty leather case with his shaving things in it.

Ravel's condition would not improve. He needed peace. He was taken to Le Belvédère at Montfort-l'Amaury. All his friends went to visit him, to pamper him, to bring him gifts. On good days he enjoyed having them as though he were well. He would show them his garden where the Japanese dwarf trees grew. He even liked to listen to music. With all this he was, however, made conscious of his own tragic incapacity. The faithful Hélène Jourdan-Morhange accompanied him on the long walks he liked to take, roaming through the Rambouillet woods together. The violinist was astonished at how accurately Ravel knew every path, every clearing, the habitat of hundreds of plants and trees.

In this way the year 1934 drew to its close. In spite of all the care, especially by his housekeeper Madame Revelot, who had loyally devoted herself to Ravel's life since 1923, his condition slowly got worse. As the doctors could think of nothing else, they advised diversion and a change of scene. Long journeys were discussed, but Ravel's passivity and incapacity for work had depleted his financial resources.

Using the pretext of his having to make Oriental studies for the ballet opera *Morgiane* Ida Rubinstein provided a large sum so that, in the company of an escort, he could go to Morocco. Léon Leyritz, who had made the portrait bust, was ready to travel with him at once. He had long studied all Ravel's habits, his little needs, and eccentricities. In fact, it was precisely as a result of this study that he had been able to choose the furnishings of the house in Levallois.

In February the two went off. Ravel wished to avoid a long sea voyage, so they took the land route through Spain.

They stayed a few days in Madrid. From a previous visit Ravel remembered there was a church in which Francisco Goya had done paintings. After several false starts and wrong directions they found the Church of San Antonio de la Florida with its Goya frescoes in the dome. Tangiers delighted Ravel. It gave him his first knowledge of Oriental life, with its colorful markets, camel drivers, and exotic goods.

But the magic of the Arabian fairy tales began for them in Marrakech. They could look down at the Arab quarter from the terrace of the Hotel Mamounia. Leyritz was always looking for new delights. He procured for his friend things he was accustomed to, such as calming peppermint tea or a chaise longue for his afternoon nap. Before Ravel came out to breakfast, Leyritz would scatter crumbs about so that the composer, who loved animals so much, would be greeted by a swarm of chirping sparrows. Ravel could read now only with difficulty. But he continued to be a tireless walker. The two men made expeditions through the Arab city, wandering through the shops of the goldsmiths and the dyers, encountering a wedding procession, the bride on a white mule, or a snake charmer displaying his art.

Ravel was known to the upper-class Arabs as a composer. They made a fuss over him, spoiled him, finally had him invited to Telouet where he was a guest of the Caid. He was fascinated with the pastel-colored horses of the Arab prince. He tasted strange dishes, which had to be eaten with the fingers, like roast chicken in rose sauce. A dance company of one hundred performed for him. This was the Mohammedan Orient, the Arab world of *Shéhérazade* that he had described with such intuition and intensity as a young man. He carried on the conversations he loved: with animals, with doves, and, most of all, with the cats, twelve of which came to see him off when he made an excursion to Fez.

A huge party was given for him in Marrakech.

Someone said to him: "This would be material for a composition by you," to which he retorted: "If I were to write Arab music, it would be much more Arab than this."

It seemed his condition was improving. During the journey he spoke hopefully to Leyritz about *Morgiane,* about ideas for the music and for the settings. He even hummed some of the melodies for his friend. After the party in Telouet something happened that Leyritz thought a miracle. Ravel, who, since the letter of condolence to Maurice Delage, had scrawled hardly more than a couple of lines, sat down and wrote his brother a long account.

They returned through Seville. They visited the café of the bullfighters, saw a running of the bulls, and heard the real *cante jondo,* the deep-throated songs of the gypsies. Young Spanish composers came to pay their respects to the master. Leyritz had to resort to deception to hide from autograph seekers the fact that Ravel was again unable to write. Once he furtively drew Ravel's monogram for him, and Ravel copied it out. Several times during the trip calls came from Ida Rubinstein, for Ravel's health worried her.

Back in France Ravel was optimistic for a while. Paul Dukas died on May 17, 1935, after having destroyed all his compositions still in manuscript. At the funeral Charles Koechlin asked Ravel how he felt and received this confident reply: "I have just made note of a theme. I can still write music in my head." But on listening to his own works, he was certain he could never write like that again. When Jane Bathori was decorated with the Legion of Honor, a celebration party was given. Ravel attended, even though he had had no respect for such recognition for himself, but he had to refuse to sign autographs. His hand no longer obeyed him.

He spent the summer again in Saint-Jean-de-Luz, again with Léon Leyritz as companion. Again they visited Spain in the autumn, this time the north: Bilbao, Burgos, and Roncesvalles. They also went back to the Basque country, halfway between Ciboure and Pamplona, from where his mother had come. Again there were unexpected gleams of light in Ravel's condition, but the improvement did not continue.

The house in Montfort-l'Amaury, standing in solitude, again received its often silent, apathetic-seeming occupant. Ravel wandered among the rooms he had decorated with such curious taste. He glanced at his writing desk, at the volumes in the very small collection he had assembled to suit his own fancy but could no longer read. On sunny days the garden gave him joy. He often rode in to Paris, where a bed always awaited him in Levallois or at the Delages'. He liked to visit Marguerite Long. A new friendship attracted him to the Jacques Meyers, to whose house in the Norman seaside resort of Le Touquet or Paris-Plage he often went as a guest. His last pupil, the composer-conductor Manuel Rosenthal, came frequently to visit him at Le Belvédère, and, of course, the Roland-Manuels were among his worried and solicitous circle of visitors.

At the beginning of 1936 his ataxia worsened. At that time, unannounced, he went to call on Colette, who lived not far from him. After his death she wrote about this visit:

Ravel lived through the worst period of the dimming of his senses toward the end of his life. I am told that his ailment granted him brief interludes of improvement and gleams of light such as deceive and destroy a condemned genius. One Sunday his steps led him, without undue effort, through the little path that connects Montfort with the little village of Menuls. He arrived after lunch at Luc Albert Moreau's. Thin, gray-white as fog, he could still smile. When he saw me, he said in a natural tone of voice: "Well, it's Colette!" But he hardly made an effort to speak, and when he sat between us he had the look of a being that is in danger of falling apart any moment. He looked as much like the living Ravel as does the picture Luc Albert Moreau made of him dead: large nose, the dark and ill-shaven beard of a dead man, shadows under the eyes and the nostrils. . . . I think that day was the last time Ravel uttered my name.

The months dragged on slowly. Ravel endured his fate without complaint. Only occasionally could one sense his inner disturbance, his feeble revolt against a state of slowly deepening isolation. He was in flight from his destiny. Sometimes he fled to the woods, often to Paris where, like a hunted quarry, he sought shelter with his friends. All useful work was denied him. His correspondence was managed by Lucien Garban, his former schoolmate, now a member of the Durand firm, his publishers. Mlle. Jourdan-Morhange found him once sitting on his balcony, his eyes taking in the view of the Ile de France in the distance. She asked him what he was doing. "I'm waiting," he replied.

The season began again. Ravel even took part in it. He was seen at the theater and at concerts. When he was in Montfort-l'Amaury, Jacques Zogheb would call on him no matter what the weather. He almost always found Ravel sitting close to the telephone in the hope his brother would call to say he was coming out to see him. His love for his brother became deeper year by year. But Edouard did not always have time to be with him. Zogheb would ring and knock. Sometimes Ravel himself would come out to open the gate, but he generally failed, and Mme. Revelot had to let him in. "How are you?" A shrug of the shoulders. "Have you been working lately?" Then the tears would run down Ravel's cheeks.

In 1937 everything remained the same. Ravel was resigned. Even the optimism of his friends, who had still believed in a repetition of a miracle, was extinguished. In June the Festival of the International Society for Contemporary Music took place in Paris. Ravel attended some of the concerts, among them one devoted to his piano music. He heard with disinterest and apathy the enthusiasm of the audience. Norman Demuth, later his biographer, tells also of an orchestral concert at the Festival, where Ravel suddenly became the object of an ovation by the whole audience, though nothing of his was on the program. He did not understand it. He thought they meant an Italian sitting beside him. "His empty expression was frightening."

The summer of 1937 that followed was a long, painful ordeal. All his friends sacrificed themselves regularly, as much in their concern for his housekeeper Revelot as for him. All of them confirm that his mind remained clear. The doctors visited him regularly. They had no other measures to suggest. As the condition was becoming continually more threatening, they called in the famous brain surgeon Clovis Vincent for consultation. His examination resulted in the following diagnosis:

No circulatory difficulty. No calcification, no atrophy. Enlargement of the skull since childhood, increasing in adult years. This signifies slight hydrocephalus.

Professor Vincent advised an operation. Ravel agreed and was taken to the surgeon's clinic, rue Boileau. Clovis Vincent was in a hurry. He performed the operation on Sunday, December 19, 1937. Only the evening before Ravel had been joking with his friends about the gauze turban on his head, which he said gave him a certain resemblance to T.E. Lawrence.

When the surgeon opened the skull he found the brain looked normal, its convolutions not weakened. Several hours after the operation Ravel opened his eyes and called for his brother. Then he fell asleep. His friends thought he had been saved, but he never woke out of this deep sleep. His friends came in every day, hoping to find him conscious. He lived eight days more, perhaps dreaming of music. One of the last sentences he uttered to his friends was: "I still had so much music to write!" It was not granted to him to do so. His agony began on Monday, December 27. His heart ceased beating in the early morning of December 28, 1937.

The news of his death excited painful attention all over the world. It was left for a Berlin Nazi periodical alone to try to degrade the French musician and scoff at him as an Eastern Jew. But in France many who in his lifetime had shown reserve about him bowed their heads in homage. Romain Rolland wrote: "Compared with his, all other music seems imperfect." Georges Auric, Darius Milhaud, and Henri Sauguet wrote words of admiration for him.

The burial took place on Thursday, December 30, in the cemetery of Levallois, beside the grave of his parents. The attendance was very large. Igor Stravinsky was present at the service. An address in the name of the government of France was pronounced by Jean Zay. (This important school reformer, a Radical Socialist, had become Minister of Education in 1936 and remained so until 1939. Later he was one of the courageous men who did not conceal their anti-Fascist convictions. Zay was condemned to death by the Pétain government and executed in 1944.) His eulogy placed Ravel's work in the context of the great tradition of French genius, along with Descartes, Racine, Voltaire, Marivaux, and Stendhal. "Greatness without vainglory was born in him. In his determination apparently not to take himself seriously lies the height of intellectual heroism."

Ravel left no will.

The diagnosis of his ailment was made by Professor Alajouanini:

No hardening of the arteries. Limited and symmetric weakening of the dura mater. Disease known as "Pick's disease." In such cases the areas having to do with the power of speech are affected.

The doctor indicated further that musical expression as the personal speech of the patient was especially restricted, the musical apathy being deeper than the vocal. Ravel composed as long as he was well. When he fell ill, his musical activity ceased.

EPILOGUE

The Basque coast with its precipitous cliffs, its coves that calm the ocean breakers, the contour of the Pyrenees in the background, the view that extends far into the Spanish mountains behind Cape Figuier, had a charm for Ravel much more than merely as a landscape. He felt at home there. His walks, hours long, led him past the lighthouse at Socoa, the Elysian fields of Chantaco, and the rocks of the promontory of Sainte Barbe. He loved to sit on the beach in cheerful talk with friends, letting the rather coarse sand slip through his fingers and listening to the murmuring of the waves. He would swim out into the bay every day, a man who, though not actively interested in sports, loved the water as his own element, a born swimmer like all the coastal Basques.

He shared his mother's sentiments. She felt more at home in Spain than in Paris. He loved the little timber frame houses on the quay at Ciboure and in the maze of crooked little streets in Saint-Jean-de-Luz more than the gigantic houses of modern big cities. Their lines and angles are bounded by white walls, which serve as places from which pelota balls can be bounced, or by blue, red-brown, or green planked surfaces.

Fishermen in pale blue washed-out costumes, with the black Basque beret on their heads. The folk dances of an evening in the Place Louis XIV. Eight girls and eight young men, dressed in green, white, and red, step out. They kneel down as a big flag is waved over them. They carry wooden swords or sticks; with these they slap the wine-filled goatskin gourds. The girls each hold a long willow wand bent into an arch. They perform dainty steps with these, and sometimes the supple arches touch each other. For this there is a bright though monotonous accompaniment of flutes and little drums. The primitive scales sometimes sound like the Dorian

minor. The rhythms are march or dance rhythms, the latter
in three-quarter time, often concealed in a syncopation difficult to grasp, with foreshortened endings or asymmetric accents.

Ravel never missed any of these evening parties on
the waterfront. He took note of the gay and almost trivial
melodies and of their internal rhythms that struck him as
usable. He never felt the same stimulus from his father's
landscape around Lake Geneva, with its magnificent, romantic views of the Mont Blanc glacier or of the Haute-
Savoie, and from the restrained clarity of Swiss folk songs, as
he did here from the chirping in wheezy thirds of two flutes
and the rat-tat-tat of beating drumheads.

Once Ravel followed the path into the upland,
where one is no longer aware of the vast ocean, where old
farmsteads lie in the valley of the tiny Nivelle, where dappled
cattle and woolly sheep quietly graze in the lush meadows.
He made the ascent up the Rhune from nearby Arcain to
enjoy the view from above, from where he could look toward
the Pyrenees horizon, beyond which lay the wide Bay of Biscay with the piers of Biarritz, Saint-Jean-de-Luz, Hendaye,
and San Sebastian. He dreamt of Spain. He felt that beyond
the Cantabrian Mountains there was a colorful, gay world
filled with dance and song. The songs his mother had sung
him in childhood came from there: habaneras, fandangos,
malaguenas, pasodobles.

Ravel was not especially gifted in languages. In this
respect he was his father's son. He knew a little school German, very little English, a few scraps of Spanish. But he
learned to understand Basque quite well from some of his
friends on the Côte d'Argent. For months he planned to
write a concerto on Basque themes. He had even chosen a
name for it: *Zaspiak-Bat.* But then he gave it up. It became
clear to him that folk tunes themselves were not well suited to

symphonic elaboration. He could, it is true, harmonize them in an incomparable manner, and in doing so he could enter more nearly into their spirit than could the natives of the races from which they sprang. But his highly sophisticated idiom, always penetrating more keenly into the actual structure of thought, was not appropriate to these little folk pictures of such limited content.

In France the highly sophisticated has never strayed too far from simplicity. French taste, for instance, in cuisine is based on the peasant cooking of the various provinces. The chefs in great cities—Bordeaux, Marseilles, Lyons, and, above all, Paris—have explored the hinterlands for ingredients and dishes to add to their menus. The climate, the soil, the old traditions of husbandry contribute immeasurably to the cultivation of raw materials. Therefore in France, more than in other countries, good cookery is a part of its culture, not only of its civilization. Like so many French artists, Maurice Ravel was a gourmet but not a snob in eating habits, an expert who prized good quality even in the simplest productions. Stravinsky spoke of this characteristic when, in writing from Ramuz, he told how Ravel loved the local wine, the well-baked bread, and the fresh cheese. What was even more striking was Ravel's love of high seasoning. He preferred the strong wines drunk in the region of his birth. He sprinkled his dishes with herbs of every kind. Pepper, paprika, salt, and mustard were indispensable to him. It was part of his physical as well as his mental makeup to require strong stimulation.

He was an inveterate smoker of cigarettes of strong black tobacco, called Caporals in France. While eating, at work, in conversation, at performances if possible, he constantly lit his next cigarette from the one he was smoking. His hunger for a smoke was so overpowering that he would often step out of a long concert for a few moments so he could take a few precious puffs. He never restrained himself in this little vice, even during his last illness.

All this is of a piece with his musical style. His harmony, his polyphony, above all his orchestration, are analogous to his practice never to allow colors to melt into each other. It is just this quality that amounts to a signature and differentiates him from Debussy. The clash of two or three half tones, the planned omission of a note in favor of its neighboring step—these intensify the aroma of a sound just as a strong condiment does that of a culinary dish. His linear instrumentation, as seen at its greatest virtuosity in his Spanish pieces, the *Rapsodie,* the opera about the pretty clockmaker's wife, the orchestral version of the *Alborada,* and especially the *Bolero,* keeps tone colors apart from each other as do salt, pepper, and vinegar the tastes of different foods. Debussy strove mostly for the opposite, the merging and running together of colors, a refinement and sublimation of the Wagnerian palette. Thus Ravel's special kind of relish for good food reveals his principles in art as well: the greatest independence of each ingredient to achieve the maximum unity of the entire production. This inner structure for the total concept was invariably of first importance to him. Once this was firmly set, a process that sometimes required months, then the choice of themes, the orchestral colors, and the harmonic idiom were governed by the requirements of contrast between tension and release.

This is like the methods of construction followed by certain painters, especially those of the Renaissance, whose first sketch was a distribution of the diagonals and proportional spaces that underlay the actual subject itself on the canvas. Only when these often inexpressive and geometrical elements were firmly established did the artist begin the execution in detail, the drawing of the objects to be shown, the laying on of colors.

It was probably the poet Léon-Paul Fargue who was the first to call attention to Ravel's ideal of technical perfection, to his industrious craft in achieving a surface of the utmost polish, behind which the internal complexity of his creative process completely disappears. Fargue also stresses the intelligence and the cultivation of the composer. Others have doubted it, presumably because Ravel's dandyism, to which he drew such attention in public, distracted from a knowledge of his intellectual life, as indeed he meant it to. His friends constantly emphasized his great shyness in regard to showing his personal feelings. Was he not equally shy in disclosing all that pertained to his art? The hiding away of books during his adolescence, when he was so highly susceptible to literature, was only the first symptom. Others followed.

We owe to Fargue's picturesque account, given after Ravel's death, our knowledge of the nickname "Rara" by which he was known in the Apache circle. This two-syllable word has several connotations. It is easy to say it comes from the first syllable of Ravel's name. This is probably how it originated. But the witty and well-schooled intellectuals around Paul Sordes were good enough Latinists to know the significance of the word as an adjective, even if they may not have remembered that it is the feminine form of a pen name used by Robert Schumann, *Rara avis,* the unusual bird. This was not inappropriate for Ravel, who often gave rise to well-meant and affectionate comparisons with members of the animal kingdom. Two ladies among his close friends saw him, one as a squirrel, the other as a fox, and Jean Cocteau later spoke of his head as shaped like that of a bird.

Ravel was also a keen observer and a brilliant portraitist, his eyes alert for the peculiarities of his fellowmen, whose company he sought and needed whenever he did not choose to withdraw into a creative period. There have been few creative personalities more gregarious than he was. He easily felt he was being neglected and abandoned by the world if, late at night or early in the morning, his companions, yawning and dead tired, had to leave him. And yet there have been few for whom the need to seek solitude and quiet was such a real necessity. This striking and unmistakable contrast was typical of his entire way of life. He looked everywhere for opportunities to mingle effortlessly with people, and he also sought ways to leave them equally effortlessly. This explains his partiality for the city life of Paris, which really became his second home, and for the bustle of a big resort like Saint-Jean-de-Luz, to which he constantly returned. It explains, too, why, in such massed collections of people, he looked for residences outside the city centers.

As he was gregarious, he studied people. He buried what he found in his subconscious, until a creative task released it and all his vigilance, all his pragmatic psychology crystallized into sound.

It is certain that Ravel discerned analogies between the animal kingdom and his friends and fellowmen, just as his friends did for him. This elevated and sharpened his gift of perception, making itself evident when, in his artistry and with great virtuosity, he attributed human reactions to an animal, as in the *Histoires Naturelles* and *L'Enfant et les Sortilèges*. He was able, by his gift of magic, to empathize completely with another creature. Analytical psychologists who look for examples of the curious relationships between men and animals in dreams can find this given quite tangible form in Ravel's work.

Ravel, the strictest and most tireless of all workers himself, was incapable of tolerating any coercion or compulsion. It is true he submitted to the laws of polite society and cultivated a manner of being well-bred and elegant. A defect in his costume could make him forget every appointment, even the departure of a train. "Impossible," he would insist, "to go about in such colors at this time of day." And yet he was capable of snapping his fingers at all good manners and, at an evening party, in London of all places, appearing in red slippers while wearing an evening jacket. To be sure, he had injured his foot so that he was not able to wear his patent leather shoes. Therefore he chose precisely the most extreme and obvious opposite to what might have been in place, something so outrageous that everyone had to conclude there was a reason for it. It was part of Ravel's psychology that in this situation he would not tolerate any half measure, e.g., to wear only one proper shoe and one slipper. That would have been less striking. He thought nothing of shocking people while playing the paradoxical role of a man who has forgotten what is proper.

One tyranny to which he refused to submit, even at the risk of hurting people, was that of the clock. Appointments at a fixed hour made him uncomfortable. He dodged them whenever he could. This was why he, who was so sociable, rarely organized parties in his own house. With friends he lost all sense of the passing hours. His prodigality with time was almost Slavic. He loved to turn night into day. Friends who wanted him to be punctual had to resort to all kinds of ruses and little deceptions. The most charming story is one that was acted out in Saint-Jean-de-Luz, probably sometime in the twenties. The little Basque town had a church choir of high quality, its Schola Cantorum. Its conductor, the church organist Charles Lebout, had prepared Ravel's three a cappella choruses *Nicolette, Trois beaux oiseaux du Paradis,* and *Ronde.* He wanted the composer to hear them sung. A performance was arranged for a Wednesday at three. As the fixing of a definite hour was painful for Ravel, he pretended he had all kinds of possible other plans for Wednesday at three—an outing, a pelota game, everything but the chorus rehearsal. He was living then in the Gaudin house in the rue Gambetta. The ladies of the house tried to persuade him that he must not keep the whole Schola Cantorum waiting or, what would be even worse, let them down. Ravel kept silent and smoked a cigarette. Then he went off to his morning swim at the beach.

The children of the house had watched all this taking place. Ravel came home at noon, his clothes over his bathing costume, as was his habit. He put his things in order and went next door to the Grotte Basque restaurant for breakfast. When he returned it was five minutes to three. Standing in front of the house was a wheelbarrow surrounded by children. Anne, the little daughter of the house—Ravel's special pet—dropped a curtsey and announced: "Mr. Ravel, the cars are ready to start. Which one do you wish to use today?"

Ravel laughed delightedly. "The Rolls Royce," he commanded. He let his little friends escort him to the wheelbarrow, took his seat in it, and rode off to where the choir was waiting for him. He did not regret it. He found the performance of the difficult choral works so perfect that he asked that nothing be altered.

Ravel's world was the world of children. Whenever daily life could be dominated by the utmost fantasy, it found him ready to share the illusion. That which was small and tender exerted great charm for him for its own sake. He yearned to be back in the protective embrace of his mother. When she was lost to him, his creativity underwent a protracted crisis. He, who alternately sought and fled solitude, felt he had been isolated from life. He had been rendered homeless, had been delivered over to the hostile powers of his environment, as bereft of hope as was the child abandoned to the menaces in Colette's imaginative libretto.

CHRONOLOGY

1832   Pierre-Joseph Ravel, father of Maurice Ravel, born at Versoix, Switzerland.

1870   He goes to Spain to work on building a railroad.

1874   He meets and marries Marie Deluarte.

1875   Maurice Ravel born in Ciboure;
family moves to Paris.

1882   Maurice Ravel begins piano lessons with Henri Ghys.

1887   He begins harmony study with Charles René.

1889   Enters Conservatoire; begins piano study with Anthiôme.

1891   Accepted in piano class of Charles de Bériot; studies theory with Emile Pessard. Napoléon-Henri Reber, and Théodore Dubois; forms friendship with Ricardo Viñes.

1893   First piano composition *Sérénade Grotesque* (unpublished).

1894   *Ballade de la Reine morte d'aimer*, voice and piano (unpublished).

1895   Father introduces him to Erik Satie; *Menuet Antique*, for piano (first published work);
Un grand sommeil noir, voice and piano (not published until 1953);
Sites Auriculaires, for two pianos: *Habanera* (never published in original form but used later by him as the third movement of *Rapsodie Espagnole*, 1907) and *Entre Cloches* (never published);
studies counterpoint and fugue with André Gédalge.

1896   *Sainte*, voice and piano.

1897   Accepted in advanced composition class by Gabriel Fauré.

1898   Unpublished *Sites Auriculaires* premiered by Schola Cantorum at Société Nationale de Musique;
piano settings for two poems by Clément Marot: *D'Anne qui me jecta de la neige* and *D'Anne jouant de l'espinette;*
Shéhérazade, an orchestral overture (never published) and parts of an opera on the same theme (never finished);
the Overture premiered at the Société Nationale in 1899;
meets the singer Jane Bathori.

1899   *Si morne,* voice and piano; *Pavane pour une Infante Défunte,* for piano two hands, later orchestrated.

1901   Begins to attend Mme de Saint-Marceaux's salon; *Jeux d'Eau* for piano solo; fails to win first prize in Prix de Rome contest.

1902   Fails second time in Prix de Rome contest.

1903   Fails third time to win Prix de Rome contest; enters circle of Paul Sordes; *String Quartet in F,* premiered 1904 by Société Nationale.

1903   *Shérérazade,* settings for voice and orchestra of three poems by Tristan Klingsor: *Asie, La Flûte enchantée, L'Indifférent.*

1904   Meets the Godebskis.

1905   Application to reenter Prix de Rome contest is rejected; moves to Levallois with family;
Noël des Jouets, piano setting to his own words;
Sonatine, for piano;
Miroirs, for piano: *Noctuelles, Oiseaux tristes, Une barque sur l'Océan, Alborada del Gracioso, La Vallée des Cloches;* orchestration of *Alborada;*
Introduction and Allegro, septet for solo harp, string quartet, flute and clarinet;
river cruise with the Godebskis to Belgium, Holland, Germany.

1906   Begins work on opera to Hauptmann's *Die Versunkene Glocke* (never finished);
Histoires Naturelles, for voice and piano, to poems by Jules Renard: *Le Paon, Le Grillon, Le Cygne, Le Martin-Pêcheur, La Pintade.*

1907   *Vocalise en forme d'habanera,* voice and piano;
Mélodies Populaires Grecques;
Rapsodie Espagnole, for orchestra;
L'Heure Espagnole, opera in one act to text by Franc-Nohain (not premiered until 1911 at Opéra Comique).

1908   Death of father;
Gaspard de la Nuit, for piano: *Ondine, Le Gibet, Scarbo* (premiered in 1909 by Ricardo Viñes);

Ma Mère l'Oye, for piano four hands: *Pavane de la Belle au bois dormante, Petit Poucet, Laideronette Impératrice des Pagodes, Les entretiens de la Belle et da la Bête, Le jardin féerique* (orchestrated in 1912, adding *Prélude* and *Danse du Rouet,* with interludes).

1909   *Menuet sur le nom de Haydn,* for piano;
begins to write for *La Grande Revue;*
meets Diaghilev in Paris;
begins *Daphnis et Chloë,* ballet for Diaghilev.

1910   *Quatre chants populaires: Espagnole, Française, Italienne, Hébraique,* for voice and piano.

1911   *Valses Nobles et Sentimentales,* eight waltzes for piano (later orchestrated);
extracts orchestral suite from unfinished score of *Daphnis et Chloë.*

1912   Finishes score of *Daphnis et Chloë;* premiere with Nijinsky.

1913   *A la manière de Borodine, A la manière de Chabrier* (two parodies for piano);
Prélude, for piano;
writes music criticism for *Comoedia Illustré;*
collaboration with Stravinsky to reorchestrate Moussorgsky's *Khovanshchina* for Diaghilev fails;
Trois Poèmes de Stéphane Mallarmé, for voice, piano, string quartet, two flutes, two clarinets: *Soupir, Placet futile, Surgi de la Croupe et du Bond.*

1914   *Deux Mélodies Hébraiques: Kaddisch, L'Enigme éternelle;*
Trio, for piano, violin, and cello;
orchestral transcriptions of piano works by Satie, Moussorgksy, Chopin., and Schumann.

1915   Settings of three poems by himself for unaccompanied mixed chorus: *Nicolette, Trois beaux oiseaux du Paradis, Ronde;*
accepted as a military driver in World War I.

1917   Death of mother;
invalided out of military service;

Le Tombeau de Couperin: Prélude, Fugue, Forlane, Rigaudon, Menuet, Toccata, for piano (later orchestrated).

1920   *La Valse,* orchestral work for ballet;
rejects Legion of Honor award;
Duo Sonata for violin and cello begun (finished 1922).

1921   Moves into Le Belvédère at Montfort-l'Amaury.

1922   Orchestrates works by Debussy and others;
Pictures at an Exhibition, orchestration commissioned by Koussevitzky.

1923   *Sonata* for violin and piano begun (finished in 1927).

1924   *Ronsard à son Âme,* for voice and piano; *Tzigane,* for violin and orchestra.

1925   *Chansons Madécasses: Nahandove, Aoua, Il est doux,* settings for voice, piano, cello, and flute of poems by Evariste Parnay;
L'Enfant et les Sortilèges, opera in two scenes to libretto by Colette (premiered at Monte Carlo Opera).

1927   American tour, ending in 1928.

1928   *Bolero,* orchestral work for ballet;
Oxford University confers honorary Doctor of Music;
Ravel Festival opens in Biarritz.

1931   Completes two piano concerti, one for left hand in D, commissioned by Paul Wittgenstein, the other in G.

1932   *Don Quichotte à Dulcinée,* three songs for voice and piano;
injured in taxi collision in Paris.

1934   Symptoms of brain damage; moves to Levallois, then back to Montfort-l'Amaury.

1935   Trip to Spain and Morocco.

1937   Brain operation in Paris;
dies there in hospital.

INDEX

Index

Index

Index

LIST OF ILLUSTRATIONS

Frontispiece. The mother of Maurice Ravel.

Following page 48
Façade of the house of Ravel's birth, March, 7 1875. From a post-card picture made at Ciboure about 1940.

First and last pages of Ravel's original manuscript of his piano composition *Jeux d'Eau*. It bears the motto "Dieu fluvial riant de l'eau qui le chatouille. H. de Regnier," and his signature at the end, dated November, 11 1901.

Following page 80
Ravel (rt.) with his pianist friend and colleague, Ricardo Viñes, 1905.

Nijinsky and Ravel at the piano playing a score from *Daphnis and Chloe*, 1912.

View of Ravel's home, La Belvédère, in Montfort-l'Amaury, from the street.

Following page 144
Ravel's balcony overlooking his garden at La Belvédère in Montfort-l'Amaury.

Ravel's piano in his study at Montfort-l'Amoury.

Ravel at Lyons-la-Forêt in 1923, with his pupil and friend Roland-Manuel.

Lyons-la-Forêt, 1923. From left: Ravel, Maurice Delage, Mme. Delage, Mme. Suzanne Roland-Manuel.

Following page 176
Ravel and conductor Paul Whiteman, in New York 1928.

Ravel at a birthday party in his honour in New York City, March, 8 1928. From left: Oscar Fried, conductor; Eva Gauthier, singer; Ravel at the piano; Manoah Leide-Tedesco, composer-conductor; and composer George Gershwin.

Ravel, shortly before his last illness, 1935.